CONSERVATION AND DISCOVERY

PETERBOROUGH CATHEDRAL NAVE CEILING AND RELATED STRUCTURES

edited by Jackie Hall and Susan M Wright

Published by MOLA (Museum of London Archaeology)
2015
Copyright © the editors and authors

A CIP catalogue record for this book is available from the British Library

Copy editing   Wendy Sherlock, Susan M Wright
Reprographics   Maggie Cox
Design and typesetting   Sue Cawood
Production   Tracy Wellman

Printed in the United Kingdom by Henry Ling Ltd
at the Dorset Press, an ISO 14001 certified printer

MIX
Paper from
responsible sources
FSC® C013985
FSC
www.fsc.org

Images and photographic credits

The following institutions are thanked for granting permission to reproduce the images illustrated (L left, R right)

Canterbury Cathedral Archives: Fig 119

Fitzwilliam Museum, Cambridge: Fig 115 upper L and R

Historic England: Fig 2, Fig 4–Fig 6, Fig 14–Fig 16, Fig 48, Fig 64, Fig 68, Fig 89, Fig 113 R, Fig 114 R, Fig 115 lower L, Fig 116, Fig 120–Fig 126, Fig 146

Society of Antiquaries of London: Fig 113 L, Fig 114 L

All remaining uncredited Peterborough images are reproduced courtesy of the various individual contributors. NB post-conservation images are noted as such in the caption

CONTRIBUTORS

The conservation project	Gillian Lewis, Julian Limentani
The wooden roof and ceiling structures	Hugh Harrison
The decorative paint	Richard Lithgow, with Helen Howard
Art-historical study	Paul Binski
Documentary research	Jackie Hall, Tim Halliday, †Donald Mackreth
Environmental survey and monitoring	Tobit Curteis
Metric survey	Paul Bryan
The masonry building	†Donald Mackreth
Paint analysis	Jane Davies, Helen Howard, Ioanna Kakoulli
Tree-ring dating	Cathy Tyers, Ian Tyers
Bayesian analysis of the tree-ring dating results	Jackie Hall
Additional text and editors	Jackie Hall, Susan M Wright

CONTENTS

FIGURES

TABLES

SUMMARY

Peterborough Cathedral's nave ceiling is an object of immense interest and significance. This wooden ceiling was erected and painted in the 13th century; it was repaired and repainted twice, once in the 1740s and again in the 1830s. In the 1990s, both the ceiling boards and the paint itself were in a fragile condition. Thus, a major conservation and investigative programme was initiated, not just on the ceiling but also on the truncated remnant of the 12th-century roof from which it is suspended. Three-quarters of the way through the programme, in 2001, a fire was started inside the cathedral, covering every surface within the building in soot. The cleaning, at least, had to be done again. Seizing the opportunity, investigation and conservation now took place on the other ceilings in the cathedral church.

This volume recounts our new understanding of the nave ceiling and its history, and of structures connected to it literally (the medieval nave roof and walls) and comparatively (the transept ceilings). All major timber structures were subject to tree-ring dating, resulting in significant adjustment to our knowledge, especially of the medieval phases, while documentary research cast light on the medieval building programme and on many of the post-medieval repairs. Structural analysis revealed medieval and post-medieval craftsmanship; paint analysis gave glimpses of medieval pigments and technique, with more revealed of the 18th- and 19th-century repaintings. So far as possible, this later work retained the medieval iconographic scheme and this is examined afresh.

The physical conservation programme is also documented here, so that best practice of the time is examined and made available for conservators and architects both of other buildings and for those who work on Peterborough in the future. Records of temperature and humidity above and below the ceiling, before, during and after the fire – the silver lining of a near-disaster – are of incomparable value to all who look after great churches but never (we hope) likely to be repeated.

ACKNOWLEDGEMENTS

Many individuals and organisations contributed to the success of the long-running conservation project described here; the team members and their roles are detailed in the 'Architect's preface' (Chapter 1.1). The authors and editors of this volume would like to express their sincere thanks to them all; our colleague, Donald (Don) Mackreth, cathedral archaeologist throughout the conservation project, contributed to this volume but died in 2014, before publication.

In addition, Hugh Harrison would like to thank the members of his conservation team, Stuart Anderson, Bob Chappell, Clare Cully, Jonathan Porter, Cameron Stewart, Brett Wright and, in particular, Peter Ferguson who contributed so much to discussions and interpretation, and some of whose drawings enhance this volume. Richard Lithgow, David Perry and Mark Perry carried out the treatment of the painted decoration, assisted by Caroline Baines, Cristina Beretta, Louise Bradshaw, Greg Howarth, Alexandra (Sasa) Kosinova, Sarah Livermore, Bianca Madden, Peter Martindale and Natalia Seggerman, with Fernando Caceres and Rachel Witt.

The editors acknowledge with gratitude the support of English Heritage and, from 2015, Historic England who funded the preparation of this book and its publication, and that of the members of the publication steering committee – Paul Binski, Gillian Lewis and Julian Limentani, and, for English Heritage/Historic England, David McComish and Linda Monckton. Paul Binski and Sarah Brown made helpful comments on Chapter 1.2, and Sarah Brown and Helen Howard on the volume as a whole. Heartfelt thanks is owed to the various members of the Anthony Mellows Memorial Trust editorial committee who discussed numerous points of documentary history with Jackie Hall, notably Tim Halliday and Nicholas Karn, and especially Edmund King, who allowed her access to early drafts of his transcription and translation of the abbey chronicle, and to John Smith for the Stukeley reference. Jackie is additionally grateful to Cathy Tyers and Peter Marshall for in-depth discussions of the Bayesian analysis (on which Phillip Lindley also usefully gave an outsider's view); and to the Paul Mellon Centre for a grant enabling her to study the west front and research Bayesian analysis. In addition, we thank Carlos Lemos (MOLA) for his redrawing of many of the graphical illustrations.

FOREWORD

'I will lift up mine eyes' wrote the pilgrim-psalmist. It is a mantra which I, among many others, often forget as I wander round historic buildings or city centres. Yet it is frequently the case that there is so much more to be seen and appreciated if we would but lift up our eyes.

When I arrived in Peterborough in March 2007, the conservation of the nave ceiling – and the clean-up after the fire of 2001 – was already complete; so I was presented with this amazing medieval artefact in its full glory. There is so much to it that, at first sight, it is impossible to take it all in. In the years since then, thanks to Julian Limentani, the cathedral architect, and Jackie Hall, the cathedral archaeologist, and many others, I have learned – and continue to learn – more and more about the ceiling: how it was made; how it is held up; what the images are; and how it relates to the rest of this wonderful cathedral church built to the glory of God.

Much of what we now know came directly from the conservation programme of 1998 to 2003. How that took place is a story in itself. This book documents the cleaning and repair process together with the many new discoveries it generated about the ceiling and other structures. I hope it will enable scholars and enthusiasts alike to explore and understand more fully this internationally important structure, which is to us, here in Peterborough, a much-loved companion to our spiritual life. More especially, I hope it will encourage you to visit or revisit Peterborough Cathedral and lift up your eyes!

Dean of Peterborough

1 INTRODUCTION

1.1 ARCHITECT'S PREFACE

Julian Limentani

The conservation project – initiation and early stages

When I became the cathedral architect in 1989, the nave ceiling of Peterborough Cathedral had been much written about but had had very little research carried out on the physical structure. It was understood to have been constructed *c* 1220 and to have had at least two interventions, recorded in the 1740s and 1830s. The central tower has been rebuilt twice, in the later 14th century and 1883–6, which was assumed to have had a significant effect on the east end of the ceiling. I inherited two inspection reports, one by Evelyn Baker from 1977, and one by Wolfgang Gärtner from 1988; the latter included a schematic plan, based on a 19th-century lithograph. Both these reports raised questions and expressed concern about the condition of the ceiling.

On inspecting the cathedral in 1991, there appeared from the clerestory walkways to be substantial gaps between the nave ceiling boards. Pamela Tudor-Craig, who had been present when Evelyn Baker had carried out her inspection, was invited to see if there had been changes, and she expressed concern at the ceiling's condition, which appeared to have deteriorated further.

I was able to persuade the Dean and Chapter to let me examine the ceiling in closer detail, with a narrow north–south bridge of scaffolding close to the east end of the nave and built up to within 1.7m of the ceiling in 1994. This was facilitated by the first of many English Heritage (EH) grants. As soon as the bridge was complete many experts came to see the problems and to offer advice.

From the scaffolding bridge it was evident that there were many problems, not least that there was a forest of nails hanging out of the ceiling, some very loose and ready to fall. There were also problems with the timber, and with the paint, which in places was very powdery and in others was flaking. A preliminary feasibility study was commissioned (Hirst Conservation 1995).

Effectively, I was responsible for one of the largest paintings of medieval origin in Europe with multiple problems and had to decide how to proceed safely to conserve it, without causing an outcry in the wall painting and art worlds. Corinne Bennett, who was at the time EH's cathedrals' architect, gave me sound advice to appoint a conservation adviser. Gillian Lewis was approached and has stayed with the project throughout.

Gillian Lewis and I decided to carry out a survey of the ceiling using a cherry picker so that the whole of it could be examined, and all the hanging nails tested (1996). The ceiling is *c* 25m above the nave floor, so a 30m 'Spider' was hired for two days. The cradle would hold two people so Gillian and I took it in turns to ride with the driver on 15 and 16 February 1996. From three positions of the cherry picker in the nave we were able to carry out sweeps from one side to the other of the ceiling and examine it at close quarters.

I was able to test each nail that was not fully secured and by the end of two days I had removed 59 nails, thus making it safe for people below; each one was put into a separate bag and its position marked approximately on the plan. Many photographs were also taken. Everywhere at ceiling level was filthy, coated with a slightly viscous grime that stuck to everything (probably nearly two centuries of soot deposits from stoves and candles).

From the cherry picker we could get a general idea of the condition of the whole ceiling. Gillian Lewis identified that there had been much replacement of boards at the west end, and that there were two areas where the paint was flaking badly, the flakes being the size of cornflakes. We then prevailed on the Dean and Chapter to carry out some emergency work on the ceiling in the area of St Peter and St Paul, where the flaking paint was in danger of being lost (Fig 1). Again this was helped financially by EH and also by the Pilgrim Trust.

In order to get permission to do this work, I felt it was important that it should be agreed by a team of experts, partly made up from the cathedral's own team of professionals, and partly from EH and the Courtauld Institute of Art, and a member of the Cathedrals Fabric Commission for England (CFCE). The first meeting of the team was on 17 March 1997, at which we defined the roles of the participants and then set timetables and priorities. Other conservators were consulted at this time to obtain as many views as possible as to the approach that should be taken to these problems.

During 1997 we went out to tender on work to refix the loose flakes as an emergency phase, partly to make sure that the paint was not lost, and partly to find out more about the ceiling and how it could be conserved. When the tenders were received an assessment panel examined the proposals,

Fig 1 The head of St Peter in 1996 before reattachment of flaking paint during the emergency treatment phase (30–31/II, bay 3)

Duration and progress of the condition survey and conservation project

There were four main phases of work between 1998 and 2001 covering nave bays 1–8 out of ten bays, beginning with the easternmost bay and working westwards (Table 1). Within four weeks of completing the phase 4 work a fire occurred in the cathedral on 22 November 2001. This filled the cathedral with thick soot from over 200 polypropylene chairs. The equipment at the nave ceiling which recorded temperature and humidity had continued to record during the fire and showed a dramatic drop in humidity to 9% and a steep rise in temperature. The scaffolding for phase 4 was still in place, so we were able to examine the nave ceiling the following morning and found that a film of soot covered the entire ceiling, as it did all surfaces in the cathedral; all the ceilings in the church would have to be cleaned. The smoke had also found its way into the roof space above, resulting in surprisingly thick soot deposits over all the ceiling and roof structures.

This was a major setback to the conservation programme. The fifth and final phase, scheduled for 2002, had to be postponed for a year and during 2002 scaffolding was reinstalled in the phase 1–4 areas so that the areas already dealt with (bays 1–8) could be re-examined and re-cleaned. We were able to bring the data from phases 1–2 up to the same level as that of phases 3–4 (and it was pleasing to find that the works had not suffered unduly), as well as undertake cleaning and some investigation of the transept ceilings which is reported here. (Work on the crossing and presbytery ceilings is not discussed in this volume.) Work on the condition survey and conservation project then resumed and phase 5 (bays 9 and 10) was carried out in 2003.

The team and the investigations

As mentioned above, all major decisions that were taken were made by a group of experts in different fields. During the period of the works, the team met twice a year. The core membership was fairly consistent, with only members from the statutory bodies changing. Linda Monckton for CFCE gave way to Maggie Goodall towards the end. Corinne Bennett handed over to David Heath, who in turn handed over to Ian Harper as EH's cathedrals' architect. Other members of the team included Donald Mackreth, then the cathedral archaeologist, David Goode, consultant structural engineer, and Paul Binski (University of Cambridge), medieval art historian and a member of the Fabric Advisory Committee of the cathedral.

English Heritage were involved in the project from the beginning and provided much expertise and resources that made a substantial difference to the amount that was achieved. It was seen as a groundbreaking project, which should be carried out using all the best practices available, in some instances pushing the use of technology further

giving scores for various areas. The combined team of the Perry Lithgow Partnership and Hugh Harrison Conservation was contracted to carry out the 'emergency works' which were done between August 1997 and May 1998 (Lithgow 1997). Before work began, Adrian Heritage and Helen Howard, then of the Courtauld Institute of Art, carried out an investigation into the phases of painting remaining on the ceiling, and the effects of cleaning on it. During this emergency phase, time was spent in finding out how to treat the paint, which was the best method of relaxing it and fixing it back in place, and which was the best method for cleaning. It quickly became clear that any form of wet cleaning would cause the paint to bloom, which left us with a dry cleaning method such as is used for wall paintings.

Having successfully achieved all that was intended with the emergency phase, we again went out to tender for phase 1 of the works to the easternmost bay of the nave. This was again won by the team of the Perry Lithgow Partnership and Hugh Harrison Conservation, as was phase 2. From then on, phases 3, 4 and 5 were by negotiated tender. Throughout, John Ward acted as planning supervisor for the project and made sure that all the health and safety requirements were met by the contractors.

forwards. At the beginning of the project identifying different areas of the nave ceiling, right down to each board, was a necessity and I had devised a referencing system for the ceiling's 160 rectangular panels, arranged in 40 north–south rows with four panels per row (following the west to east numbering in Gärtner's 1988 inspection report: this system is detailed below, 1.3). An immediate problem was to find a suitable way of recording the work by the conservators. Paul Bryan was brought in from the metric survey section of EH (Chapter 6.3). He devised a system of superimposing over metric survey a greyscale photograph of the ceiling so that all patterns and details showed on each board, employing a computer with one of the largest available memories at the time, fitted with a military software program for mapping and targeting missiles. The system was very successful and has since been used with many other projects. In addition the upper side of the ceiling was surveyed with reflectorless electromagnetic distance measurement (REDM) equipment so the upper side of the ceiling could be directly superimposed on the lower or underside; again this was the first time these methods of recording had been put together. EH were able both to carry out some of the survey work and to specify how further work was to be carried out.

A tree-ring survey was also commissioned by EH of the timbers by the Sheffield University Dendrochronology Laboratory under Cathy Groves (later Cathy Tyers, and of EH scientific dating team), who pioneered the use of a new technique for dating the boards of the ceiling without the removal of any timber, using FIMO to obtain impressions of the boards which were then baked and measured without any damage or removal of historic material (Chapter 4.2). Cathy Tyers worked on the oak and conifer nave ceiling boards, while Ian Tyers carried out the rest of the EH-funded tree-ring work at the cathedral. Many of the structural timbers of the nave ceiling and the north portico (ie, the north bay of the west front) were dated to give an overall picture of building sequences in the late 12th and 13th centuries (Chapter 2.3; Chapter 4.2). Post-fire, an 'informed conservation' programme was undertaken in parallel with the programme of grant-aided repairs that used the opportunity afforded by the comprehensive clean-up programme and new scaffolding. A series of tree-ring recording and sampling programmes covering many different groups of timbers in the north and south transepts, as well as the apsed presbytery and the central crossing tower, was requested by EH in order to help elucidate the dates and the sequence of modifications of the structures.

The Courtauld Institute of Art took a considerable interest in the project from the beginning and were instrumental in the determination of techniques which should be tried to clean the ceiling. Sharon Cather was a member of the advisory team from the beginning through to completion, with David Park and Adrian Heritage also being involved. Subsequently, when Adrian Heritage joined EH he became involved again as head of the wall paintings section; this position was then taken over by Robert Gowing. The work of paint sampling and analysis was initially carried out by Helen Howard at the Courtauld Institute and then by independent analysts and conservators Jane Davies (Jane Davies Conservation), Catherine Hassall and Joanna Kakoulli, under the direction of Richard Lithgow. Analysis of iron nails was undertaken by Brian Gilmour at the Archaeology Laboratories of the Department of Materials, University of Oxford.

Treatment of the ceiling boards and ceiling structure was the responsibility of Hugh Harrison; treatment of the painted decoration was carried out by Richard Lithgow and Mark Perry (The Perry Lithgow Partnership). The graphic documentation for the technical survey was based on photogrammetric drawings of the underside of the ceilings plotted by the Downland Partnership.

A conference was held following the emergency works to disseminate the details of what had been done. This drew international interest and the concluding discussion indicated that more was needed in the way of environmental monitoring; it was as a result of this that Tobit Curteis (Tobit Curteis Associates) was brought into the team. He performed two functions: firstly, carrying out the environmental monitoring and, secondly, managing the documentation that the project was producing.

Throughout the project a high priority was to record in detail as much as possible, and to record it both graphically and in written form so that in future exactly what was found would be known and thus form a benchmark for the future. From the beginning the intention was to consult and share information widely. During the project, visits were made to see other churches and cathedrals, either of this age and nature or with associated problems. Gillian Lewis and Julian Limentani visited the conservators at St Martin's church, Zillis, in Switzerland in 1996, where the problems were different but the age and nature of the nave ceiling were similar, that is painted timber from the 12th century. As part of the European Community's Raphael programme, a project under the acronym COMPOTEC (Conservation of medieval painting on timber through European cooperation) was developed with NIKU (Norwegian Institute for Conservation) in Norway (the equivalent of EH) and the Historiska Museum in Stockholm, Sweden. In Norway, Kristin Solberg, Jørgen Solstad and Mille Stein were looking at the use of true and synthetic sturgeon glues which had been used in Vestre Slide church 20–30 years before and the effects. In Sweden, Sonia Leon and Håken Lindberg were looking at the conservation of painted staves of Björsäter church which were dismantled in the 19th century and stored in the museum; the intention was to conserve and display them. The grant included visits to each other's projects and discussion on the work, thus broadening our knowledge. Hugh Harrison visited Dädesjö church in Småland, Sweden, after our visit to Stockholm in May 2000, and was able to examine the structure of the ceiling of this church, which again is 12th century. At the end of the projects there was a conference in Peterborough at which each party presented their findings, ending with a summary by Mille Stein. As a result of COMPOTEC many friends have been made and many useful discussions held with colleagues from within the UK and Europe.

Funding for the conservation project

Towards the beginning of the project, the cathedral launched a major appeal to raise £7.3 million between 1996 and 2000 for a number of projects including the nave ceiling. The appeal was successfully led by Sir Stephen Hastings and achieved its goal. The fact that the cathedral thus had matching funds meant that it could make use of a series of generous grants from EH; these started with the investigative work at the beginning and the emergency work phase, and then all five of the main work phases. In addition the project was supported by the Pilgrim Trust and the Cripps Foundation with substantial grants in the development period. Without support of this nature, it would not have been possible to have carried through this work (Table 1).

Phase 2 of the works was also helped by a European Community grant under the Raphael programme, which involved complementary projects in two other community states; this was the COMPOTEC project (above).

1.2 THE BUILDING AND THE CEILING

Jackie Hall

Destruction and rebuilding

Now highly prized as a rare medieval survival, the painted ceiling at Peterborough Cathedral was also the culmination and effective completion of an extended building project at what was then the abbey church. More was to follow – the bell tower and Lady chapel also in the 13th century and the new central tower and 'New Building' (retrochoir) subsequently – but the provision of the nave ceiling, with other furnishings, properly finished the church and made it fit for worship. As such, the place to begin is not the nave and the time not the mid 13th century, but instead 4 August 1116.

On this night, the abbey's chronicler Hugh Candidus tells us, the whole monastery was burnt and the whole town, because the abbot had cursed the monastery and 'rashly commended it to the devil' (Mellows 1949, 97; Halliday 2009). Unusually for a great Benedictine abbey of Peterborough's wealth and stature, two generations after the Conquest the church still belonged to the Anglo-Saxon era (along with nearby Crowland). Large, well-appointed and probably renovated after the Conquest, the church clearly served its purpose well (Hall 2008, 22). Nonetheless, it is hard to suppress a suspicion that the fire created a welcome

Table 1 Conservation work on Peterborough Cathedral nave ceiling, 1994–2003

Year	Work undertaken
1994	pollution tests by B Knight of English Heritage (EH) indicate much soluble acid present in the wood; tests for chlorides and sulphates also gave weakly positive results (Lithgow 1997, 10)
1995	Hirst Conservation undertakes feasibility study, involving cleaning and consolidation tests, with basic visual pigment identification (Hirst Conservation 1995)
1996	G Lewis and J Limentani inspect the ceiling from a hoist; paint samples taken by GL at this time are subsequently examined and photographed at EH laboratories; some of the samples were also subjected to analysis by SEM/EDXS at EH (Lewis 1996)
1997–8	phase of emergency conservation treatment and documentation of condition by the Perry Lithgow Partnership in the zones around St Peter, St Paul and the dulcimer player (Lithgow 1997)
1998	phase 1 of condition survey and treatment by the Perry Lithgow Partnership and Hugh Harrison Conservation consisted of the four east rows of panels, that is, a total of 16 panels (rows 39–36; bay 1; Harrison and Lithgow nd a)
1999	phase 2 of condition survey and treatment by the Perry Lithgow Partnership and Hugh Harrison Conservation consisted of the next eight rows, a total of 32 panels (rows 35–28; bays 2 and 3; Harrison and Lithgow nd b)
2000	phase 3 of condition survey and treatment by the Perry Lithgow Partnership and Hugh Harrison Conservation consisted of ten rows, a total of 40 panels (rows 27–18; bays 4, 5 and 6a; Harrison and Lithgow nd c)
2001	phase 4 of condition survey and treatment by the Perry Lithgow Partnership and Hugh Harrison Conservation consisted of ten rows, a total of 40 panels (rows 17–8; bays 6b, 7 and 8; Harrison and Lithgow nd d)
2001 (Nov)	fire in the north aisle causing widespread smoke damage
2002	restoration of fire damage by the Perry Lithgow Partnership and Hugh Harrison Conservation (bays 1–8; Harrison and Lithgow nd f)
2003	phase 5 of condition survey and treatment by the Perry Lithgow Partnership and Hugh Harrison Conservation consisted of eight rows, 32 panels (rows 7–0; bays 9 and 10; Harrison and Lithgow nd e)

opportunity to build anew rather than repair, especially since new claustral buildings had already been begun (Mellows 1949, 90). Two years after the fire, John de Seez, abbot 1114–25, laid the foundation stone of the new church (ibid, 98; Table 2). Services were first held there in 1140, when the presbytery was finally completed by Martin de Bec (abbot 1132×33–55) (Plummer 1952, i, 265; Mellows 1949, 108). With its four-bay aisled presbytery and stilted apse, massive galleries and clerestory passages, Peterborough was very much following local expressions of Romanesque architecture, as for instance at Ely and Norwich (Fernie 2000, 152) (Fig 2; Fig 3).

The location of the old church (Irvine 1894) meant that it was not necessary to finally dismantle it until the presbytery of the Romanesque church was complete; the Anglo-Saxon church must have been repaired sufficiently for services, given the 22 years it took to complete the first section of the new one. Despite a suggestion that work on the Norman church may have started from east and west simultaneously and before the fire of 1116 (Reilly 1997, 13, 15 and passim), there is no evidence in the masonry to doubt the salient facts

of the chronicler's account (Peers 1906, 431–40; Fernie 2000, 148–52; Thurlby 2006).

After the completion of the east end, William de Waterville (abbot 1155–75) is credited with finishing both transept arms (Fig 4), building three stages of the tower and constructing the choir (as well as erecting many other buildings around the precinct; Mellows 1949, 130). Prior to this point, the monks must have worshipped in the presbytery, perhaps in makeshift stalls, but, since the nave was not yet built, William de Waterville's choir, that is the monks' stalls, must have been either in the presbytery or in the crossing.

Abbot William, or rather his unnamed mason, must also have been responsible for the nave bays buttressing the tower, so clearly visible in the fabric. On the south side, Mackreth suggests that construction of the arcade started earlier, in the time of Martin de Bec, along with the south aisle wall to enclose the cloister (Chapter 2.1). On the north side, at the time the crossing tower was finished, the first bay of the nave was completed to clerestory level, along with two bays of the gallery (ie, the middle storey) and more bays of the arcade

Fig 2 Aerial photograph of Peterborough Cathedral from the south, taken in c 1960, showing the Romanesque church, with later additions, at the heart of the extensive precinct of the former abbey

N

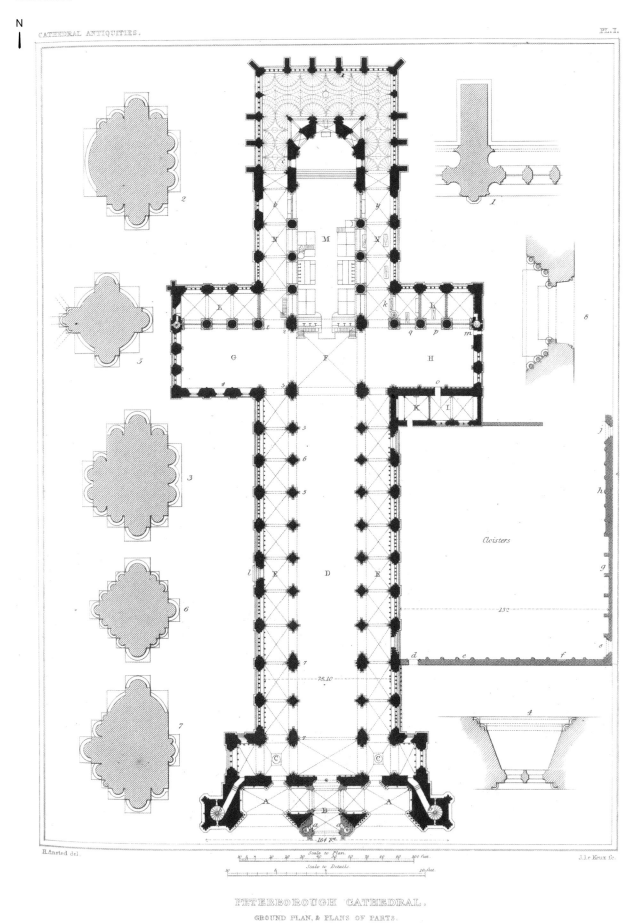

H. Ansted del.

J. le Keux sc.

PETERBOROUGH CATHEDRAL.

GROUND PLAN, & PLANS OF PARTS.

Printed by Barnett &.

Fig 3 Plan of the cathedral church when the choir was in the presbytery, whereas earlier and later the choir was further west (Britton 1828, pl 1; cathedral shown here at scale 1:700)

0   25m

Fig 4 General view of transept interiors, looking south

(Fig 5). The very plain wall arcade in the south aisle wall, so different from the north aisle wall arcade, strongly suggests that this too was built at an early date, as soon as the Anglo-Saxon church was dismantled, in order to provide enclosure for the cloister.

The nave and the west front

After the erection of the crossing tower and its buttressing there may have been an extended building break, since at this time a decision was made to abandon the motif of decorated tympana in the gallery (Fig 5) and another was made to vault the nave (eventually changed in favour of the painted wooden ceiling). The second abbey chronicler, Robert of Swaffham (writing *c* 1256; Mellows 1966, ii), tells us that Abbot Benedict (1177–93) 'built the whole of the nave of the church in stone and wood from the tower of the choir right up to the front and built the pulpitum' (Sparke 1723, 99; translation Halliday 2009). Although the fundamental style and proportions of the Romanesque nave are retained, Gothic features appear for the first time: water-holding bases in the main arcade from bay 6 on the north side; occasional Gothic capitals and bases in the galleries and clerestories. Given Benedict's previous post as prior of Christ Church Canterbury, and the major works taking place there in the new style, this is apposite (Peers 1906, 440; Mackreth 1994; Thurlby 2006, 82–7).

The nave was initially intended to have nine bays with the ninth having twin towers over the aisles (for the evidence see Mackreth, Chapter 2.1). There is no evidence to tell us whether this was finished or not, but there was a change of plan, with a decision to extend the nave by a further bay with a western transept in front of that, again surmounted by twin towers in line with the nave aisles. During the next major building break, again stepped to support the earlier work, another change of plan was made – perhaps coincident with the death of Abbot Benedict – to extend westwards once more, and add the iconic three-arch galilee, covered in statues and with turrets at either end (Fig 6).

The 1998–2003 conservation programme (above, 1.1; Table 1; Chapter 6) examined not only the nave ceiling but a number of related structures either because they also required conservation, such as the medieval nave roof and the transept ceilings, or because it was felt that their examination would significantly aid our understanding. This was the case for the whole programme of tree-ring analysis, carried out by Cathy Tyers and Ian Tyers, which included the nave ceiling, the medieval nave roof, the transept ceilings and the original roof above the north bay of the west front as reported here (Chapter 2.3, 2.4; Chapter 3.2, 3.3; Chapter

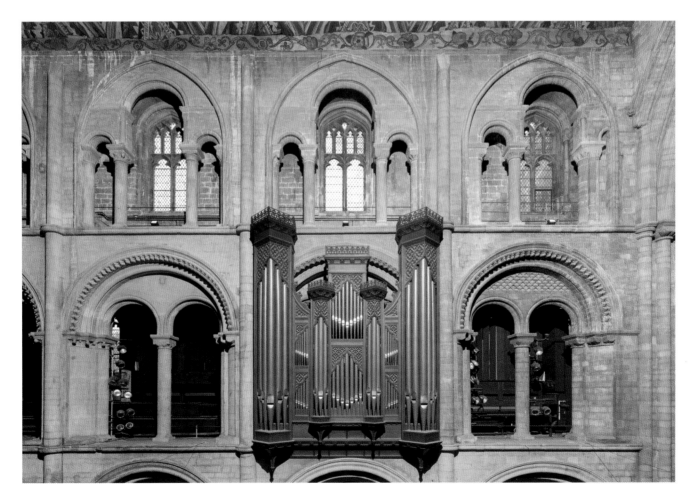

Fig 5 View of the gallery and clerestory of nave bays 1–3, north side, showing changes in design between bays 1 and 2 (right) at clerestory level and between bays 2 (obscured by organ) and 3 at gallery level

Fig 6 The west front

4.2), as well as other structures not reported (Tyers 2004). The tree-ring dates strongly confirm the documentary history and support the view that the roof of the west bay of the nave significantly post-dated Benedict. Lack of medieval timber in the western transept means that the next significant tree-ring date is that over the north portico: the combined felling date range of *c* 1225–30 (OxCal Combine *1224–34)* shows it to have been completed after the main nave roof (Chapter 2.3, 2.4). This is the most important observation on the west front in the last half-century and completion of the front may have taken place at the same time as, or only very shortly after, completion of the west nave bays and western transept. Discussion of the many remaining design and construction questions surrounding the west front, however, must await the publication of the results of the recent conservation programme there.

Vault or ceiling?

The next significant documentary reference to the church building concerns Robert of Lindsey, abbot 1214–22 (Sparke 1723, 107; King forthcoming). During the time Robert was sacrist (ie, pre-1214), he glazed 30 or more windows in the church, which were before filled with straw and twigs, as well as glazing other conventual buildings. The 30 windows are sometimes taken to mean the western transept and front, although some portion of the nave is also a possibility.

Also while he was sacrist, Robert of Lindsey had the images of SS John and Mary above the high altar renewed, and the 'vaults' whitewashed in the retrochoir (*fecit dealbare volsuras in retro choro*), the location of which is subject to debate but most probably lay west of the monks' choir (Chapter 2.1).

Donald Mackreth, cathedral archaeologist throughout the conservation project, strongly favours a location in the crossing for the choir, which would make the whitewashed vault cover the nave (Chapter 2.1). He suggests that the putative vault there must have failed – hence its replacement with the wooden painted ceiling. There is certainly plenty of evidence from the east end to the west that a vault was intended (Chapter 2.1). However, if William de Waterville's choir lay east of the crossing in what became the presbytery, perhaps to avoid the proximity of building works, the whitewashed vault would have been above the crossing itself (or perhaps *volsura* was not used in an architecturally precise way). Malcolm Thurlby (2006, 86–7) has suggested that a decision to abandon the vault was made before it was built, in favour of the wooden ceiling we have now, an outcome fitting both the archaic restraint of the nave and the liturgically more important east arm, which, apart from the apse, was also ceiled in wood.

A visual examination alone does not resolve the issue. Save in the rare (in England) cases where tiles or slates are laid directly on a stone vault, the latter, just like a wooden vault or a wooden ceiling, would not have been built prior to the roof. And, once the roof has been erected and covered, there is no urgency to complete the vault or ceiling. Like the choir stalls or screens or other fitments, it could, if necessary, wait until other urgent works – perhaps the west front, the infirmary or other works around the precincts – were completed and money, masons and carpenters became available again.

The detailed studies that formed part of the nave ceiling conservation programme did not prove or disprove whether the intended stone vault was ever erected. The studies did, however, importantly, demonstrate that considerable parts of the medieval transept ceilings survive and Hugh Harrison and Richard Lithgow have been able to reconstruct for us the original structural design and some of the decorative elements (Chapter 3.1), while they have also been successfully dated (Chapter 3.2, 3.3), although without precise felling dates. All of these are of relevance to the nave ceiling. In the first place these ceilings are now shown to have been built in the early 13th century (combined felling date range south transept c 1203–31, north transept c 1200–25; OxCal Combine 1203–15), that is prior to the construction of the nave ceiling. Like the nave ceiling, they are made up of rows of lozenges and thus they are its most relevant precursor, albeit both structurally and decoratively simpler. Also like the nave ceiling, the transept ceilings post-date their walls/roofs by as much as two generations since the transept was built in the third quarter of the 12th century; like the nave, there are also signs that transept ceilings of different design were originally intended (Chapter 3.1). Once again, there is no evidence to prove or disprove whether or not these early ceilings had been built. If they and the nave vault had been built, this would show either a remarkable major refashioning of the interior space even before the church was complete or a rather careless loss of three expensive ceilings. On the other hand, if the lozenge pattern ceilings were the first to be built in both transept arms and nave, then this would show a cautious approach to the works on the church, one subject to the availability of resources – surely more likely. Thus, two views on the nave vault are present in this volume: here and in Paul Binski's section (Chapter 4.5) an intended but never-built vault is preferred, while Donald Mackreth (Chapter 2.1) favours a nave vault that was built but probably collapsed, thus necessitating a new ceiling.

Other building works

Although this volume is focused on the church – and just a few aspects at that – it is useful to remember the sheer quantity of building work going on elsewhere throughout the precincts, and on the abbey's other properties. Aside from his work on the presbytery, for instance, Abbot Martin de Bec focused on improving the town. During the building of the transept and crossing tower, Abbot William built the infirmary, and a chamber, chapel and other offices in the court, and began the chapel to St Thomas, as well as covering many of the claustral buildings with lead (Mellows 1949, 122 and 130–1; King forthcoming). While the nave was being built, Benedict built the great gatehouse, a great hall (probably one of the guesthouses) and completed the chapel and hospital of St Thomas, we are told (Sparke 1723, 101; King forthcoming). The next abbot (Acharius, 1200–10) was not noted for his building work, although, like Benedict, he gave the church many vestments, hangings and vessels, and also a new reliquary for the arm of St Oswald, the most precious of the abbey's many relics. As well as his work glazing the church and many other buildings, Robert of Lindsey enlarged the dormitory, covered the abbot's hall with lead, erected a marble (ie, local Alwalton (Hunts) marble) laver, started a new gateway, stables, fishponds and a 'great house'. It is clear that, if not stretched, then the available resources were well utilised. The following abbot, Alexander (1222–6), is only remembered for one building (a solar for himself) and a handful of vestments and precious vessels, while Walter of Bury St Edmunds seems to have been much more active (1233–45). As well as many vestments and precious vessels, he contributed most of the large timbers and 10 marks (£6 13s 4d) 'to the work of the stalls'. He also made the entry into the new refectory and built many buildings in the court and on the manors and granges of the abbey (Sparke 1723, 119–20; King forthcoming).

Walter of Bury St Edmunds

The church was consecrated in 1238, during Walter's abbacy (Sparke 1723, 117; King forthcoming). Matthew Paris, however, records Peterborough in a list of churches that were consecrated following a decree made at the 1237 Council of London, which directed that all completed churches should be consecrated within two years (*Chron Majora*, iii, 517; Powicke and Cheney 1964, 245–6; Binski 2003, 46). That is, the consecration may only be casually related to the completion of the church since this decree prompted a flurry of overdue consecrations.

The tree-ring dating is crucial to our new understanding of the ceiling (Chapter 4.2); from the 1930s, it was thought to date to c 1220 (Cave and Borenius 1937, 297; Tristram 1944, 58 and 141–2); before the 1930s, it was thought to be co-eval with the walls and roof, that is, late 12th century (eg, Peers 1906, 446). The ceiling boards may represent a single intensive felling period or a continuous longer felling period spanning a number of years. If all the boards were purchased at the same time, then the ceiling could not have been begun before 1238, and could have started some years later. If they were purchased in batches, then the ceiling could, theoretically, have started a few years earlier, but still could not have been finished any earlier than 1238. Either way, this suggests that completion of interior fittings, such as the choir and ceiling, was not relevant to the 1238 consecration (above).

Thus Abbot Walter of Bury St Edmunds (1233–45) is highly likely to have played a role in the construction and completion of the ceiling. Paul Binski furthers the case for this by pointing out that Walter's other activities, such as giving money and timbers towards the stalls, form part of a larger programme, while his stylistic analysis of many elements also points to a mid century date (Chapter 4.5). This hypothesis receives further confirmation in a hitherto barely noticed part of Swaffham's chronicle:

Ipse quidem quando ultimo mare transiturus erat dedit feretris trium uirginum et celature ecclesie duo paria bacinarum noua et preciosa de precio septendecim marcarum et dimidii; et duas nouas cuppas de argento deauratas et artificiose operatas de precio sexdecim marcarum. Que omnia successor eius abbas Willelmus mutuo accepit. (King forthcoming)

When he [Walter] crossed the sea for the last time he gave to the shrines of the three virgins and to the ceiling of the church two pairs of lamp-basins, new and most precious, worth 17½ marks [£11 13s 4d]; also two new cups of silver gilt, very finely worked, worth 16 marks [£10 13s 4d]. All of which his successor Abbot William gave as security for a loan.

The meaning of the crucial phrase, *celature ecclesie*, is far from certain: *celatura* has several meanings. 'Carving' is hardly likely here, but 'canopy' is certainly possible. The context suggests that Abbot Walter is securing a safe crossing by donations to altars, so perhaps the lamps were intended to hang from the ceiling of the sanctuary of one of the altars, or the choir. It is highly unlikely that lamps would have hung from the excessively high nave ceiling, but it is likely that the *celatura ecclesiae* was the nave ceiling, since *ecclesia* often implies nave (P Binski, pers comm). As Binski demonstrates, the 13th-century nave ceiling covered part of the liturgical choir as well (Chapter 4.5) so this wider meaning may be particularly appropriate here (and at many other great churches with similar arrangements). In this case, the lamps could be providing lighting for a just-finished painted ceiling. It is not likely that they were intended to be sold to defray the ceiling costs, despite the fact that Walter's successor pawned them.

This is far from unambiguous, but it certainly adds a tantalising primary documentary reference to the body of other evidence – tree-ring dating and art history – pointing towards a date in the 1240s; Abbot Walter's last journey was in June 1245 (King forthcoming; *Cal Pat R 1232–47*, 453–4). If some of the goods *were* meant to be sold, it should be noted that 33½ marks (£22 6s 8d) would barely have touched the costs involved in creating the nave ceiling. If they were not meant to be sold, but gifted to the altars then the lack of a clear reference to Walter contributing to the ceiling is frustrating but hardly conclusive, given that medieval chronicles were not written for buildings historians. Either way, it is worth suggesting that, as with the majority of works on the church, the ceiling was in the care of the sacrist and that the majority of money came out of the sacrist's revenues, whether from estates or from gifts. Like his predecessor Robert of Lindsey and his successor Richard London (abbot 1274–95), Abbot Walter was previously sacrist but, unlike in those cases, the chronicle does not make much mention of what he did during this time, save for a journey to Rome to defend the abbey's rights in Castor church (*Cal Pat R 1232–47*, 20; Sparke 1723, 117; King forthcoming).

Oak

A slightly unusual feature of the documentary evidence is the complete absence of gifts of oak from the king (the abbey's patron) for the building of the church, although relevant records do not survive prior to the reign of King John. This compares unfavourably with many other major churches. Salisbury, for instance, received over 200 trees in the 1230s, while Wells received 60 oaks in 1220; Lincoln received even more (Ayers and Sampson 2000, 34; Sampson 1998, 45; Laxton et al 2001, 70). York Minster, though, also received very little from the king (Rackham 2006, 123–4). As at York, Peterborough Abbey must have been able to supply the need from its own woodland. Indeed, the tree-ring analysis shows that in the late 12th and early 13th centuries, when the nave roof and north portico roof timbers were felled, the abbey had access to straight slow-grown oaks, possibly local (Chapter 2.3).

A hint of the importance to the abbey of its woodland is given in the chronicle, which notes many cases of dispute with the king's foresters. So, Abbot Benedict, 'builder' of the nave and its roof, '… wisely and munificently fortified the whole abbey of Peterborough with all the liberties contained in the charters of King Richard, both against the sheriffs in respect of the lands and against the foresters concerning the woods, which belonged to the abbey' (King forthcoming).

Benedict's successor, Acharius (1200–10), suffered 'from a severe king, from unfettered tyrants, and from forest officials'. The sorry tale continued in the time of Robert of Lindsey (abbot 1214–22) since 'in those days the foresters and the beasts of the forest lorded it over men' (King forthcoming; for abbey lands in the Forest of Rockingham see Foard et al 2009, 16–19). His solution was, with the knights and free tenants, to pay King John 1220 marks (£813) for the disafforestation of Nassaburgh (the double hundred of the Liberty of Peterborough) (King forthcoming). The benefits of this were multifarious (and certainly related to assarting: King 1973, 72–83), as indicated by the vast cost, but better access to timber must have been one of them. Certainly, around this time, the abbey was still able to supply oak from England for the transept ceilings, but only a generation later, when timbers were needed for the nave ceiling, they were imported, probably from north Germany, no doubt due to more plentiful supplies of oak and to their greater suitability as boards (Chapter 4.2). This was one of the most dramatic findings of the conservation programme and showed it to be the earliest importation of boards then known. Analysis of timbers since then, for example from Salisbury Cathedral and Westminster Abbey, shows that importation of boarding and structural timbers from a variety of sources was becoming routine in the 13th century, although Peterborough remains the earliest large-scale example of importing from Germany (Chapter 4.2). Scarcity of timber is shown in the chronicle from the mid 13th century: William Hotot (abbot 1246–9) promised not to sell woodland without the consent of the convent, and 50 years later William Woodford promised not to sell woodland cheaply 'for he dared not use up the treasure of his church' (King 1973, 84).

Disputes between the abbey and the king over timber continued after the nave ceiling was completed. In 1260 the king issued a letter to his justiciar of forests south of the Trent to ensure that the full force of the law would fall on the abbot and convent if they exhausted or sold timber from their lands within the areas of the king's forests (*Cal Close R 1259–61*, 51). At last, however, the abbey began to receive gifts of timber: in March 1256, the king gave ten oaks 'for timber' for the infirmary; in July 1261 he gave the abbot 'four good oaks' without naming the building works; but in 1262 only four dead trees (or coppices) for his hearth (*Cal Close R 1254–6*, 284; *1259–61*, 414; *1261–4*, 24). A further gift, of four oaks, was made to the almoner for the repair of almshouses in 1263 (*Cal Close R 1261–4*, 363–4).

Three of these four gifts were in the time of John of Caux (abbot 1250–63, also known as John of Caleto), who served as the king's treasurer from 1260–3. It is hard to avoid the thought that these gifts of oak were as much to do with John of Caux's good standing with the king as with need, since the abbey can never have needed oaks more than during the construction of the church and its fitting out with stalls, screens and ceilings. This supposition is strengthened by the fact that Henry III gave eight oaks to the abbot's nephew, at the request of John of Caux (*Cal Close R 1259–61*, 414).

Appreciation of the painted ceiling

Appreciation of the ceiling is only apparent from the late 18th century with a letter from Thomas Pownall on 'Ancient Painting in England' written in 1788. Though this did not go beyond identifying the paint as oil-based, and a few of the figurative elements (Fig 7; cf Fig 122–Fig 125), it remains the primary source of our knowledge of the 1740s repainting (Chapter 5.2). Pownall appreciated the ceiling as a Norman painting, although he 'could not but observe the difference between the Spirit of the drawing, and the wretched daubing of the colouring' (1789, 149), a view which has in different

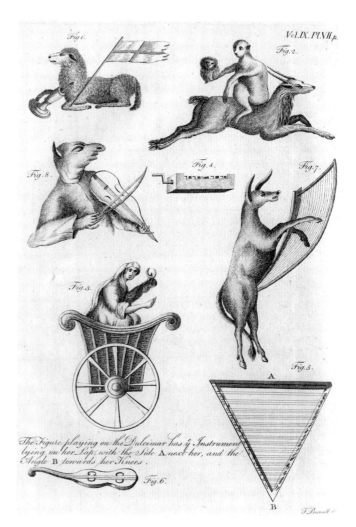

Fig 7 Figurative elements in the nave ceiling as recorded by Thomas Pownall in 1788: from top left, clockwise – fig 1 'the lamb triumphant in death, bleeding into the holy chalice'; fig 2 'goat … running … rider … face to the tail'; fig 7 'Assinus ad Lyram'; fig 5 dulcimer; fig 6 mandoline/guitar; fig 3 'a woman riding in a self-moved cart'; fig 8 'caricature of a musician, … playing on a violin'; and centre: 'viol' (Pownall 1789, pl VII opp 147)

forms echoed through the centuries since. Luminaries such as Thomas Rickman admired it as a rare 12th-century example of 'a real flat-boarded ceiling' and thought it carefully repainted (Rickman 1817, 53), while John Britton, writing in the 1820s, deplored the wooden ceilings in the cathedral as a whole: 'Thus not only the architectural character of those lofty parts are deteriorated, but the obtrusive and spotty style in which they are painted offend the eye and injure the apparent magnitude and effect of the building' (Britton 1997, 55).

Only 20 years later, and 13 after another major repaint, the ceiling was considered to be of sufficient beauty and curiosity to justify the production, paid for by subscription, of a coloured lithograph by the local artist William Strickland (1849; Fig 8; cf Fig 124 and Fig 125). In the short accompanying text, Strickland follows Davys's 1846 guide to the cathedral, and the structure of the ceiling is

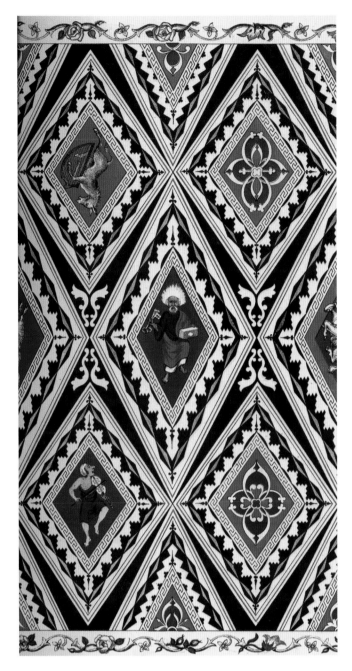

Fig 8 A portion of Strickland's lithograph of the nave ceiling, showing (top left) the harp-playing ass, (centre) St Peter and (bottom left) a semi-naked fiddler (Strickland 1849)

finally considered, as well as its painting: the lapped planks are noted and the method of constructing each lozenge. Consideration of the structure, however, led to some strange conclusions, notably the belief that the ceiling was originally 'flat' (ie, horizontal), and then raised when the crossing tower was rebuilt in the 14th century, in order to clear the new pointed arches (also Poole 1855, 214–15). By the end of the 19th century, this had been revised to the view that the ceiling was always canted but the whole had been raised in the 14th century (Sweeting 1898; 1932, 84; Peers 1906, 446). Meantime, although not consistently, the nave ceiling made it into popular guides, as 'unique' and 'remarkably interesting' (eg, King 1862; Sweeting 1898;

Dry 1906).

A real leap in understanding the ceiling and its various contexts was not made until 1937 with the publication of C J P Cave's and Tancred Borenius's major paper. They at once argue against the idea of the ceiling having been raised, for the first time discuss the roof as the structural support to the ceiling and introduce a wide range of comparative material – psalters originating in Peterborough, the few remaining near-contemporary ceilings elsewhere, contemporary wall paintings and Limoges caskets – in order to better understand Peterborough's ceiling and its context. As a consequence, its date moved into the early 13th century. Only a few years later, E W Tristram published the first part of his great catalogue of *English medieval wall painting* (1944), drawing on similar material, and coming to similar conclusions, suggesting it was painted *c* 1220 despite its 'essentially Norman' character. In an echo of older less well-informed studies, he describes the painting as 'virile and almost barbaric', no doubt a consequence of the repeated unsympathetic repaintings.

By comparison with Cave and Borenius, and Tristram, Folke Nordström's paper of 1955 advanced a number of highly speculative theories, including: identifying some of the figurative elements as part of an Aristotelian schema; relating others to medieval number symbolism and aspects of medieval theology; and the whole to Bishop Grosseteste's optical theories. The latter is most unconvincing since it is only possible to 'see' the optical illusion after it has been pointed out, and then only with difficulty. The speculation, though, masked genuine advances, for instance in increasingly accurate identification of the figurative elements, including recognising the Liberal Arts for the first time.

Conservation and discovery

The next major advance in understanding the ceiling and related structures stems from the conservation programme of 1998–2003, as reported here (Chapter 6). As in the 19th and 20th centuries, neither the earlier structures, such as the nave roof, nor the ceiling itself can be properly understood without also grasping the difficulties through which we see them today. The transept roofs do not survive at all; only fragments of the transept ceilings remain. Of the nave roof, to which the ceiling is attached, only truncated scissor braces and the truncated lower collar of each scissor truss survives; the ceiling itself contains numerous replacement timbers and has been comprehensively overpainted; the upper surface cannot be viewed at all without removing the hessian backing applied in 1926–7. By a miracle, the north portico roof survives almost intact, and the iconography of the nave ceiling has barely changed despite the near-obliteration of the medieval paintwork. What survives does so both because of, and in spite of, a series of minor and major interventions: principally significant repainting in the 1740s and 1830s, and significant structural works in the 1830s, 1880s and 1920s (Table 2; Chapter 5).

The conservation programme was also, naturally, a programme of investigation. Each of these complex, truncated, restored, overpainted structures is now better understood; the discoveries are set out in full in the following chapters and some have already been referred to. The tree-ring analysis has been crucial for establishing a new chronology for ceilings and roofs and for understanding timber supply (Chapter 2.3, 2.4; Chapter 3.2, 3.3; Chapter 4.2; Chapter 5.4). The truncated nave roof is fully realised in its medieval form (Chapter 2.2; Fig 20). The structural analysis of the ceiling by Hugh Harrison shows that far more of the medieval timbers survived than anticipated (Chapter 4.1) and also allows us to appreciate fully for the first time the sheer complexity of the object, and the importance of that complexity in contributing to its aesthetic quality. The master carpenter chose not to insert flat tie-beams, so the ceiling is radically different from the horizontal design of the earlier transept ceilings. Instead it is a three-dimensional object, much of whose life and beauty stems from the interaction between the lozenge shapes and the constraints imposed by the canted structure, with rows of differently sized lozenges forcing tapering spaces between them.

Although the medieval painting is heavily overlaid by later repaints, thorough sampling and careful examination by Richard Lithgow and the paint analysts revealed much about the original aesthetics of the ceiling (Chapter 4.3, 4.4), for instance the use of a sophisticated palette including azurite for flesh tones, which hints at a much higher degree of artistic skill than we can see today. Most of the ceiling's area may, in probability, have remained unpainted. Raking light showed lost elements in low relief. Paint was found underneath original nails, implying both that the boards were painted before being fixed and that there was a high degree of collaboration between the carpenters and the painters.

Using the new discoveries and looking at the images afresh, Paul Binski's authoritative art-historical analysis re-examines date, style and patronage, and shows the iconography mirrors popular medieval themes: founders (the kings and bishops); proto-humanist subjects (the Liberal Arts, sun and moon – the only such English monumental representation); musicians (foolish and good); and vice (the drolleries), as well as religious subjects directly relating to the liturgical arrangements below (Chapter 4.5).

The post-medieval repair phases were also examined by the conservation team, and many documents looked at for the first time (Chapter 5). This not only provides a valuable account of these structures through time, but was necessary in order for the team to understand the original phases. Similarly, their conservation was also sometimes necessary in order to preserve the whole, and the repair history of all structures is brought up-to-date in the final chapter (Chapter 6), a record of the 1998–2003 conservation programme and the recording strategies adopted. We hope these sections will be of use not just to future custodians of Peterborough Cathedral but to those of other great medieval buildings.

Table 2 Chronological outline of building work and repair to the main body of Peterborough Cathedral, from the laying of the foundation stone in 1118 to the 1920s, where relevant to the nave ceiling and related structures

Period	Building work/repair
Medieval	
1118	foundation stone laid of new church (from Hugh Candidus's chronicle: Mellows 1949, 98)
1140	first service held in new presbytery (from Hugh Candidus and the Anglo-Saxon Chronicle: Mellows 1949; Swanton 2000)
Mid 12th century	based on architectural evidence and masons' marks, the nave south aisle wall built now in order to enclose the cloister, along with parts of the nave arcades (Chapter 2.1)
1155–75	building of the crossing tower and transept, along with some of the principal nave walls, in order to buttress the tower (from Hugh Candidus and masons' marks: Mellows 1949; Chapter 2.1)
1177–93	the nave completed 'right up to the [west] front' (Robert of Swaffham's chronicle: Sparke 1723, 99; translation Halliday 2009), that is, the first eight bays and some or all of bay 9, with its twin west towers; tree-ring analysis supports this date (Chapter 2.3, 2.4)
1193–1220s	the west front built, along with bays 9–10 and the western transept; in general, dating and phasing unclear but now tree-ring analysis shows that the west front roofs were put on in the late 1220s (Chapter 2.3, 2.4; Chapter 4.2)
1203–15	Bayesian analysis of tree-ring dates shows that this is when the main transept was ceiled with wood (Chapter 3.3)
1238	the church was consecrated (recorded by Robert of Swaffham and Matthew Paris: Sparke 1723, 117; King forthcoming; *Chron Majora*, iii, 517)
1238	tree-ring analysis indicates that either a) the nave ceiling cannot have been begun before 1238 or b) the nave ceiling cannot have been completed before 1238 (Chapter 4.2)
1372 or later	crossing tower rebuilt using timbers felled in winter 1371–2 (Tyers 2004)

Table 2 (cont)

Period	Building work/repair
Post-medieval	
1662	repairs to the 'painted roofe over the quire' costing 17s (CUL, PDC MS 52, ann 1662)
1660s	numerous repairs to roofs around the cathedral including to the 'north ile' and the 'south ile' which may indicate the transept rather than the nave aisles; often it is not possible to tell from the accounts where has been repaired although 'holes over quire body of church where it rained in' were repaired in 1669 (CUL, PDC MS 52, ann 1669; also tie beam with 1668 date in south transept: Chapter 5.1)
1671	whitewashing of upper part of church (for £25) and £8 for 'mending all the seeling of the church' (CUL, PDC MS 52, ann 1670–1, fo 4v)
1676–7	scaffolding was taken down 'from the peece of work in the cieling in the quire'; also repairs to 'the ceiling over the Bps seat', 'the ceiling over the altar' and 'the cieling in the quire', when 81ft of board was used and 9 yards painted (CUL, PDC MS 53, ann 1676–7, fos 2–3)
1677–8	'work don in the roof of body of church', total spend £23 3s 4d; plumbing work in 1678 (CUL, PDC MS 53, ann 1677–8, fos 2v and 4v)
1678	reconnection of south transept 'isle' roof to the crossing tower, total spend £25 1s 11d (CUL, PDC MS 53, ann 1678, fo 3v)
1679–80	repairs to roofs at east end of church and north transept 'isle' costing £9 2s 11d, including new boards and timbers (CUL, PDC MS 53, ann 1679–80, fo 2)
1694	plumbers' work on north aisle and body of church (CUL, PDC MS 35, ann 1694, fo 43)
1740s	repair, washing and repainting of nave ceiling, recorded by Pownall some 30 years later and also in Stukeley's diary entry for 17 August 1747, although it is not clear to which ceiling he is referring (Pownall 1789, 149; Stukeley 1887, 70)
1761	south end of roof of south transept at least replaced and whole re-covered with Westmorland slates (PCL, PDC MS 54, fo 115; NRO, PDC Box X5157, ann 1761)
1763	decision made to replace lead with Westmorland slate over 'quire' (PCL, PDC MS 54, fo 118v)
1767	'part of the roof of the south isle … latterly fallen in' and required urgent repair – not clear whether this is nave aisle or south transept (PCL, PDC MS 54, fo 124v)
1824	roof of south transept repaired and about half the timbers new as recommended by Wilson of Lincoln (CUL, PDC MS 35, fo 64; NRO, ML 874, ann 1824)
1825	painting of south transept ceiling, possibly only in white (NRO, PDC Box X5052, ann 1826–7)
1827	north transept roof replaced to plan by Blore (NRO, PDC/E. 211 [X505]; PCL, Irvine Papers, v, fo 41); ceiling subsequently repainted in white and umber (NRO, PDC Box X5052, ann 1828–9)
1834–6	nave ceiling repainted; inscriptions on boards (1834 on the new archbishop figure; 1835 and 1836 on the ashlar boards); list of paints given in a receipt (NRO, PDC Box X5053, ann 1834–7 and ann 1836)
1835	roof of nave rebuilt by Ruddle to plans by Blore, and re-covered with slate not lead (NRO, PDC Box X5053, ann 1834–7 and ann 1836)
1847–8, 1850–1, 1852–3, 1856, 1862	minor repairs to south transept ceiling in each year, with replacements in deal (NRO, PDC Box X5054, ann 1847–8, ann 1850, ann 1853, ann 1856, ann 1862)
1863	minor repairs to nave ceiling by Ruddle (NRO, PDC Box X5055, ann 1863)
1875	minor repairs to nave roof and ceiling (NRO, PDC Box X5055, ann 1875–6)
1877	minor repairs to south transept ceiling (NRO, PDC Box X5055, ann 1877–81)
1883–6	central tower taken down and rebuilt, causing minor disruption to east end of ceiling (Chapter 5.4)
Late 1880s	major modifications to south transept roof and major restoration of north and south transept ceilings by Pearson (NRO, PDC Box X5096 PDC RP18; PDC Box X5097 PDC RP42)
1924	major repairs to north transept roof and hessian backing to ceiling (Moore 1925)
1926–7	major repairs to nave roof and hessian backing to ceiling (Moore 1925)
1927	major repairs to south transept roof and hessian backing to ceiling (Moore 1925)

1.3 RECORDING AND TEXTUAL CONVENTIONS

For the conservation project, the following conventions were adopted for recording and referencing material relating to the nave roof and ceiling (Fig 9). The nave bays were numbered 1 to 10 from east to west, in accord with the usual practice of counting from the crossing outwards; piers are similarly numbered, with pier 1 being the pier west of the crossing pier. The truncated nave roof trusses, comprising sections of the lower collar and scissor braces, were numbered 1 to 81 from east to west (the timbers of the 81st truss are inaccessibly embedded in the modern firewall). The nave ceiling is physically made up of a total of 160 rectangular panels, arranged in 40 north–south rows with four panels per row; each row comprises one panel on the canted area each side and two in the central area. In terms of the overall design, a quarter of each of two lozenges appears on each panel. A grid reference system was used to locate each nave ceiling panel and individual boards. Starting from the west and working east, the ceiling was divided into the north–south rows, numbered 0–39 (following the numbering in Wolfgang Gärtner's 1988 inspection report). The four panels in each north–south row were numbered from north to south I–IV. In addition, the boards within each panel were located alphabetically, with 'a' being always the easternmost board, giving an individual board reference of, for example, 23/II/e. The north and south ashlar boards (the vertical boards above the wall plate, also referred to as the frieze) were numbered sequentially by side (1–45 on the south side, 1–54 on the north side), and associated with adjacent ceiling panels. The west end vertical boards were simply assigned numbers 1–50, from north to south. At the east end there is an additional row (row 40) of panels infilling between the end of the 13th-century ceiling (row 39) and the 14th-century crossing arch.

Although the wooden ceilings in the transept arms are the precursors of the nave ceiling, the transept ceilings were investigated secondarily, in 2001–2 after the fire. The north and south transept ceilings are almost identical in terms of dimensions and layout and so were numbered similarly for recording purposes (Fig 10). Each transept ceiling is made up of a total of 130 panels, arranged in rows, referred to alphabetically from north to south as A–N and numbered 0–9 from west to east. Individual boards within each panel are located alphabetically, with 'a' being the easternmost board. In this volume, for example, a panel is referred to as south transept M/5 and a specific board as south transept K/2/f. The perimeter boards were numbered according to which side of the ceiling they were on and then sequentially, that is n1– (north side board 1 onwards), e1–, s1–, w1–.

Both the transept and nave ceilings are described in this volume as 'clinker-built', a term normally used in relation to boats made with a skin of overlapping boards. 'Shiplap' is another term for skins of overlapping boards but generally refers to boarded exterior walls. 'Clinker' is the term used here (eg, Chapter 3.1; Chapter 4.1) as it was felt it best describes the construction at Peterborough.

Felling dates obtained from tree-ring analysis are quoted following the accepted conventions: empirically derived individual felling date ranges are 95% confidence intervals but combined felling date ranges (using what is also called the 'truncation method' in Chapter 2.4) from empirically derived individual felling dates are not (these are cited as, eg, c 1225–30). Those using the Bayesian OxCal Combine function are 95% probability estimates and are cited in italics (1224–34) (eg, Chapter 2.4; Chapter 3.3). The north portico roof trusses were numbered from east to west for sampling purposes.

The paint samples referred to in this volume are listed in

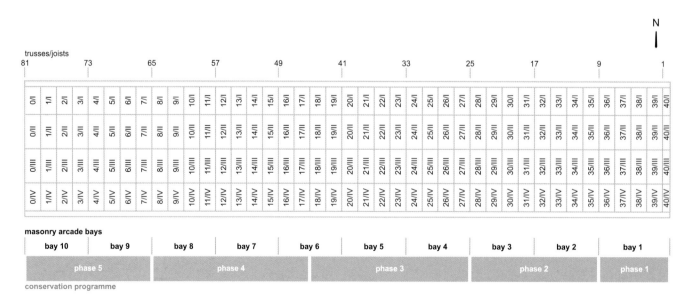

Fig 9 The recording conventions for the nave ceiling (reflected view, ie as if viewed in a mirror below, thus keeping the cardinal points in their usual relationship, north to top) (not to scale)

Table 9, appended to Chapter 6.

The core of the archive comprises the five phase reports for the nave (each a volume of text and graphics, a volume of colour plates and a volume of colour slides), as well as the report on the transept ceilings (a volume of text, graphics and plates, and a volume of colour slides) (see Harrison and Lithgow nd a–f). In addition, there are numerous short reports and an archive of correspondence. The hard copies may be found in the Northamptonshire Record Office (NRO) and digital records (including of photographs, board-by-board database and film footage of conservation) at the Archaeological Data Service (ADS).

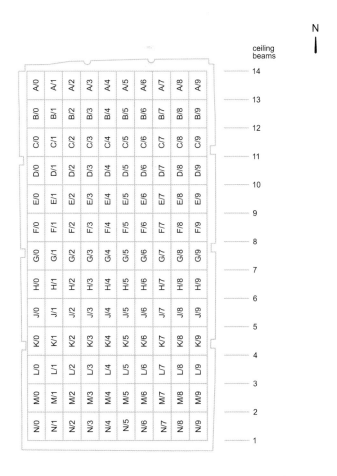

Fig 10 The recording conventions for the transept ceilings (reflected view of the north transept, ie as if viewed in a mirror below, thus keeping the cardinal points in their usual relationship, north to top) (not to scale)

2 THE MEDIEVAL NAVE AND NAVE ROOF

The raison d'être of the conservation project, the painted wooden ceiling, is suspended from the timber structure that forms the nave roof, which is itself supported by the stone walls of the nave. Discussion of the form (below, 2.2) and date (below, 2.3 and 2.4) of the medieval nave roof is preceded logically here then by an examination of the chronology and sequence of construction of the masonry nave itself (Fig 11; below, 2.1). The question of to what extent the builders fulfilled what was evidently their original intention to erect a vault over the nave below the roof is also considered. Mackreth (below, 2.1) argues in this chapter that a stone vault was indeed built, but fairly rapidly demolished and replaced by the ceiling that we see now; elsewhere Hall (Chapter 1.2) and Binski (Chapter 4.5) take an alternative view, suggesting that the idea for a vault was abandoned before anything other than the springers and wall ribs were in place.

2.1 BUILDING THE NAVE

Donald Mackreth

The masonry

A study of the masons' banker marks has revealed much which, when read with the account of chroniclers, allows the divisions in the construction of an apparently seamless building to be discerned. The accessible masons' marks, from the apse to the beginning of the western transept, have provided welcome information that, accompanied by the analysis of the seemingly monotonous Romanesque capitals, allows clear stages of construction to be seen (Fig 12).

As we have seen (Chapter 1.2; Table 2), Martin de Bec (1132×33–55) finished the presbytery and William de Waterville (1155–75) completed the transept, built the three storeys of the central tower and laid out the choir. He also covered the cloisters with lead (Mellows 1949, 130). He or his master mason changed from the habits of the masonic lodge up to this time by restricting the use of banker marks on the exposed faces of the ashlar blocks.

The style of scallop capitals used under Martin de Bec (Fig 12) is rather similar to that of the simple cushion capitals which appear generally in the blind arcading assignable to him. Also shown in Fig 12 are the more individual masons' marks belonging to the piers. The latter contain common marks such as the broad arrow, linked Vs,

Fig 11 View of the interior of the nave in 1898, looking east (*The Architect* 1898, no. 136)

pentagrams and crosses. The more individual ones are the initials, buckle and bow and arrow. Fig 12 shows the same kind of elements assignable to William de Waterville. The capitals, with facets and fluting, contrast markedly with those made before and after him. There are few masons' marks of common types but the leaf tip and 'IUo', or occasionally, 'IoU', are distinctive.

Fig 13 shows in diagrammatic form the sequence of construction identifiable in the south and north elevations of the nave. If the successive stages of construction on each side are considered, there is a contrast. Martin de Bec hardly did anything on the north, his main thrust being on the south to close the north side of the cloister where the late Saxon monastic church had stood. The masons' marks suggest that at the same time he built the main part of the south aisle and arcade. This phase of the arcade ended against the west wall of the intended twin-towered west front. William de Waterville completed the cloister and began the next stage of

Martin de Bec, 1132–55

south arcade, pier 5, respond capitals

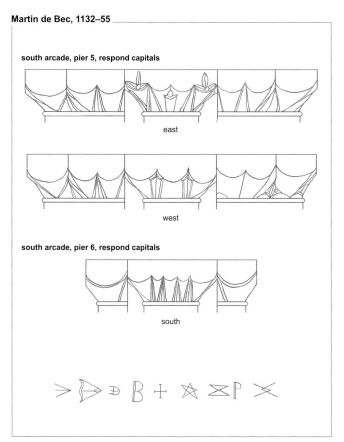

William de Waterville, 1155–75

north transept clerestory

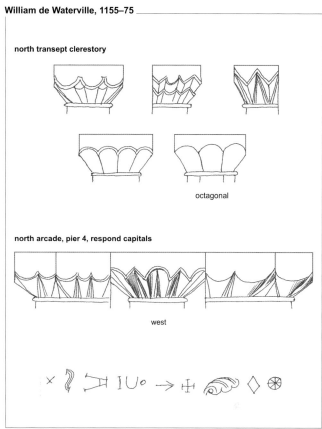

Benedict phase 1, 1177–85/90

north arcade, pier 9, respond capitals

north arcade, pier 5, respond capitals

north arcade, pier 8, respond capitals

'signature pier', pier 3, north gallery

pier 4

north clerestory

south clerestory

additional marks in nave

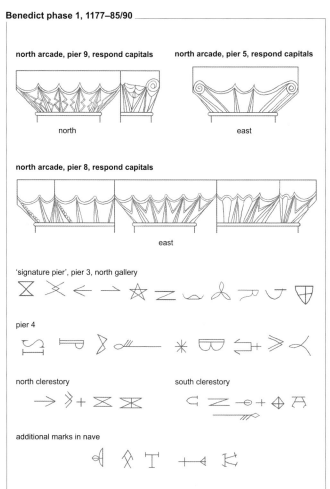

Benedict phase 2, 1185/90–3

north aisle, pier 10, north wall arcade

north gallery, pier 10, respond capitals

south arcade, pier 10, respond capitals

the only mark in bay 10 on the south gallery

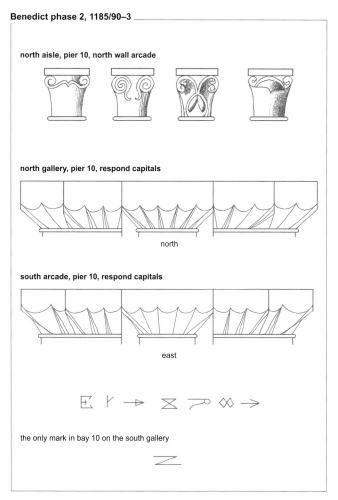

Fig 12 Sample capitals and masons' banker marks from the time of abbots Martin de Bec (1132x33–55), William de Waterville (1155–75) and Benedict (phase 1, 1177–85/90; phase 2, 1185/90–3) (not to scale) (drawn by Donald Mackreth)

the south tower. However, his main effort was to support his new tower and this is especially clear on the north (Fig 5; Fig 13 lower).

It is clear that the wall rib for a vault was inserted into bay 1 of the clerestory on each side, and this was carefully retained, or rebuilt, during the rebuilding of the central tower in the later 14th century (timber vault felling date of winter 1371–2: Tyers 2004) and in the 1880s (Table 2; Chapter 5.4). Furthermore, J T Irvine noted during demolition of the crossing tower that the wall rib on each side had been inserted into a pre-existing ashlar wall (PCL, Irvine Papers, iv, fo 89). In other words, Waterville intended there to be a horizontal ceiling as was also intended in both transepts. Any roof he had put up in the first bay was replaced under the

south elevation　　　　　　　　　　　▨ de Bec　　▨ de Waterville　　▨ Benedict phase 1　　▨ Benedict phase 2　　▨ refaced

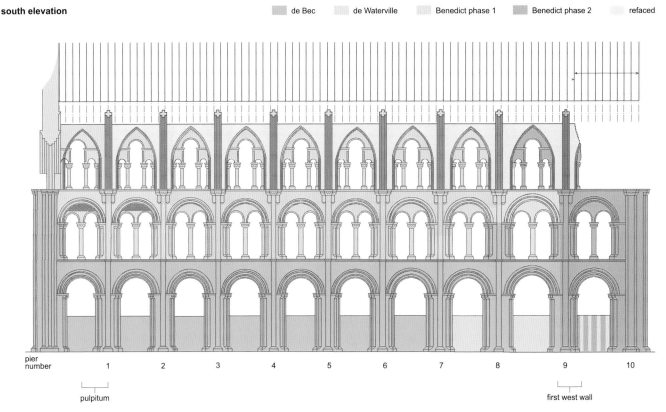

Fig 13 The sequence of construction seen in the nave elevations (drawn by Donald Mackreth)

next abbot, Benedict.

Waterville was deposed in 1175, and it is possible that his masons' lodge was disbanded. Benedict, prior of Christ Church Canterbury, was appointed abbot in 1177 and almost certainly re-established work; we have seen that Benedict built the whole of the nave *ad frontem* – 'up to the front' (Chapter 1.2; Table 2). Fig 12 gives designs of capitals and masons' marks under Benedict. These divide naturally into two sequential groups, with a dramatic change between the two. In the first phase, there are many masons' marks and a distinctive capital form not seen hitherto. In the second phase, there are few masons' marks and the capitals tend towards plain and regular scallops. In bay 10 on the north side there is the introduction of a new style of capital in the blind arcading.

Benedict had been effectively head of the priory at Canterbury, Thomas Becket being busy elsewhere for much of the time. When a disastrous fire burnt out the east end at Canterbury in 1174, Benedict began the rebuilding with French master mason William de Sens. He, therefore, had first-hand knowledge of the new French style, with its high vault, as it was being applied at Canterbury. Certainly, from his abbacy, Gothic elements appear and it is possible that he had a suite of capitals carved in the new style, which, in the event, were placed within a still-Romanesque building campaign. The chief elements are in pier 3 in the north gallery; the masons' marks in the pier supporting them are given in Fig 12, along with others. There was a change in the style of the bases from simple earlier Romanesque forms to a water-holding form in the main arcade. These, with the masons' marks, show that the central nave walls continued to be built in stepped sections, each buttressing the earlier work, as the earlier work buttressed the central tower. This is a standard method and can be seen, for instance, in Ely Cathedral, Wells Cathedral or Binham Priory (Fernie 2003, 100–2; Sampson 1998, 13–18; Pevsner and Wilson 1997, 389–92; Hall and Atherton 2011, 155).

The nave was initially intended to have nine bays with the ninth having twin towers over the aisles (Chapter 1.2). There should be no doubt that *ad frontem* refers to the aborted twin-towered front. The clerestory wall walks were brought to an end in the middle of piers 8, there being termination arches in the passages. More clearly, piers 8 and the east sides of piers 9 are much wider than the other arcade piers (Fig 3). Additionally, in the south gallery there are clear signs that a tower was started – the remains of an arch projecting from behind pier 8; and a small staircase tower built against a pre-existing wall, since removed (Fig 14). The remains bear the marks of the removed west wall, as well as of the later medieval floor. The west façade of the church may also have been started, suggested by a long vertical building break in the nave side of south pier 9. It is possible to argue that the south tower had been completed at least to the top of the clerestory to serve as a belfry. The west side disappeared when the nave was extended. The east side at gallery level survived complete until Dean Monk (dean 1822–30) tidied

up the area where the abbot's lodging once abutted the nave, the springing of the east arch surviving. Aside from the greater width of the pier, no evidence survives of a north tower, and opinion is divided as to whether or not the planned twin towers were completed (eg, Peers 1906, 440 and Reilly 1997, 82 versus Fernie 2000, 150).

A decision was made to extend the nave a further bay and finish with a west block with projecting transept and new twin towers again aligned with the nave aisles. The masons' marks suggest that this plan is also attributable to Benedict; the clerestory in bay 9 on both sides belongs to him. Within this work there is another building break. This break would not be visible at all were it not for an obvious change in tooling from diagonal to vertical on plain ashlars (on shafts and round piers, there is vertical tooling from an early period). It was this change that Peers observed, when he traced the building break:

the ninth bay was complete to the top of the clearstory, and the tenth bay to the sills of the clearstory windows. At the junction with the transepts the work had reached the floor of the clearstory passages, and at the eastern angles of the transepts it was some 6ft. below that point. In the gable

Fig 14 Evidence for a tower in the south gallery: the springing of the arch can be seen on the left-hand side and the rough back of the stair tower on the right-hand side

ends of the transepts the wall was only as high as the springing of the large north and south windows, and at the west angles of the transepts had sunk to the level of their sills. (Peers 1906, 440)

Some of this break is now difficult to observe – the north-west transept, for instance, was panelled in the 1930s to create a new baptistery. It would seem that the pause marked by the tooling started out as a planned building break (like the one at the east end of the nave), stepped to buttress the earlier work. The abrupt change in tooling may suggest that in the event the break was longer than planned, long enough for a complete change of masonry technique (and personnel?) either at the quarry or at the banker. However, no obvious stylistic changes mark the break – as opposed to the much greater stylistic difference between the nave and the western transept, which deliberately melds Romanesque and Gothic elements before reaching the distinctively Gothic west wall – so it is possible there was little pause between the two styles of dressing.

The clerestory levels of the north and south walls of the western transepts are typical of the openings in the nave, the south one with stylistically earlier elements, and so older than that on the north, its detailing being closely related to that of the nave. There is a suggestion that the lower part of the central west wall might also owe something to Benedict, if not actually completed by his death. It must have been during this building break that the decision was made to extend westwards again, this time to create the astonishing triumphal arch west porch, which has become such an icon of the City of Peterborough (Fig 6). Certainly, the stylistic uniformity of the western transepts with the west front at gable level would support this view.

It is tempting to suppose that the beginning of the west front is Benedict's 'magnificent work next to the brewery' (*et illud mirificum opus juxta Bracinum incepit*) (Sparke 1723, 101). The site of the brewery is not known, but can be surmised. The undercroft of the abbot's lodging (the west range of the cloister) was commonly given over to the cellarer and the brewery is likely to have been close by, most probably at the east end of what became the north range of the abbot's curia, the area where the palace and its grounds lie. It was clearly unfinished at the death of Benedict in 1193 (*sed morte preuentus consummare non potuit*).

Evidence for a vault and its date

Benedict's biggest innovation was, this author would argue, the introduction of a nave vault. To accommodate this, the roof consisted of rafters and scissor trusses, with a high collar to take the crown of the vault. Only the lowest elements of this roof survive because the painted ceiling was attached to it. Tree-ring dating has shown that bays 1 to 7 belong to the time of Benedict (there being no heartwood/sapwood boundaries in the bay 8 samples; below, 2.3). He built all the clerestories

save for that in bays 1 and 10, and the clerestory passage had haunching put in behind the bay divisions to buttress a stone vault. One haunch which was removed in the 19th century showed that the walling ashlar rode over it, evidence that the haunching and the passage were constructed *pari passu*; no-one wastes ashlar by covering it over.

Other indications of a vault include the cutting back of the vault capitals. This can be seen in Fig 15, which shows the head of the shaft at pier 8 on the south side just under the clerestory string (also Thurlby 2006). The regular coursing is interrupted by larger stones, three at the top and a make-up stone at the base to level up. In all, five courses are disrupted. The wall surface shows coarse reworking leaving the profiles of capitals and short shafts clearly demarcated.

On the string-course the profile of the abacus above the now cut-back triple capital is suggested where the redressing had not been efficiently carried out. The section of the abacus is similar to that over the capitals of the west closing arch of the nave (Fig 16). The form of the capitals there is that of phase 2 of Benedict's abbacy (Fig 12), the whole of bay 10 of the nave, save the arcade level on the north, being part of the extension (Fig 13). That set of capitals is set over a triple wall shaft to suit the major terminal arch of the nave. The ordinary wall shaft with capital or 'mast' was supplemented with short shafts to suit the diagonal ribs (here of Gothic design) of the vault. Fig 16 also shows the junction of the abacus with the string to the east suggesting that the remains seen in Fig 15 must be part of a similar arrangement.

Fig 15 The head of the shaft at nave pier 8 on the south side, showing the cutting back

Fig 16 The west end of the nave, north side, with the western transept on the left; note the projecting diagonal vault rib

to be the location of the retrochoir at, for example, another Cistercian house, Bordesley Abbey (Stopford and Wright 1998, 307). This seems to have been accepted, but cautiously and in relation to Cistercian houses (Friar 1996, 380). At Benedictine Peterborough the term could be applicable to the nave as a whole.

Taking this interpretation forward then, the documentary evidence for Peterborough would strongly suggest that the vaults would have been completed before 1214, when Robert of Lindsey formally became abbot. They are unlikely to have been constructed until the west works were well advanced. The Pope imposed an interdict on the kingdom in 1208 which effectively meant that the church ceased to function in the country at large. When Acharius died, no successor could officially be appointed to fill his place until 1213 when the interdict was lifted. However, the monks had the right to elect and it seems likely from his acts before formal election that the sacrist, Robert of Lindsey, was chosen abbot in 1211 (Sparke 1723, 107–8) and before he was confirmed by King John in 1214.

The inner face of the clerestory outer walls has putlog holes at floor level, some now plugged with stone at the behest of J L Pearson. These would have secured the ends of timbers running out into the nave. They would have supported timber staging from which the vault could be put up; and used again when the vault was taken down. The latter would have required the face of the walls outside the wall ribs to be refaced, it having previously been faced in rag as it had not been visible from the interior. As work advanced west, the less frequent the reuse of diagonal dressing becomes. Fig 17 shows some of the facing above the

The assessment of when the vaulting was completed depends on the monastic chronicle. After Benedict there came Andreas (1194–9) who had been prior and was greatly respected and aged. He was succeeded by Acharius (1200–10), prior of St Albans. Neither is recorded as having done anything in the church. The next abbot after Benedict to be credited with work on the church is Robert of Lindsey (1214–22), and much depends on understanding where the work might have been. While sacrist, he whitened the vaults in the retrochoir (*fecit dealbare volsuras in retro choro*: Sparke 1723, 107). 19th-century ecclesiologists called any area east of the high altar the retrochoir, a usage which continues (eg, Peers 1906; Reilly 1997, 99n; Chapter 4.5). Peterborough had no space beyond the apse until *c* 1500, therefore there must be another meaning. To any monk sitting in the choir, all attention was to the east, therefore what lay behind him was to the west, in the nave and beyond.

The term occurs in modern literature in the discussion of the context for a pulpitum at Tintern where it is bluntly stated that the retrochoir lay between the choir proper and the rood, the latter being at the east end of the lay brothers' church (Harrison et al 1998, 249–51). This is also understood

Fig 17 Vertical dressing on the facing above the south wall ribs in bay 8

wall ribs and vertical dressing which cannot have been there as part of the Benedict phase 1 work. The date at which the vault was removed, the facing of ashlar inserted and the present ceiling put up is indicated by the tree-ring dating of the latter (below, 2.3, 2.4). If the staging was needed to take out the vault, it was also needed to put up the ceiling, an operation which could not have been completed before 1238 at the earliest (Chapter 4.2). In conclusion then, there is potentially a gap of some 40 years between the dating of the scissor truss roof and that of the wooden ceiling during which this author believes the nave vault would have been largely in place.

2.2 THE STRUCTURE OF THE MEDIEVAL NAVE ROOF

Hugh Harrison

The original medieval scissor truss nave roof structure comprised 81 scissor trusses, each composed of two scissor braces, two collars (upper and lower) and two common rafters. Samuel Ware's *c* 1805 drawing of the nave roof (Ware 1809, pl 18: Fig 18), and that of H Ansted in 1827 (Britton 1997, pl XIV), both show, albeit with inaccuracies, a scissor brace roof having existed prior to the cathedral architect Edward Blore's reconstruction of the roof in the 1830s. Blore dismantled the old roof except for the timbers to which the ceiling is attached, and built the new roof using some of the original timbers (Fig 19); this destroyed all evidence of the construction of the base of the roof, at wall plate level, including the ashlar posts or pieces. What remains of the medieval (12th-century: 2.3 and 2.4) scissor truss roof are the lower sections of the scissor braces (transformed by Blore into sloping ceiling joists) and the lower collars (transformed into horizontal ceiling joists) (Fig 20; Fig 21). The location of the lower collar exposes a considerable length of the bottom of the scissor brace which creates the sloping or canted sides of the (later) ceiling (the ceiling structure is described in detail in Chapter 4.1). Significant numbers of medieval timbers – including original rafters – are evidently incorporated into the rafters of Blore's reconstructed roof but study of the extant roof structure per se was not part of the original project brief.

The medieval oak roof is reconstructed in Fig 20 (lower). A few reused timbers found in the present ceiling structure were measured and those with sufficient constructional details were recorded (eg, trusses 71, 73 and, embedded in the firewall, 81) and carefully projected on to the reconstruction study for the original roof, allowing also for the adjusted pitch measured from the weathering course (the sloping string course) discovered on the exterior of the west transept north tower east wall. The results of this projection were inconclusive for truss 73 south scissor brace and truss 81 horizontal lower collar, but an excellent match was obtained for truss 71 south scissor brace; however, the

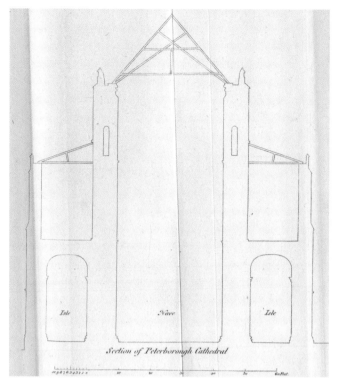

Fig 18 Section of Peterborough Cathedral: drawing by Samuel Ware, *c* 1805 (Ware 1809, pl 18)

Fig 19 General view inside the nave roof space, showing the existing roof structure largely of the 1830s

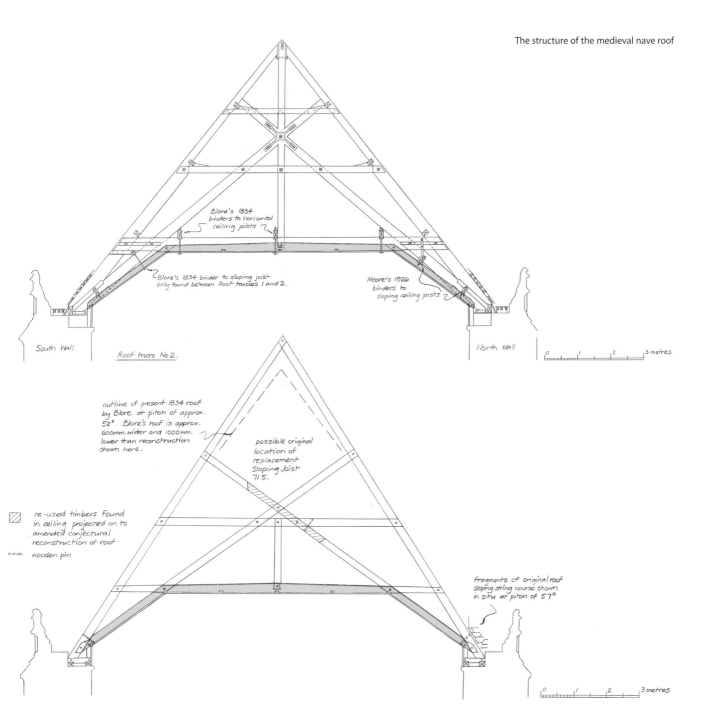

Blore's 1834 binders to horizontal ceiling joists

Blore's 1834 binder to sloping joist only found between Roof trusses 1 and 2.

Moore's 1926 binders to sloping ceiling joists

South Wall

Roof truss No 2.

North Wall

0 1 2 3 metres

outline of present 1834 roof by Blore at pitch of approx. 52°. Blore's roof is approx. 600mm wider and 1000mm lower than reconstruction shown here.

possible original location of replacement sloping joist 71 S.

re-used timbers found in ceiling projected on to amended conjectural reconstruction of roof

wooden pin

fragments of original roof sloping string course shown in situ at pitch of 57°

0 1 2 3 metres

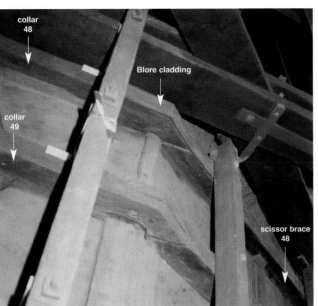

Fig 20 (upper) The existing nave roof structure (truss 2) showing the medieval ceiling suspended from the 1830s roof; (lower) reconstruction study of the medieval nave roof, suggesting original placement of some reused timbers, with the surviving section to which the ceiling is attached shown pink (general configuration of roof as Ware's 1805 drawing, here Fig 18) (drawn by Peter Ferguson)

Fig 21 Part of the existing nave roof structure, showing the truncated junctions of scissor braces (right) and the south ends of collars (left) of trusses 49 (lower; original) and 48 (original plus Blore cladding of halving joint), looking east

25

Fig 22 A surviving original square peg in the centre dovetail of collar 48; original pins are typically more oval than square

Fig 23 Halving joint of scissor brace (left) and lower collar: 'A' and 'B' are pinnings; 'C' is a hole bored for tree-ring analysis (truss 75)

reconstruction shown in Fig 20 must remain tentative. None of the existing ashlar posts have so far been definitely identified as original. The surviving lower collar lengths are now around 7m, but it seems likely these were 10m long prior to truncation.

An examination of the remaining sections of the 81 scissor braced trusses of the original roof showed that all of the medieval lower collars, which subsequently served as the horizontal ceiling joists, from east to west as far as and including 71 measure nominally 9in deep × 5in wide (c 230 × 130mm) in the centre and 7 × 5in (c 180 × 130mm) at each end. In the centre of the west face of each collar is a single-sided dovetail pinned joint (Fig 22) into which would have been fitted a post linking this lower collar to an upper collar of the old roof. Where the scissor braces cross the lower collars, they are half-jointed and pinned, both vertically through the centre line of the joint ('A' in Fig 23) and horizontally through the centre of the halving joint ('B' Fig 23).

Truss 73 lower collar (part of the westernmost truss of bay 9), however, measures nominally 6 × 6in (c 150 × 150mm) with very little taper (camber) (north end c 150mm wide × 150mm deep, centre 160 × 170mm, south end 155 ×

160mm) (Fig 29). Importantly, all the medieval lower collars from here to the west end (ie, 73 in bay 9, 74–76 and 78–80 in bay 10; collars 72 and 77 are 1920s replacements) are over 1in (>25mm) wider in cross section than the average lower collar. Lower collar 73 is original, with bird's beak (or 'bird's mouth') joints for noggins (short pieces of timber between each truss) and a (unusually wide) dovetail joint in the centre, but has a different section, has very little camber, nor has it a halving joint at the south end (Fig 24). This suggests that the timber might originally have been temporarily placed there as part of an end truss for the roof, pending a decision on the final configuration of the west end and its transepts, and when bay 10 was added it was found unnecessary to remove it (below). Unfortunately, tree-ring analysis produced no useful data for lower collar 73, only a tree-ring date of after 1163 (bay 9, collar sample 28M; below, 2.3).

At their lower (bottom) ends the braces were found to have been shaped and pinned to the rafters of the roof trusses, terminating in a pinned side lap joint (Fig 25; Fig 26 illustrates this arrangement). On the underside at this point, mortices remain into which the original ashlar posts were

Fig 24 Truss 73: joint between south scissor brace (left) and lower collar (right), looking west and showing a beautifully fashioned pin securing the joint driven from the east side

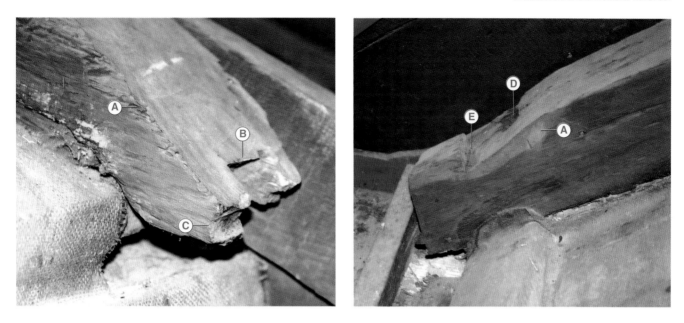

Fig 25 Trusses 63 and 64: left – shaped ('A') bottom end of north scissor brace 64, with mortice 'B' into which the original ashlar post was tenoned and pinned 'C'; right – bottom end of north scissor brace 63: 'A' shaped shoulder to former medieval rafter; 'D' pinhole and 'E' notch for the attachment of the rafter to the scissor brace

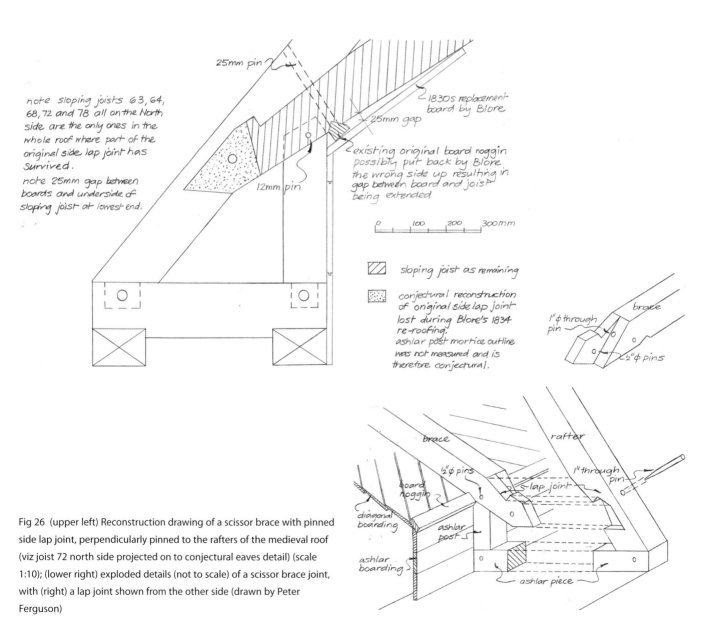

Fig 26 (upper left) Reconstruction drawing of a scissor brace with pinned side lap joint, perpendicularly pinned to the rafters of the medieval roof (viz joist 72 north side projected on to conjectural eaves detail) (scale 1:10); (lower right) exploded details (not to scale) of a scissor brace joint, with (right) a lap joint shown from the other side (drawn by Peter Ferguson)

tenoned and pinned. All the surviving roof joints were fixed with either ½in (c 12mm) or 1in (c 25mm) oak pins and examination of remaining pins shows them to have been beautifully made, with square shanks and widened heads. The north portico roof (c 1230; see 2.3) has a near-identical example of a pinned side lap joint (Fig 27).

No reliably identifiable carpenters' marks have been found on the surviving medieval roof structure which supports the ceiling. A selection of roman numerals can be found on timbers reused in the 1830s roof which one assumes come from the medieval roof, though their character is quite different from deeply cut carpenters' marks found on some other 13th-century timbers (eg, at St Albans: Harrison et al 2012; Munby 1996, 169). The structural timbers are well squared, and the joints accurately made with attention to fine detail such as the shaping of the pins (above). All the medieval timbers observed in bays 1–8 and in bay 9 as far west as truss 71 were converted in the same manner, that is, hewn on all three visible sides. They bear evidence of long striated marks or splits parallel with the edges of the beams (Fig 28), which suggests that the same workshop got out all these roof timbers.

An inspection of the timbers westwards from truss 73, the westernmost truss in bay 9, showed differences of

technique, which would imply that new carpenters had taken over. This would be understandable after a generation or so, the interval suggested as occurring before the construction of the roof above the extended nave, viz bay 10. On these original timbers (westernmost bays 9 and 10) see-sawing was found, for some timbers on all visible faces, with change points occurring from 20in (c 510mm) to 5ft (c 1.520m) from the centre of the length of the timber and sawing angles ranging between 60° and 75°. Fig 29 shows see-sawing on truss 73 lower collar, the westernmost truss of bay 9 (above). Some of these timbers are still hewn on one or two complete faces, truss 80 for example, exhibiting broad axe signatures, clear tool marks, and several instances of blade edge and travel signatures. Other faces are part sawn, part hewn, and on truss 80 lower collar a score mark can be seen near the junction of the sawing and hewing. Almost straight tree rings indicate that some timbers were obtained from large logs capable of providing four timbers (below, 2.3). To conclude, both the dimensions and conversion characteristics of timbers in bays 9/10, from truss 73 westwards, would suggest a different provenance. Sampled timbers with late dates in bays 9 and 10 which show significant variation in felling date

Fig 28 Striated marks or splits parallel with the beam edge, indicating hewing with an axe

Fig 29 See-sawing (arrowed) on a complete face of lower collar of truss 73; 'A' shows an empty bird's beak where the noggin is missing

Fig 27 A pinned side lap joint in the north portico roof

Discussion

The structural oak timbers are all of native English origin and generally derived from quartered or halved trees. The trees are of a quite slow-grown nature and are remarkably straight grained, with the earliest recorded ring dating to AD 887. The site master chronology constructed is extremely well replicated and matches well to tree-ring chronologies from across Europe as well as to virtually every contemporaneous data set from England and Wales. However, the best matches (Tyers 1999 for details) are mostly to other eastern and central English data and there seems little doubt that the timbers were derived from somewhere within this area. The unexpected dating of 69 of 70 measured sequences from the medieval roof timbers must be partly a reflection of the great length of the sequences derived from many of the samples, but may also be indicative of the exploitation of a common or at least remarkably similar woodland area for both the nave and north portico building works. This suggestion is potentially supported by statistical analysis of the tree-ring series using cluster methods (H-H Leuschner and T Reimer, pers comm), principal components analysis (J Spain, pers comm), and the Litton-Zainodin grouping procedure (Litton and Zainodin 1991) which all fail to indicate there are any consistent subgroupings within the data. If this is the case, a single woodland type or area was continually exploited for long straight slow-grown timbers for 40 to 60 years for the construction of these abbey roofs. This conclusion fits with the lack of documentary evidence for gifts of timber from the crown to the abbey in this period (Chapter 1.2).

The vast majority of the timbers in the truncated trusses in the nave are of late 12th-century date with the only later material identified in the nave roof being restricted to the west end of the nave, in bays 9 and 10 (above). The construction of the new west front and towers would have disturbed any pre-existing roof structure over nave bay 9 (above, 2.1). The tree-ring evidence appears to suggest that timbers from a putative roof over bay 9 may have been reusable, but it was also necessary to incorporate at least some fresh or stockpiled timbers during the roofing/reroofing of bay 9 and roofing of the extended area, that is bay 10 (Chapter 1.2). Three, or possibly four, of the sampled timbers from bays 9 and 10 are likely to be contemporary with the reconstruction of the end section of the nave. Assuming the nave ceiling was inserted only after all of this construction work was completed, this appears to suggest that the earliest possible date for the ceiling is *c* 1222–31 (the combined felling date range for the four later roof timbers in bays 9 and 10), a date further refined by the tree-ring analysis of the nave ceiling itself (Chapter 4.2). The trusses in the north portico appear to be contemporary with this disturbance, and construction there occurred probably shortly after felling of these timbers in the period *c* 1225–30.

2.4 THE BUILDING PROGRAMME AND THE TREE-RING DATING: AN INVESTIGATION USING BAYESIAN STATISTICS

Jackie Hall

Introduction, methodology and aims

It is clear from the preceding pages how valuable the tree-ring study of the early roofs at Peterborough has been. It has characterised the oak, given us estimated dates for the first phase nave roof (bays 1–8), and the north portico roof, and suggested that the roof over bays 9 and 10 may also be contemporary with the west front roof.

Despite the large numbers of samples, though, there was no bark and very little sapwood was found, therefore no precise felling dates for the primary timber of the nave or north portico. Thus, the given date ranges for each timber and structure are estimates rather than 'facts'. The desire to maximise the information from this large data set prompted the attempt by this author (as cathedral archaeologist) to further exploit the data. This was achieved by using a Bayesian approach, for both single date ranges and combined date ranges, developed by Dan Miles and Christopher Bronk Ramsey incorporating the methodology set out by Andrew Millard, available within OxCal (OxCal 2014; Millard 2002; Miles 2006; Bronk Ramsey 1995; 2008). Despite the recognised need for further research (Tyers 2008), the results for Peterborough detailed below are remarkable, agreeing extremely well with the documentary record and with the structural evidence, and throwing new light on some aspects of the building campaign.

As noted above by Ian Tyers, where only heartwood exists, there can only be a *terminus post quem* (tpq) for felling. Where the heartwood/sapwood (h/s) boundary survives, the felling date cannot be identified but, instead, quoted date ranges, at 95% confidence, are based on sapwood estimates. Before beginning the Bayesian analysis, it is important to review how sapwood estimates are made and, where there are several samples from single structures (as at Peterborough), how these estimates may be combined to give a single date range for each structure. Beyond that, we need to consider the problems of each combination method, and the difficulties of applying any method to major medieval building campaigns.

Sapwood estimates

The given felling date range for a sample with an h/s boundary but incomplete sapwood depends on an estimate of the number of missing sapwood rings. This sapwood estimate is based on empirical data using samples with complete sapwood. However, the number of sapwood rings varies – with side and height of the same tree; with age of tree; and regionally and temporally with climatic conditions.

Consequently, as more data have become available, sapwood estimates have changed. In 1987, 197 oak samples were used to propose a 95% confidence sapwood estimate of 10–55 rings for the whole of the British Isles (Hillam et al 1987). Thus, a sample with an identifiable h/s boundary dated to 1210 would have a felling date estimated to be within 1220–65, at 95% confidence; if the sample additionally had 20 sapwood rings, the felling estimate would be reduced to 1230–65. In 1997, Dan Miles used 920 samples from England and Wales to propose three different (but similar) estimates for three different regions (north and midlands; Wales and borders; south of England). In each region the 95% confidence range was narrowed by more than ten years. Although the new estimates were widely used, other laboratories developed estimates based on their own data and the particular region that a sample is from; this can be seen clearly in the round-up of tree-ring dates in recent issues of *Vernacular Architecture*. More recent research by Miles, using over 3000 samples, suggested that the material from England and Wales is relatively homogenous, although many of the data came from the south and west (Miles 2006).

Individual laboratories, however, continue to use their own estimates. Miles himself did not suggest a unified revised sapwood estimate, but instead a method of improving estimates for individual samples using the number of heartwood rings and the mean ring width as well as sapwood data. The extra data were incorporated using Bayesian statistics, the mathematical endpoint of Bayes's theorem, which is used to calculate how the degree of belief in a proposition changes with additional evidence. While the principle is straightforward, the mathematics will remain opaque to all but a few. (For an account of its relevance to buildings historians, see Bayliss 2007; also see Hamilton et al 2007.) The use of Bayesian statistics to produce individual felling date estimates, as developed by Miles and Bronk Ramsey and applied later in this section, is not yet routinely used (for the mathematics see http://c14.arch.ox.ac.uk/oxcalhelp/hlp_analysis_inform.html#dendro). The 95% probability range obtained from OxCal for a given sample with no precise felling date is analogous to the 95% confidence range of the conventional estimates. Put another way, with a large number of samples, our expectation should be that 1 in 20 of these samples will fall outside the given date range and will represent an outlier of the mathematical model.

Whatever method of estimating sapwood is used, it is vital to remember that a date range is just that, an estimate.

Date-range combination

Where a number of samples without complete sapwood are believed to come from a single-phase structure the date ranges may be combined, but this is not straightforward. There are three methods currently in use – two have been around for a long time and one is relatively new. They can briefly be described as the truncation (or common overlap) method, the h/s boundary mean method and a Bayesian statistical method.

In order to provide an example of each technique, a single bay of the nave – bay 1 – is used, representing part of a structure that might reasonably be assumed to be single phase (although see analysis below). Six samples were dated from nave bay 1 and three of these had an h/s boundary (Fig 32) Although shorter sapwood estimates had recently been introduced by the Sheffield laboratory (10–46 years), Ian Tyers used the long estimate of 10–55 because the Peterborough nave timbers appeared to be cut from very long-lived and slow-grown trees, both factors known to increase the number of sapwood rings (Tyers 1999, 6; above, 2.3).

TRUNCATION METHOD OF DATE-RANGE COMBINATION: 'PERIOD OF COMMON OVERLAP'

Ian Tyers calculated the combined date by using the period of common overlap, giving a date range of *c* 1169–88 for nave bay 1 (Tyers 1999, 10 and fig 6). This is the method

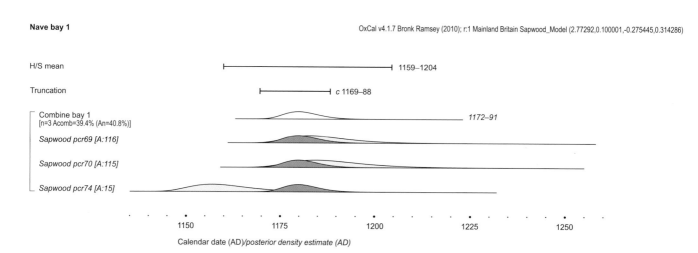

Nave bay 1

OxCal v4.1.7 Bronk Ramsey (2010); r:1 Mainland Britain Sapwood_Model (2.77292,0.100001,-0.275445,0.314286)

H/S mean — 1159–1204

Truncation — *c* 1169–88

Combine bay 1 [n=3 Acomb=39.4% (An=40.8%)] — 1172–91

Sapwood pcr69 [A:116]

Sapwood pcr70 [A:115]

Sapwood pcr74 [A:15]

Calendar date (AD)/*posterior density estimate (AD)*

1150   1175   1200   1225   1250

Fig 32 Nave bay 1 combined felling date ranges: the truncation and the h/s mean methods of combination are shown at the top with the Bayesian derived results below (individual felling date distributions are shown in light grey); here, the combined distribution is shown in outline, because the model failed

shown in the English Heritage guidelines of 1998 (Hillam 1998) and in many of the results listed in *Vernacular Architecture* around that time. This straightforward approach does not produce a definable confidence level and actually discards much of the information (also Miles 1997, 48; 2006, 92). One way of grasping this intuitively is to see the three date ranges as giving us six pieces of information (three start dates and three end dates). It is then clear that this truncation method uses only two of those pieces of information (the latest start date and the earliest end date) – two-thirds of the information has been discarded. If ten date ranges are combined using this method, then 90% of the information will be discarded. Also, as individual date ranges become further apart, the combined date range grows narrower, rather than reflecting the more widespread data.

H/S MEAN METHOD OF DATE-RANGE COMBINATION

Another method of combining date ranges, used by many dendrochronology laboratories, is to average the h/s boundaries and then to add on the sapwood estimate. In the example of nave bay 1, the average of the h/s boundaries is 1149 and the addition of the 10–55 year sapwood estimate gives a date range of 1159–1204. This uses all the information, and weights it correctly – the two later date ranges having twice as much impact as the earlier range – leading to a result with greater validity. Compared with the truncation method, the midpoint has changed from 1179 to 1182. However, the precision has not increased and will not increase, however many results with an h/s boundary are combined, because the same sapwood estimate is always added on to the mean. Ideally, the more times the observation is repeated, the better the result should be with respect to precision, while still maintaining accuracy, if the assumption that the timbers were felled at the same time is correct.

BAYESIAN METHOD OF DATE-RANGE COMBINATION

The straightforward answer to these issues is to use a statistical method of combining results, although things are rarely as straightforward as they seem. This means going back to the original mathematics used to model the data. In this case, the mathematical model successfully used to describe the number of sapwood rings is a log-normal distribution, as used for a long time in tree-ring dating, and the 95% confidence mid range estimate can be worked out from this (Hughes et al 1981).

Unfortunately, it is not easy to intuitively grasp statistical combination methods. It might best be shown by expressing each of our three date ranges for nave bay 1 as a graph where the shape of the graph is defined by the mathematical model and the area underneath it is equal to 1 (because we know that the tree has been felled, therefore the probability that it has been felled is 1). If the three graphs are 'factored' together then a much larger graph will be the result, but with a narrower taller profile. This must then be normalised

so that the area under the graph is again 1. Lastly, the 95% probability estimate is worked out from the new graph, giving the quoted combined range (cf Fig 32). Compared with the other methods, this should have the advantage that accuracy is maintained while precision is increased. However, until recently, no statistical method has been available for tree-ring data, probably because tree-ring date ranges are seen as sufficiently precise in themselves.

Coincidentally, at the same time as these questions were raised by the Peterborough data, Dan Miles and Christopher Bronk Ramsey developed a Bayesian method of predicting felling date ranges (above). This is publicly available in OxCal via the Sapwood function, while the output from two or more samples thought to represent a single felling event may be combined using the Combine tool (Miles 2006, 92–5). In our Peterborough nave bay 1 example, this method produces a *combined felling date range* of *1172–91*, significantly narrower than the h/s mean method. The midpoint is the same as with the h/s mean method, unsurprisingly, since all the information has gone into the calculation.

The Bayesian method also usefully provides 'indices of agreement', 'A' (and a Student's *t* test); A_{comb} are shown by the numbers with % signs in the graphs returned by the OxCal Combine function (eg, Fig 32) but they are not percentages and can go above 100 (Bayliss 2007, 79–81; Bronk Ramsey 2008, 48). The individual agreement indices show how well the individual date range fits with the model – in our bay 1 example, the assumption that all three timbers were felled at the same time. The combined agreement index (A_{comb}) shows how well the whole model works. For two samples, a threshold of 50% for A_{comb} is used as a guide to acceptability, but this threshold decreases as the number of combined samples increases (in order to keep to the ideal of 95% probability). Within the combined group, individual agreement indices lower than 60% may indicate samples that are outliers of the mathematical model (remembering that 1 in 20 results should be outliers for 95% probability). If the combined index of agreement is lower than the threshold, the model definitely needs to be re-examined. Perhaps the samples do not belong to a single felling date or period. For instance, one or more of the timbers may have been stockpiled, reused or introduced as a later repair. Alternatively, they may have anomalous growth characteristics. In the example of nave bay 1, A_{comb}=39.4% (the guide threshold for three samples is 40.8%), so it might be sensible here to question the underlying assumption that the three timbers were felled together (this is addressed later in this section).

In fact, within the Combine function, there is also the option of assuming that a few years of stockpiling has taken place, that is, the assumption that the collection of enough timber to build a given structure has taken more than a year. This – 'stockpiling prior' – has not been used in the following analysis since, although this is likely to be true, adding this further layer of interpretation might have obscured larger differences. Instead, knowledge of how well the model works for each bay is used here (below) to help develop different models of tree-felling.

When developing and testing Sapwood and Combine against many groups of timbers from single felling events of known date, Miles found that *combined felling date ranges* produced from large groups of samples are over-precise and drop below the ideal of 95% probability. He concludes that the optimum number of samples is seven to nine (Miles 2006, 93–4; Tyers 2008, 99, suggests 5–9 samples is ideal). This issue is a significant failing, but one that is likely to be ameliorated as further work goes into the programme. Bronk Ramsey (pers comm 2008) comments that the reason for this is probably due to the assumption of uncorrelated errors. The statistical method used for combination assumes that the uncertainties in each sample are independent. At some level this is clearly not the case – for example, some of the trees may come from adjacent locations or there may even be wood from the same tree that has not been identified as such.

Evaluation of Bayesian interpretation of tree-ring dates

In 2008 Cathy Tyers published an evaluation of the Bayesian interpretation of tree-ring dates, especially as expressed in the output of OxCal Combine. Using 13 case studies from ten locations, all with timber with known felling dates, she compared the known felling date with four date range combination methods: the period of common overlap (truncation method); the OxCal Combine function; and two h/s mean methods, using different sapwood estimates. Of these 13 examples 'specifically selected to illustrate some of the potential limitations of the [Combine] method' (Tyers 2008, 91), for only four does Combine produce acceptable results. For the other seven examples, Combine produces a date range, at 95% probability, that does not overlap at all with the known felling date, compared with only one non-overlapping result for the other three methods together. Tyers highlights, in particular, potential deficiencies in the temporal and geographical distribution of the data used to develop the underlying sapwood model, which Miles had also recognised (ibid, 99–103).

The Mainland Britain model (currently the only one publicly available) used in the Sapwood function was developed from empirical data mainly derived from relatively short-lived tree-ring series (25–100 rings) from vernacular or supra-vernacular buildings of the later medieval and early post-medieval periods. It is also dominated by material from south and west England. It is therefore potentially markedly different from the Peterborough assemblage, notably derived from much longer lived trees. However, the use of the Mainland Britain model through the Sapwood function on the nave roof samples produced results in close conformity to I Tyers's original individual date ranges (above, 2.3) based on the 10–55 sapwood estimate, that is, the model appeared to work, as will be seen below (Fig 33).

Major building campaigns and Peterborough

It is well known that major medieval building campaigns frequently used stockpiled timber or reused timber from earlier campaigns (Miles 1997, 50–5; Hillam 1998, 14–17; Hillam and Groves 1996). It was standard for institutions to buy the materials and pay the carpenters, plumbers, masons and so on separately. Since timber was extremely valuable – woodland was the 'treasure of his church' according to a late 13th-century abbot of Peterborough (Chapter 1.2) – it would always have been conserved, with any leftover timbers being saved for the next phase of building. Additionally, it may often have been necessary to gather very large timbers over a few years, if enough were not available from a single source at a single point in time.

Dan Miles's analysis of stockpiling showed that more than 75% of large high-status churches used stockpiled timbers and that a peak (across all building types) was reached in the 13th century (2006, 85–7). Although most stockpiled timber is only a few years old before it is used, there are examples of longer storage. At Lincoln, the roof over St Hugh's choir (built after 1196) contains many early timbers that pre-date the 1185 earthquake and which may have been felled but not yet used (Laxton et al 2001, 40–6). At Salisbury, the three main post-medieval phases of nave roof replacement, with many precise felling dates, all clearly used stockpiled timber, particularly for difficult-to-obtain tie beams, ranging from six to nine years old (Miles 2005).

What these examples show is the potential hazards of interpreting tree-ring data with no felling dates, since the story behind the data can be much more complex than that implied by a simple single combined date range, especially in major buildings. Despite these hazards, and the issues raised by C Tyers (above), the Combine function is used here to explore the nave roof tree-ring data further. This is based on the apparent success of using the Mainland Britain model in Sapwood function (on which OxCal Combine builds) and a strong desire to exploit available statistical methods, as well as the conventional combine techniques already discussed.

Bayesian analysis: results

Bayesian date range estimates for nave bays 1–8

Fig 33 shows the date range estimates for the single samples with h/s (and possible h/s) boundaries using both the OxCal Sapwood function and the original sapwood estimate; it also shows late tpqs (samples with late heartwood). For individual samples the Sapwood estimated felling dates hover around 36 years in range and, with one exception, sit within the long sapwood estimate recommended for the Peterborough material. Satisfyingly, then, these new results are broadly in agreement with Ian Tyer's view that the trees were slow growing and long lived (above, 2.3).

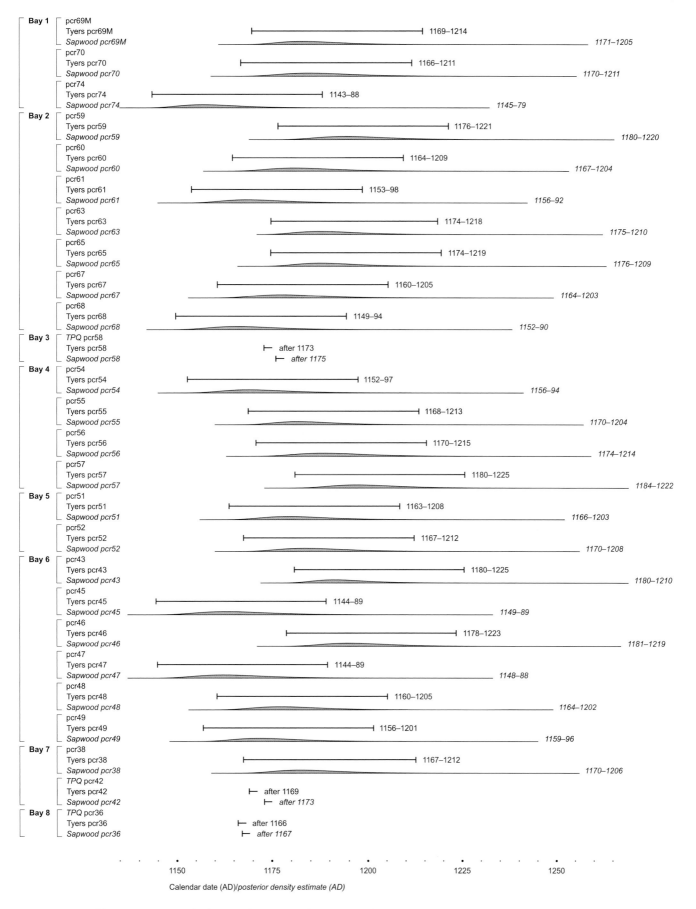

Fig 33 Individual felling date estimates for the 23 timbers with h/s boundaries and two timbers with late tpqs, in bays 1–8: the 10–55 year empirical sapwood estimate used by Ian Tyers is shown together with the Bayesian distribution derived using Mainland Britain in the OxCal <u>Sapwood</u> function for each sample

Nave bays 1–8 Bayesian analysis 1: assuming all bay 1–8 timbers to have been felled around the same time

Given the architectural history of the masonry, Hugh Harrison's observations on the roof structure (above, 2.2) and the clear evidence of the original tree-ring analysis, it would be bizarre to make the assumption that roof bays 9 and 10 were built at the same time as bays 1–8, let alone that the timbers were felled together, or in the same few years. This

analysis, then, uses the results from bays 1–8 only (effectively bays 1–2 and 4–7, as no samples with h/s boundaries were dated in bays 3 and 8) (Fig 30; Fig 33).

The analysis was undertaken initially to ascertain whether it was feasible that the relevant 23 samples with h/s boundaries could represent a single felling event. It was additionally decided to analyse the data on a bay-by-bay basis for two reasons. Firstly, to see if OxCal <u>Combine</u> would replicate Ian Tyers's conclusion that there was no evidence

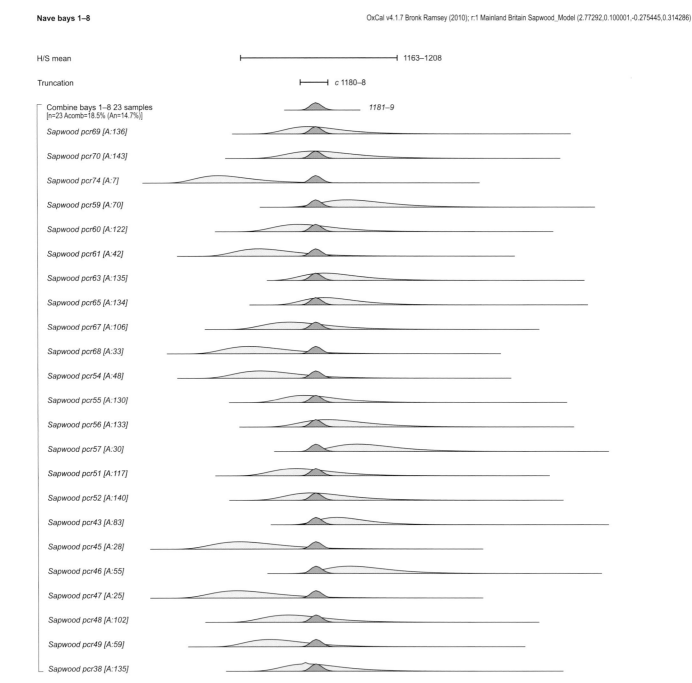

Fig 34 Nave bays 1–8 combined felling date ranges: the truncation and the h/s mean methods of combination are shown at the top with the Bayesian derived results below; individual felling date distributions are shown in light grey with the combined distribution shown in dark grey

that the east end was built noticeably earlier than the west end, up to bay 8 (one of the original hypotheses of the project). Secondly, this naturally limits the number of date ranges combined, which might otherwise produce overly narrow results (above). Note also that Ian Tyers did not observe any anomalous growth characteristics that would have the potential to give falsely low individual indices of agreement, and so this factor will not be considered further below.

Combining all 23 dated samples with h/s boundaries from bays 1–8 using <u>Combine</u> shows that in principle all the samples could represent a single felling event within *1181–9* (Fig 34). It is interesting to note that nine samples have low individual indices of agreement (ie, below 60%), seven on the early and two on the late side of the distribution, which will be discussed further below.

NAVE BAY 1

Combining all three samples, it is possible to see the advantages and disadvantages of the different methods (Fig 32). The truncation method produces a narrow date range (*c* 1169–88), in this instance skewed by the early h/s date of sample 74. The h/s mean combination (1159–1204) is reasonable but too broad to be of much use in understanding the nave. <u>Combine</u> produces a *combined felling date range of 1172–91* and draws our attention to something we are likely to have spotted anyway – the very poor individual agreement index of sample 74 compared with the other two samples. In this case, the lack of agreement is so great as to lower the combined index of agreement below the acceptable level (just). This should therefore lead to re-examination of sample 74 and the underlying assumption made when employing the <u>Combine</u> function, namely that the three samples represent a single felling event.

NAVE BAY 2

The same comments apply to the combination methods and their results as in nave bay 1 (Fig 35). <u>Combine</u> has produced the narrowest date range of *1179–92*. Here, the combined index of agreement is above the threshold and thus all six samples could represent a single felling event. There are two samples (with the earliest h/s boundaries) with low individual agreement indices.

NAVE BAY 3

A result was obtained for only a single sample (58) in bay 3 (Fig 33), without h/s boundary, but with late heartwood; the <u>Sapwood</u> function produced a tpq of *1175*.

NAVE BAY 4

Both <u>Combine</u> and the truncation methods produced narrow date ranges, of 17 years (*1181–98* and *c* 1180–97 respectively; Fig 36). As in bay 2, the combined index of agreement is acceptable, indicating that all four samples could represent a single felling event. One sample (54) has a very low individual agreement index.

NAVE BAY 5

In this instance, with only two samples, which are clearly in agreement with one another, the conventional combination methods produce broad date ranges (Fig 37). <u>Combine</u> produces a narrower range, of 25 years (*1172–97*).

NAVE BAY 6

The truncation method gives a very narrow range (*c* 1180–9) and OxCal <u>Combine</u> produces a slightly broader one (*1180–93*) but showing an unacceptably low combined index of agreement, strongly suggesting that the underlying

Nave bay 2

OxCal v4.1.7 Bronk Ramsey (2010); r:1 Mainland Britain Sapwood_Model (2.77292,0.100001,-0.275445,0.314286)

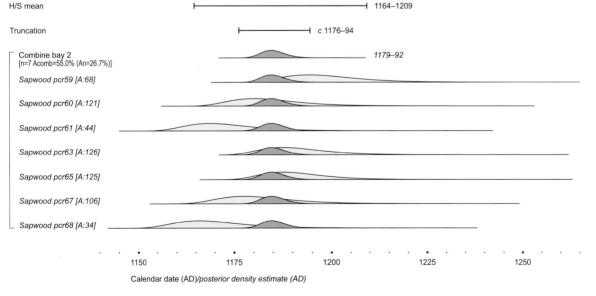

Fig 35 Nave bay 2 combined felling date ranges: the truncation and the h/s mean methods of combination are shown at the top with the Bayesian derived results below; individual felling date distributions are shown in light grey with the combined distribution shown in dark grey

The medieval nave and nave roof

Nave bay 4

OxCal v4.1.7 Bronk Ramsey (2010); r:1 Mainland Britain Sapwood_Model (2.77292,0.100001,-0.275445,0.314286)

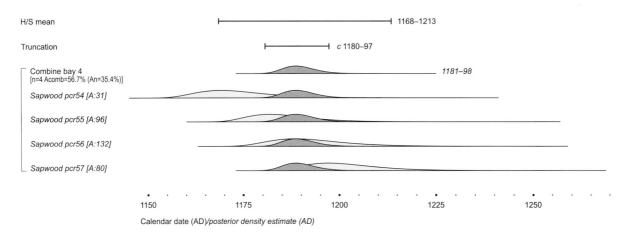

Fig 36 Nave bay 4 combined felling date ranges: the truncation and the h/s mean methods of combination are shown at the top with the Bayesian derived results below; individual felling date distributions are shown in light grey with the combined distribution shown in dark grey

Nave bay 5

OxCal v4.1.7 Bronk Ramsey (2010); r:1 Mainland Britain Sapwood_Model (2.77292,0.100001,-0.275445,0.314286)

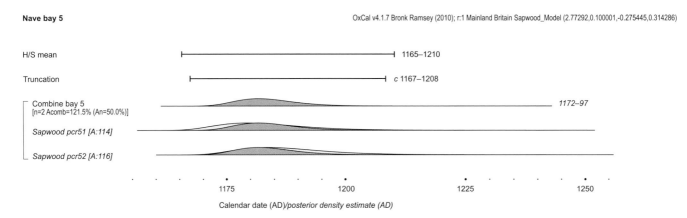

Fig 37 Nave bay 5 combined felling date ranges: the truncation and the h/s mean methods of combination are shown at the top with the Bayesian derived results below; individual felling date distributions are shown in light grey with the combined distribution shown in dark grey

assumption that the timbers were felled at the same time is wrong (Fig 38). Three samples, all with early h/s boundaries, have low individual indices of agreement.

NAVE BAY 7

One sample from bay 7 had an h/s boundary and a further sample had later heartwood (Fig 39). Combined, the felling estimates are *c* 1169–1212 (truncation method) and *1172–1204* (<u>Combine</u>).

NAVE BAY 8

No samples from bay 8 had h/s boundaries and the latest heartwood was not late enough to affect the interpretation of the nave in any way. For the record, the latest tpq for the three dated samples given by <u>Sapwood</u> is *1167* (Fig 33).

Discussion: Bayesian analysis 1

Looking at the A_{comb} measure alone, <u>Combine</u> suggests that the model of all the timbers being felled around the same

time works for four bays (bays 2, 4, 5, 7) and fails for two bays (bays 1 and 6), while the remaining two bays had no dated samples with h/s boundaries (bays 3, 8). As with the original bay-by-bay analysis by Ian Tyers, the Bayesian analysis also saw no clear progression of felling dates between the timbers of each bay. Using the results from bays 1, 2, 4, 5, 7 (bay 6 failed too badly to be used), the probability that the timbers for bay 1 were felled before those for the other bays is 31%. The probability that the timbers were felled sequentially for bays as they progressed from east to west is 8%. All results concur with the documentary record, namely that the nave was finished by Abbot Benedict, who ruled 1177–93 (Chapter 1.2; above, 2.1).

The number and distribution of samples with low individual indices of agreement (potential outliers) is, perhaps, of more interest, as already indicated in the combination of all samples with h/s boundaries from bays 1–8. The total number of samples in the bay-by-bay analysis with h/s boundaries is 23 and a total of seven samples with low individual indices of agreement (ie, 30%) was identified,

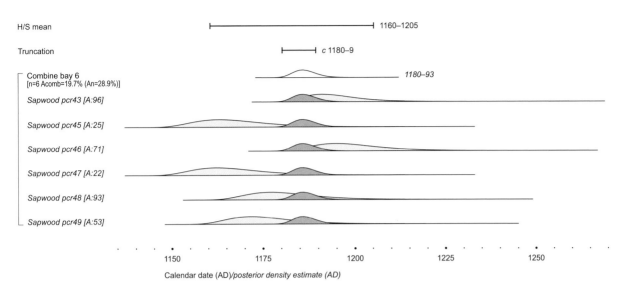

Fig 38 Nave bay 6 combined felling date ranges: the truncation and the h/s mean methods of combination are shown at the top with the Bayesian derived results below and individual felling date distributions are shown in light grey; here, the combined distribution is shown in outline, because the model failed

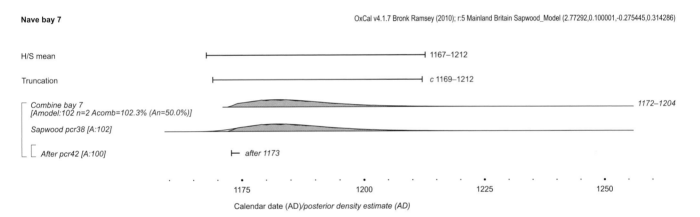

Fig 39 Nave bay 7 combined felling date ranges: the truncation and the h/s mean methods of combination are shown at the top with the Bayesian derived results below; the individual felling date distribution is shown in light grey with the combined distribution shown in dark grey

all on the early side of the distribution, that is, a very high proportion of the assemblage. Identifying why samples may be outliers is problematic, although in this case long-term stockpiling, as already discussed, may be an important factor.

Nave bays 1–8 Bayesian analysis 2: an alternative model

Aside from the large number of samples with low individual indices of agreement, the wide spread of h/s boundary dates (from 1133 to 1170) may suggest that the assemblage comprises timbers with widely spread felling dates, that is, potentially indicative of long-term stockpiling. Although comparative evidence (above) indicates that major structures may use timber that has been stockpiled for more than a few

years, in the absence of felling dates it is not currently possible to identify or date phases of stockpiling. However, creating a model that contains a prior belief that the sampled timbers were felled over a potentially long period of time can be used to estimate the earliest and latest felling dates in a group (Bayliss 2007). This model, using the 23 samples with h/s boundaries (Fig 40), was chosen to reflect the possibility that timber was left over from the previous major roof building campaign on the church, namely in the transept and crossing, completed during the rule of Abbot William de Waterville 1155–75, as well as in the few years immediately prior to construction.

The model shows good overall agreement (A_{model}= 94%) and provides an estimate of *1155–86* for the 'first' felling date. This demonstrates that a proportion of the timber

Nave bays 1–8

OxCal v4.1.7 Bronk Ramsey (2010); r:1 Mainland Britain Sapwood_Model (2.77292,0.100001,-0.275445,0.314286)

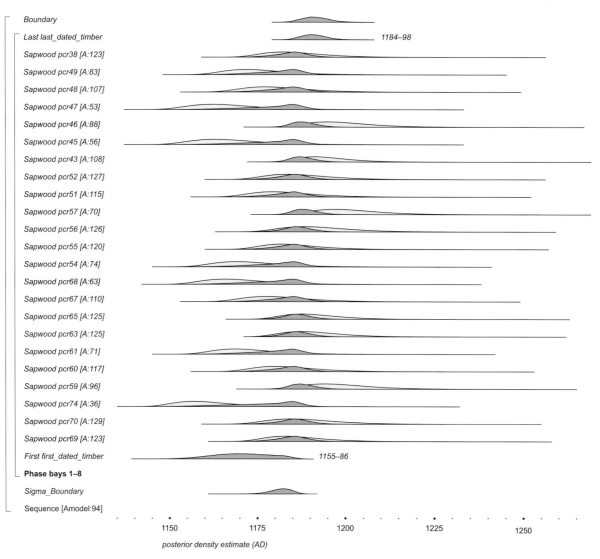

Boundary

Last last_dated_timber   *1184–98*

Sapwood pcr38 [A:123]

Sapwood pcr49 [A:83]

Sapwood pcr48 [A:107]

Sapwood pcr47 [A:53]

Sapwood pcr46 [A:88]

Sapwood pcr45 [A:56]

Sapwood pcr43 [A:108]

Sapwood pcr52 [A:127]

Sapwood pcr51 [A:115]

Sapwood pcr57 [A:70]

Sapwood pcr56 [A:126]

Sapwood pcr55 [A:120]

Sapwood pcr54 [A:74]

Sapwood pcr68 [A:63]

Sapwood pcr67 [A:110]

Sapwood pcr65 [A:125]

Sapwood pcr63 [A:125]

Sapwood pcr61 [A:71]

Sapwood pcr60 [A:117]

Sapwood pcr59 [A:96]

Sapwood pcr74 [A:36]

Sapwood pcr70 [A:129]

Sapwood pcr69 [A:123]

First first_dated_timber   *1155–86*

Phase bays 1–8

Sigma_Boundary

Sequence [Amodel:94]

1150   1175   1200   1225   1250

posterior density estimate (AD)

Fig 40 Nave bays 1–8, a model allowing for the potential use of stockpiled timber: for each of the samples two distributions have been plotted, one (light grey) which is the <u>Sapwood</u> felling date estimate and one (dark grey) based on the model used; the model here is not based on a uniform pattern of felling over a number of years, but instead assumes that the majority of felled timbers derive from close to the period of construction, but with allowance for some to be felled earlier; the model also calculates distributions for the first and last dated timbers

could have been felled during the works in the crossing and transept undertaken by Abbot William, as suggested by the documentary evidence. Similarly, the 'last' felling date, *1184–98*, is in agreement with the later years of Abbot Benedict, documented to have completed the nave.

Discussion: Bayesian analysis 2

Overall, this model fits the data very well, and the Bayesian analysis of the data strongly reinforces the documentary record that the nave roof was built during the rule of Abbot Benedict (1177–93), apparently in one campaign, with no obvious progression in the dates of the timbers from one end to the other. Moreover, it demonstrates the real possibility that timbers may have been stockpiled for decades from the previous major building campaign (the

transept, 1155–75) and may have been used throughout the roof, given the lack of progression of felling dates. The latter also implies a swift campaign, rather than one with a number of building breaks.

Plausibly, excess oak trees were collected while the main transept was being built, in the knowledge that many more would soon be needed for erecting the nave roof. In the event, it seems as if the nave was not ready for roofing until quite late in the rule of Abbot Benedict, perhaps 20 or more years later. In a large, rich abbey like Peterborough, we should not rule out the possibility that the stockpiled timber was left over from the erection of another major building, other than the church. Abbot William is credited not only with the transept and tower, but also with the infirmary, the cloister, chambers, chapels and other offices (Chapter 1.2). However, few of these buildings would

3 THE MEDIEVAL TRANSEPT CEILINGS

Between the late 12th-century building of the nave roof and the mid 13th-century construction of the nave ceiling the north and south transept ceilings were constructed. The transept ceilings are not only the chronological precursor of the much better-known nave ceiling – all three are rare and important 13th-century survivals – but are crucial prototypes for both the structure and the design of the nave ceiling. The transept ceilings are almost identical to each other in terms of dimensions and layout (Fig 45). Both are horizontal and covered with a clinker-built overall lozenge design, employing techniques used on the nave ceiling subsequently, although the latter is far more ambitious in both its construction complexities and paint scheme. Despite repeated structural interventions, repaintings and stripping, sufficient survives of the 13th-century transept ceilings to appreciate their original construction and appearance. (The referencing system adopted for the conservation project is described in Chapter 1.3 and illustrated in Fig 10.)

3.1 THE STRUCTURE OF THE MEDIEVAL TRANSEPT ROOFS AND WOODEN CEILINGS

Hugh Harrison

The layout and dimensions of the two transept arms are almost identical. The crossing tower and transept were constructed in the period 1155–75 during the abbacy of William de Waterville. A fine drawing of the south transept roof as it existed in the 1880s survives in the Northamptonshire Record Office, possibly by J T Irvine, J L Pearson's clerk of works (Fig 46). Elements of the medieval roof were also photographed by Leslie Moore (then the cathedral architect) during works in 1924 (Table 2; Chapter 5.4, 5.5; Moore 1925).

No structural timber or boards from an earlier, 12th-century, ceiling have been identified. The small number of tree-ring dated noggins from the south transept ceiling includes only three that are potentially from a 12th-century structure (below, 3.2; Fig 61). The only evidence for a 12th-century ceiling, or an intended one, are a row of empty pockets 325mm above the present ceiling level in the north gable wall of the north transept, which could have supported longitudinal beams (Fig 47), and masts (wall shafts) in the same wall that project above the level of the ceiling. Transverse beams could have used the dressed masonry

pockets at approximately 400mm centres in the east and west walls, subsequently (or originally) utilised for the 13th-century ceiling (Fig 48). These pockets indicate a beam size of *c* 250 by *c* 275mm which would have had not only to span a transept width of over 10m but also to support longitudinal beams spanning the length of the transept arm. The 12th-century wall capitals are rebated to accommodate a ceiling (Fig 49).

The intention may have been to construct coffered ceilings, each divided into twelve principal panels. To form a coffer both sets of beams need to be in the same plane and this can only be achieved by using halving joints. The beams, already under-specified it seems in terms of size, would also have been weakened by the pockets for joists. Any such plan may not have been realised, indeed it probably was not and instead efforts were focused on the west end of the nave (Chapter 1.2).

Irvine shows the 13th-century ceilings as being constructed of closely spaced transverse (east–west) beams, 340 × 210mm × 11.415m in length, at approximately 750mm centres (Fig 50). This was confirmed on site by measuring filled pockets still discernable in the masonry of the east and west walls of the south transept and those visible to a more limited extent in the north transept. The Irvine drawings show these transverse beams to have been recessed 60mm above the underside of the transverse beams to receive noggins 135mm wide (Fig 50). The ceiling boarding would then have been nailed to the underside of the transverse beams and noggins, as it was in the (later) nave ceiling (Chapter 4.1). The 13th-century construction thus employed transverse beams, without longitudinal beams, and a lightweight ceiling, consisting of the lozenge patterned boarding, parts of which survive today, clinker-built and complete with the characteristic grooves parallel to the edges of some boards.

Some noggins from the 13th-century ceilings appear to have survived, incorporated within the present structure. Short pieces of oak, varying in length from 570mm to 700mm and of average girth 100 × 60mm, were reused by Pearson in both transept arms for the construction of perimeter ceiling traps and for supporting perimeter boarding (Fig 51). The timbers conform in length to the original setting out of the transverse beams: measurements taken off reused timbers where original joints survive (eg, Fig 51) show that these timbers would have fitted into the recesses recorded by Irvine as present in the 13th-century ceiling transverse beams. They would have fitted between the

Fig 45 Overall images taken from below of (upper) the north and (lower) the south transept ceilings, following conservation (east to bottom)

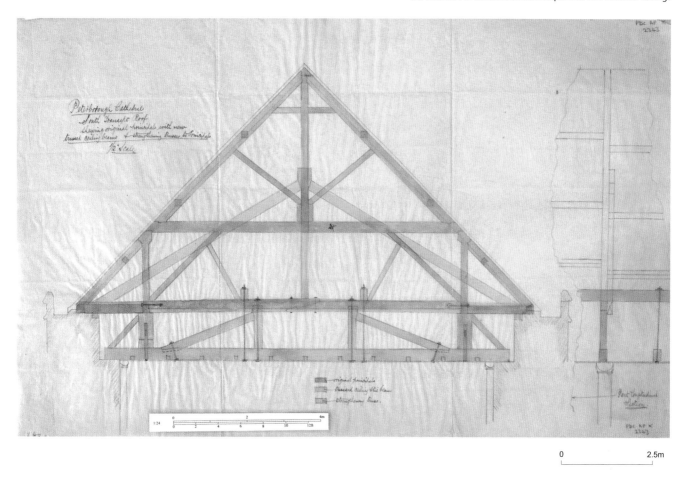

Fig 46 Drawing of the south transept roof, perhaps by J T Irvine, showing earlier (medieval or 1760s) principals (in blue) with new trussed ceiling beams (brown) and strengthening trusses (yellow) to principals (drawn at ½in to a 1ft, ie 1:24) (NRO, PD/DC/AP 2343) (scale 1:100)

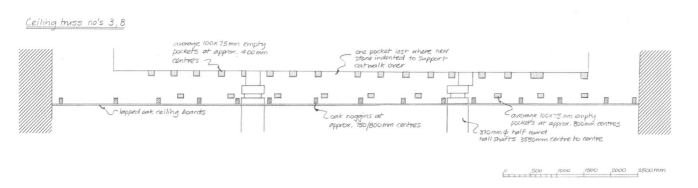

Fig 47 North transept: elevation of the north wall at ceiling level, showing wall shafts and row of empty pockets, and lower row of pockets (drawn by Peter Ferguson)

old beams as recorded by Irvine (Fig 52). The pockets for the noggins in the north transept gable wall (Fig 47) were similarly positioned 60mm above the ceiling boards.

Some of these timbers still have their original bird's beak joints (now disused) on at least one end. There is no evidence of nailing in the joints of the surviving noggins. The slots in the original transverse beams suggest that the noggins would have been carefully made fractionally oversize to fit between each beam and offered into the slots at an angle, then tapped into position at 90° to the joists at

positions to suit the board ends. This method would have ensured a tight fit without the requirement to nail or pin.

Double rows of original nail holes have been recorded on the underside of these noggins (visible where the reused timbers have been laid upside down or on their sides). The nails are set 25mm from the edge of the timber at 125–150mm spacings. The nails appear to have been finely tapered and flat shanked and almost certainly supported the original boarding.

Each transept ceiling is composed of an overall regular

Fig 48 Empty pockets and top of mast in the north wall of the north transept

Fig 49 Detailed view of south transept 12th-century west wall capital, showing rebate for a ceiling timber; taken before treatment, showing fire damage (flaking limewash and loss) and following cleaning tests

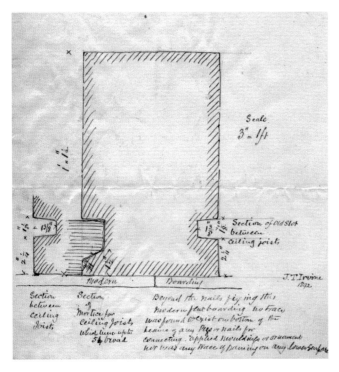

Fig 50 J T Irvine's record of transverse beams in cross section showing the end of a noggin mortised into the transverse beam (south transept west wall) (PCL, Irvine Papers, v, fo 46)

Fig 51 Two oak noggins from the medieval ceiling reused in an 1880s perimeter ceiling trap adjacent to the west wall of the south transept (row L); note disused bird's beak joints in the ends of each (arrowed)

pattern where the size does not vary, comprising 130 panels in total per transept ceiling in ten rows by 13 rows (Fig 10). All the boarding was taken down during Pearson's restoration of the 1880s and ceiling traps – eight small square hatches – created in the perimeter boarding, running down both north–south edges, that is four per north–south edge. Nevertheless, a substantial number of boards survive from the 13th-century transept ceilings (referred to henceforward in the text as 'original' boards): 42 boards remain in the north transept (out of *c* 1340) and 243 in the south transept (out of *c* 1330) (Fig 63). In addition to these original boards, a further 56 'intermediate' boards belonging to the 17th century remain in the south transept only; these boards were retained by Irvine as part of Pearson's ceiling (Chapter 5.1, 5.4). Irvine recorded the painted decoration and grooves on fragments of medieval boards removed, noting that the ceiling woodwork was 'remarkable' and the ornamentation 'singular' (Fig 53).

Sufficient original and intermediate boards survive in the

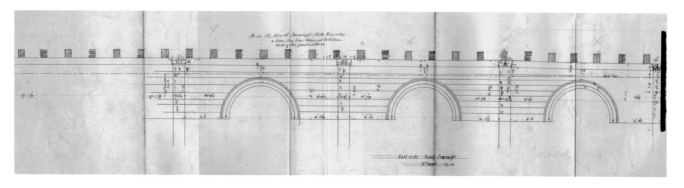

Fig 52 J T Irvine's archaeological record drawing of the east side of the south transept showing masts which might have supported a 12th-century coffered ceiling and the closely spaced transverse beams of the 13th-century ceiling (PCL, Irvine Papers, v, fo 49)

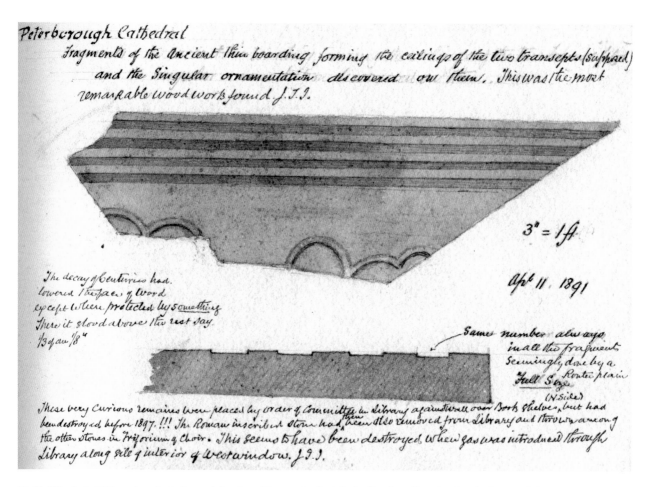

Fig 53 J T Irvine's 1890s archaeological record drawing of fragments of original ceiling boarding, showing the four parallel grooves along the edge of the board and 'ornamentation' (PCL, Irvine Papers, v, fo 48)

south transept to provide a number of complete or near-complete panels, enough to determine the general pattern of the original board layout. This is indicated on Fig 54, but it should be appreciated that there is none the less considerable variation in detail.

Panels M/5 and M/6 in the south transept were measured and drawn (Fig 55) and may be said to be fairly typical. Each panel consists of a flat baseboard spanning the longest diagonal ('d' on M/6, 'f' on M/5), with an average of two to three boards either side which are shiplapped over the

baseboard and each other, being nailed at approximately 125–150mm spacings each end and randomly clench nailed at approximately 300mm centres along the leading edge. Many of the principal boards either side of the baseboard are of considerable width, up to 500mm, with the outermost boards formed out of the end offcuts from these middle boards, resulting in their being laid across the grain in a number of instances (Fig 56).

Board overlaps, where examined, indicated considerable variation of width in a panel from 25mm to 85mm. Unlike

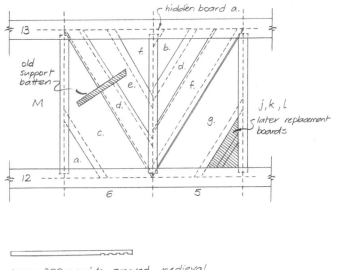

approx 320mm wide grooved, medieval

approx 260mm wide, chamfered on one edge, 17th C.

approx 430mm wide, tapered and grooved, medieval

approx 360mm wide plain, medieval / 17th C.

Fig 54 South transept ceiling details: upper – part plan from above showing typical board layout as reconstructed in the 1880s from reused boards; lower – original and intermediate board profiles (for location see Fig 10; for diagonal sections see Fig 55) (drawn by Peter Ferguson)

the nave ceiling boarding, there was no evidence found to suggest that the board edges had been carefully worked to produce a tight fit. Both nave and transept ceilings were clinker-built, but, overall, the construction of the transept ceilings was considerably less complex and sophisticated.

The original boards appear to be nearly all radial and very straight grained and generally flat, 6–9mm thick, and remarkably wide (up to 500mm, 19¾in) (Fig 57). A few of the very widest boards are tapered from 12mm to 4mm and one 430mm-wide board noted was feather edged (cf 'c' on M/6, Fig 55). The boards are generally thinner and wider than those of the nave ceiling (Chapter 4.1). It was not possible to determine absolutely how the original boards were manufactured: only a small number of boards had hessian removed from the back and these did not produce enough usable evidence.

The baseboards which form the outer boards of each lozenge are not grooved but a number of boards bear the four characteristic parallel grooves along the board edge which are also found in the nave (Fig 58). Three original boards in each panel bear a set of grooves ('a', 'c', 'f' on M/6, Fig 55). The effect was that each lozenge was defined by two sets of grooves – the outer set being shared with the adjacent lozenge – but the exact position varied depending on the width of the boards in each lozenge. The grooves are uniformly 9mm wide and are spaced 9mm apart. The depth is nominal, possibly 1–2mm. Grooving would appear to have been done after the panel boards were cut (Fig 55) and their relationship to the paint scheme suggests that their function was to provide a lining-out guide for the painters (below, 3.4;

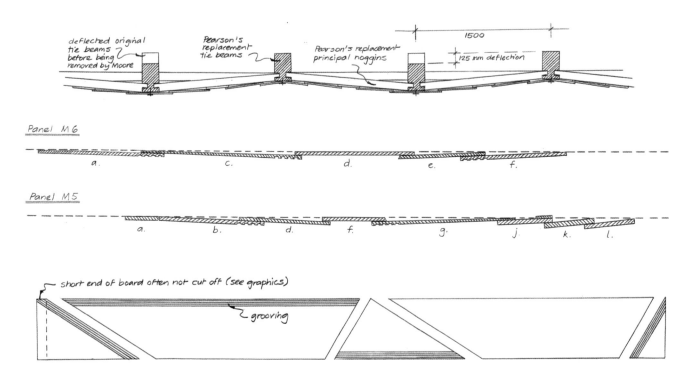

Fig 55 South transept ceiling details: top – reconstructed longitudinal lozenge centre section to show underside board profile at point of maximum deflection before Moore's 1920s intervention; middle – diagonal sections through south transept panels M/6 and M/5 (Fig 54); bottom – diagram to show the different types of panel board profiles extractable from a complete board length (drawn by Peter Ferguson)

Fig 56 The north transept ceiling following conservation, showing the overlapping construction

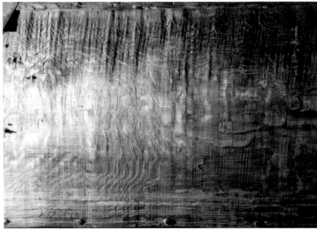

Fig 57 Original grooved wide board showing surface weathering with rays and saw marks (south transept panel M/7/f, post-conservation)

Fig 58 South transept ceiling panel G/4 shown following the fire but before cleaning (cf Fig 59)

Fig 59 South transept ceiling panels G/3–G/4 (post-conservation): detail of ends of two original south transept boards showing (left, G/3/a) with-grain grooves and (right, G/4/g) cross-grain grooves; note impression of large headed original nail in G/4/g (top, centre) which does not transfer to G/3/a, indicating that boards might have been matched rather than replaced in original position in the 1880s

Fig 60 Detail (south transept panels J/1–2, boards a–c, post-conservation) showing cross-grained grooved original board (J/1/a, centre and right) not in correct position; note also surface weathering of boards and Pearson nails and empty nail holes

Fig 64). Like the nave ceiling, all the boards would have been painted before they were finally fixed (Chapter 4.1). Where boards forming the inner lozenges are laid cross-grained, the grooves have been cut across the grain (Fig 55; Fig 59; Fig 60).

It would appear that in the 1880s Pearson de-nailed the original boards and renailed mostly into the original holes, very little damage occurring to the woodwork in the process. Spacing is approximately 125–150mm at the ends and about 250–300mm along the board edges. There was no evidence found to suggest that Pearson took down and reused original boards in pairs (or more) without releasing original nails, though a few original nail heads remain embedded in the boards.

3.2 THE DATE AND ORIGIN OF THE MEDIEVAL TRANSEPT CEILINGS AND ROOF STRUCTURES

Ian Tyers

Tree-ring dating of the medieval transept roof structures and ceilings

Tree-ring sampling was undertaken on various structural and decorative timbers in the roofs and ceilings of the north and south transepts during the conservation programme following the fire of 2001. The methodology is described in Chapter 2.3 and in Tyers (2004).

A total of 72 timbers were selected from all periods for sampling, by coring tie-beams or, in the case of noggins, by shortening their ends where they overlay the masonry walls (no. = 33), and by direct measurement of boards (no. = 39) (Table 4). Fifteen of the boards had been already identified as

original. In the case of the original and intermediate boards (above, 3.1), the board end mitred joints were found to be so tight and the boards so thin that *in situ* measuring was not possible; it was therefore decided to release specific boards. These were measured in the cathedral, using a measuring stage, microscope and computer set up in a walkway over the south transept. The benefit of this unusual approach was that it reduced the risk of damage to these somewhat fragile items during their movement. Seventeen of the measured sequences were derived from hatches within the north and south transept roofs and this work in particular involved minimal intervention to the structure. All the measured boards removed during the repair work were subsequently returned and replaced in their original location.

Due to the condition of the transept ceiling boards, many had inner and outer sections that were impracticable to measure and estimates of the numbers of unmeasured rings in each board were made to assist with the interpretation of this material. The transept ceiling diamond panels are constructed from trapezoidal boards with a *c* 33° angle at one end and its reciprocal 57° at the other. The ring widths in these boards were directly measured along their shortest exposed ends; subsequently these angled ring width series were converted to true ring width series (ie, as if they had been measured in the original horizontal plane of the tree) by multiplying each value by the cosine of 33°. The sapwood estimates applied to the English-sourced material from the transept (since they had a different growth profile from the nave roof timbers: Chapter 2.3) are a minimum of 10 and maximum of 46 annual rings, where these figures indicate the 95% confidence limits of the range (Tyers 1998b). These figures are applicable to oaks from England and Wales.

Of the 72 selected timbers, 64 were successfully measured and 19 (six south transept boards, five north transept boards and eight south transept noggins from the perimeter traps) of them formed the sequence PCF1, which is dated AD

Fig 67 Conjectural diagrammatic reconstructions of the early 13th-century painted design on the transept ceilings, (left) with cross bottony and (right) with cross fleurie; there is firm evidence (ie, surviving shallow relief) only for the crosses and the inner and outer band of four parallel lines

edges of boards and smeared residues on some 1880s and earlier retained boards. Documentary evidence indicates a repainting of the transept in the 1820s, by the same firm which painted the nave ceiling in 1835, and another repainting in the 1740s (Chapter 5.2, 5.3).

Fig 67 provides two speculative reconstructions of the early 13th-century lozenge paint scheme, both with the inner and outer bands of four parallel lines. That on the left has the cross botonny, accompanied by a border pattern of cusped trefoils (the 'bun' pattern, above); the other (right) shows the cross fleurie and a different border pattern based on dog-tooth as in the 1740s transept paint scheme (Chapter 5.2).

4 THE MEDIEVAL NAVE CEILING

The painted wooden nave ceiling of Peterborough Cathedral measures *c* 204ft (62.2m) east–west by *c* 35ft (10.7m) north–south and covers all ten nave bays, at a height of over 80ft (*c* 24.5m) above the nave floor. It is a marvellous and extremely important survival, the largest in a medieval great church in Europe and one of the very few English 13th-century examples of painted vault or ceiling figurative decoration. The lozenge design, so dominant viewed from the nave floor (Fig 68), conceals a complex construction where each lozenge comprises four triangles, each of which is half of a rectangular panel. The flat central portion of the ceiling is one lozenge (two panels) wide, with subsidiary smaller interlocking lozenges split between the horizontal ceiling and the canted (sloping) sides. Each of the canted sides is one panel wide, with half-lozenges alternating with the smaller lozenges. Along the centre of the ceiling there are 20 lozenges (40 rows of abutting panels). The lozenges required considerable attention to detail in the techniques employed as part of the original construction process. The many phases of 'restoration' and repair undertaken in subsequent centuries turned it into a rigid structure and radically altered its appearance (but not its iconography) in ways that were more obvious close to than viewed from the floor of the nave. Now, secured and cleaned, its skilful design and construction, and its colourful decoration and story are more readily appreciated.

The roof structure supporting the ceiling as originally built is described above (Chapter 2) and subsequent modifications below (Chapter 5). The referencing system used to record work and observations on the panels and boards during the conservation project is described in Chapter 1.3. The 20th- and 21st-century recording methodology and conservation programme in practice are detailed in Chapter 6.

4.1 THE STRUCTURE AND DESIGN OF THE MEDIEVAL WOODEN NAVE CEILING

Hugh Harrison

The design of the nave ceiling structure

A lozenge design is common to both the nave ceiling and the earlier transept ceilings (Chapter 3) but an architectural eye cleverly switched an overall diaper-like pattern in the transept into a design that seamlessly cloaked the rather more awkward shape of the nave ceiling. This was achieved by changing the scale of the lozenges: the main, central, lozenges occupied the width of the horizontal part of the nave ceiling; the secondary lozenges were centred on the angle of the ceiling thus masking the change of angle of the canted sides (eg, Fig 69; Fig 70). Without the decision to centre these secondary lozenges, the actual shortening of the lozenges on the sloping ceilings combined with the visual foreshortening would have emphasised the irregularity of the shape of the whole lozenge if the other half of the lozenge continued to the centre line on the horizontal ceiling. This change of length and width of lozenge created tapering spaces between adjacent lozenges which are flat boarded (with a 'baseboard') in contrast with the clinker boarding of the lozenges themselves. These tapered spaces are also found separating the half-lozenges on the sloping ceilings. There are thus three lozenge shapes and sizes and this diversity, with none of the lozenges actually fitting each other, adds variety to an otherwise repetitive design. The three lozenge shapes which reduce alternately in length and then in width form a diminishing progression of size from the centre lozenges outwards to the wall plates.

Construction

The nave ceiling as it survives today is in very large part – joists, noggins, ceiling boards, nails – made up of original elements which carry with them evidence of how they were made and assembled (Figs 69–71). The structure remains remarkably consistent despite the ceiling bulging outwards 15in (0.38m) in the centre. The ceiling, including the sloping sides, is formed of boards placed clinker-fashion (Fig 88) and nailed directly to the underside of the roof structure and noggins, with additional nails spaced along the edges of adjoining boards. The medieval scissor truss nave roof structure itself – comprising 81 sets of scissor braces and collars – is examined in detail in Chapter 2.2 and its dating in 2.3 and 2.4. The original sloping ceiling 'joists' are the former lower sections of the scissor braces and the horizontal ceiling 'joists' the lower collars (Fig 72); for ease of reference the truncated lower collars and scissor braces are frequently referred to in this and subsequent chapters as 'joists' since this is how they function in relation to the ceiling. (The scissor trusses are referred to as 'joists' throughout the archive reports where the focus is on the ceiling.) The unusually high lower collar beam exposes a considerable

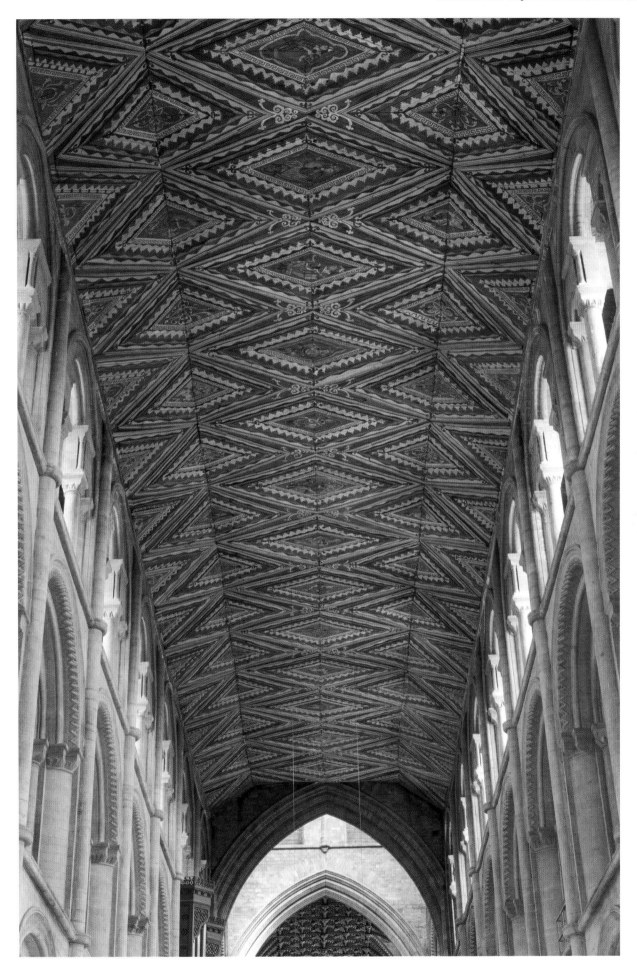

Fig 68 The nave ceiling, viewed from the west

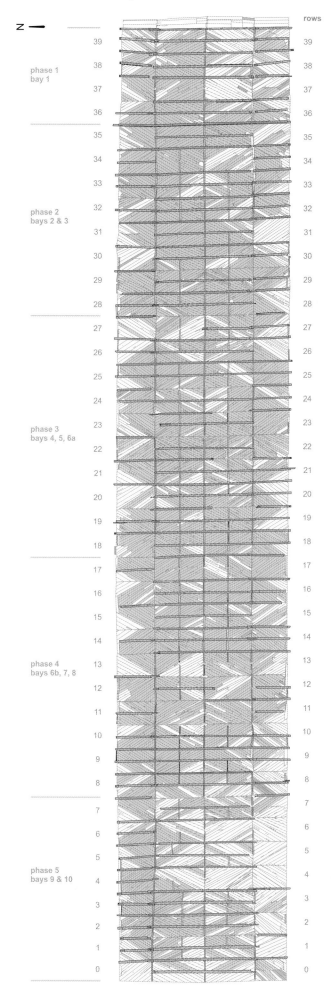

length of the bottom of the scissor brace which creates the sloping sides of the ceiling. The sloping joists project beyond the lower end of the boards by a similar distance throughout the ceiling.

The horizontal part of the ceiling widens from row 3 in bay 10 towards the west, but it stays the same height, so here the sloping sides steepen. The shape of the lozenges was dictated by the spacing between the scissor braces to which the boards are nailed. The visible edge of each board is moulded with one of three different moulds and the sequence for these moulds remains constant with every lozenge (below and Fig 77). The centre boards in each lozenge, on which the figurative painting has been applied, have a different, flatter profile than the patterned boards.

It is presumed that butt-jointed vertical boarding ('ashlar boarding') filled the space between the masonry wall head and the lower edge of the sloping sides (as it does now with much later timber: Chapter 5), since two boards reused in the ceiling have a very different painted design to the ceiling boards (below, 4.3, 4.4). The bottom ends of the sloping boards frequently stop short of the wall line, sometimes by as much as 8in (200mm) (Fig 73). This is not just individual boards but whole rows of boards, and even then the distance swings from nothing to the maximum figure given, as though the original vertical ashlar boarding waved in and out. However, the haphazard completion line must remain open to speculation (Chapter 2.2).

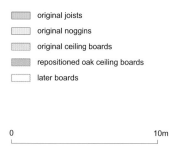

original joists
original noggins
original ceiling boards
repositioned oak ceiling boards
later boards

0   10m

Fig 69 Combined survey record from conservation phases 1–5 of surviving original elements in the nave ceiling: overall 'reflected view', that is, with the ceiling boards as if viewed in a mirror below, thus keeping the cardinal points in their usual relationship; the trusses are as seen from above (scale 1:250)

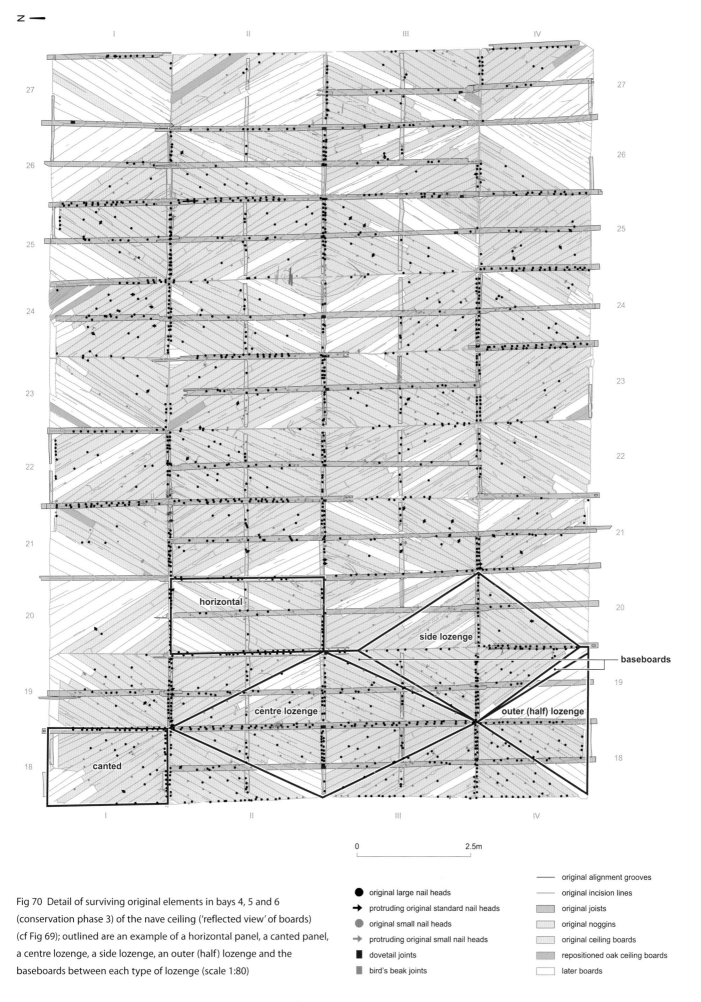

Fig 70 Detail of surviving original elements in bays 4, 5 and 6 (conservation phase 3) of the nave ceiling ('reflected view' of boards) (cf Fig 69); outlined are an example of a horizontal panel, a canted panel, a centre lozenge, a side lozenge, an outer (half) lozenge and the baseboards between each type of lozenge (scale 1:80)

0   2.5m

● original large nail heads
→ protruding original standard nail heads
● original small nail heads
→ protruding original small nail heads
■ dovetail joints
■ bird's beak joints

—— original alignment grooves
—— original incision lines
▨ original joists
▨ original noggins
▨ original ceiling boards
▨ repositioned oak ceiling boards
□ later boards

63

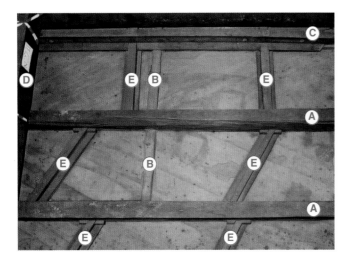

Fig 71 Detail of the nave ceiling from above: 'A' – original joists; 'B' – original noggins; 'C' – a 1920s composite joist; 'D' – an 1840s binder; 'E' – 1920s noggins

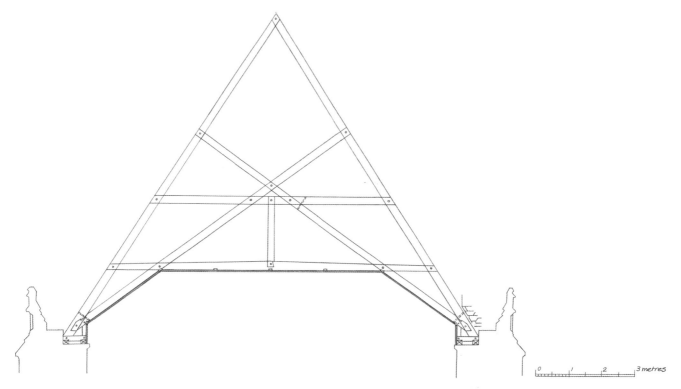

Fig 72 A reconstruction of the original nave roof with the ceiling shown pink (drawn by Peter Ferguson)

Fig 73 An example of the original nave ceiling boards ending some distance above the present ashlar boards, with the gap filled by later boards (4/1, bay 9, north side)

Noggins

Before boarding could be fixed securely to the roof timbers (joists) many short pieces of oak, known as noggins, had to be inserted between each truss. The oak noggins at the ends and middles of the panels had to be inserted before the boarding could be fixed. The noggins (Fig 74, 'A' and 'B') were fitted from below, between the elements of the underside of the roof structure (that is, between the scissor braces and lower collars), being jointed to the underside of the joists ('C') with a simple bird's beak joint and nailed using either one or two flat-headed nails (Fig 75). This suggests that these small timbers, average cross section 3 × 2in (75 × 50mm), were not added until the underside of the roof was about to be boarded in to form the new ceiling. The purpose of these noggins was obviously to support the board

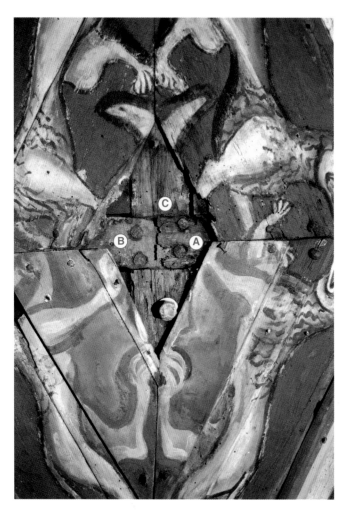

ends which were nailed to them (below). One observation was the curious absence of noggins between horizontal joists 1 to 9 (row 34); and they were little used for supporting the centre span of the boards for at least a further bay west.

Boards

As it survives, the ceiling boarding comprises original, probably north German, oak boards (below, 4.2) and 18th- to 19th-century softwood replacements; the ashlar boarding is 19th-century tongue and groove softwood (Chapter 5.2–5.4). The original ceiling boards are radial and 'riven' ('cleft') oak and therefore vary in thickness and length, and mostly have a tapered section. To acquire this tapered section the boards would have come from near the centre of a log of slim girth (but one large enough – probably *c* 600mm in diameter – to produce boards clear of sapwood). The boards are also planed and smoothed down after riving on at least the lower (painted) surface (cf the upper surface of one board adzed after riving: Fig 82). These boards are on average 200mm (*c* 8in) wide and with a thickness of 15–22mm on one edge

Fig 74 Noggins ('A' and 'B') jointed to the underside of a joist ('C') (at the junction of 38–39/II–III, four lions circling a fish, and below the centre of joist 3); also visible is a temporary bolt and washer inserted to carry the joist while the original was being conserved

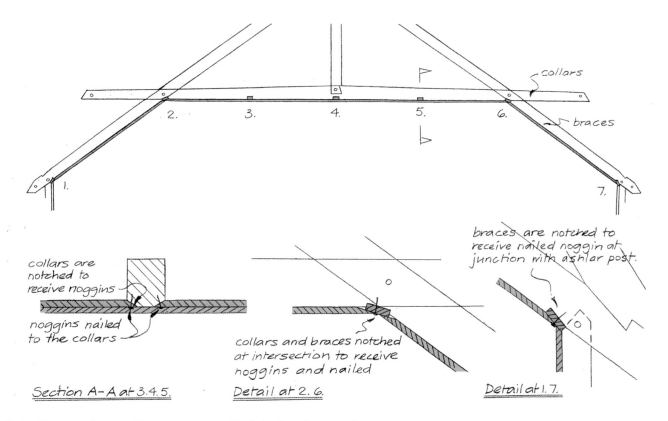

Fig 75 Diagrammatic views of the support noggins (shaded red) for the nave ceiling (shaded green): upper – part section through the roof structure showing the distribution of seven original board noggins; lower – section and details of noggins at the junction of horizontal section and canted/sloping sides and at the junction of canted sides and ashlars (not to scale) (drawn by Peter Ferguson)

and 3–9mm on the other – an average of ½in (19mm).

It was found that a pattern of board widths exists within the panels, there being two roughly equal groups, one measuring approximately 7in (175mm), and the other 8½in (220mm) wide. The widest board found was 11½in (290mm). The two original oak ashlar boards (above, and 4.3, 4.4) reused in the ceiling are flat square-edged boards located together with oak dowels in their edges.

Measurements taken from a large sample (409 boards) suggest that there was a standard length of board between *c* 6ft 6in and 7ft 1in (1976mm and 2176mm) (Table 5). As the maximum length of diagonal across each panel is nearly 13ft 0in (3950mm) and the maximum length of board used is less than 9ft 0in, it suggests that no boards anywhere near the desired length were available to form the baseboards for example. Long boards were therefore made up by scarf jointing two boards (Fig 76 upper). In the case of the sloping panels, the additional length was made up using random lengths, probably offcuts, as no attempt was made to place the scarf beneath a structural timber. However, in the case of the central horizontal panels, the majority of scarves are made to coincide with either a noggin or joist above, suggesting that the extension pieces were cut to a predetermined length and therefore mostly from whole boards.

Throughout the ceiling a variety of techniques was used to form the scarves, resulting in beautifully fitting joints and

Table 5 Average length of original nave ceiling boards

Nave ceiling boards		% of total
No. of boards measured	409	
Average length	6ft 9¾in (2076mm)	
No. of boards within 2in (50mm) of average length	210	54%
No. of boards within 4in (100mm) of average length	350	86%
Maximum length board	8ft 8½in (2650mm)	

feathered edges. A notable number of instances are found where only 2–3in (50–75mm) are added to the end of a board. It should be remembered that, including a scarf 3" (75mm) long, the added piece has to be 6in (150mm) long (Fig 76, lower). In a very few instances, very short pieces, say only 1in (25mm), were butt-jointed on to the end of a board. This seems to indicate the value of the timber and the lengths the carpenters went to in order to use every possible fragment of timber.

The baseboards of the lozenges on the horizontal part of the ceiling are each made up of three separate boards, all untapered in section; this is quite unlike the clinker design of the rest of the ceiling (Fig 77). The single board at the narrow end is scarfed to twin boards at the wide end (Fig 78; egs can be seen on Fig 70). The twin long boards are dowelled along their butt-jointed length at approximately 1ft 6in (450mm) centres using square oak dowels, the position of some being indicated with location marks on the surface of the board (Fig 86). The dowel holes are made with a spoon bit, which has a rounded end. The baseboards in the sloping sides are one board wide, but scarfed in length with one short board at the narrow end and a long board from there to the bottom end.

Although the *visible* surfaces of the baseboards taper to a narrow point below the ceiling, they are quite wide above the ceiling. When a sample board was revealed by removing the hessian above, it measured approximately 5in (125mm) at its narrowest point. What is noteworthy is the extent of the overlap, which requires the outer edges of the lower surface of the baseboard to be chamfered down to allow the first border board each side to lie flat (Fig 77). In section it shows the chamfer may continue across the lower surface of the board, producing a ridge down the centre.

One recurring aspect of the twin boards at their wide end is that, although they are often unequal in width where they scarf with the single narrow end board (see the widths of boards 'A' and 'B' in Fig 79), they are always cut in their width so that the joint comes in the middle of the mitre with the other twin boards coming from the other side of the lozenge (shown arrowed in Fig 79). As it would never be noticed from ground level if the two centre joints did not

Fig 76 Forming scarves: upper – two scarf-jointed boards (38/II, bay 1); lower – adding to the end of a board (36/III, bay 1)

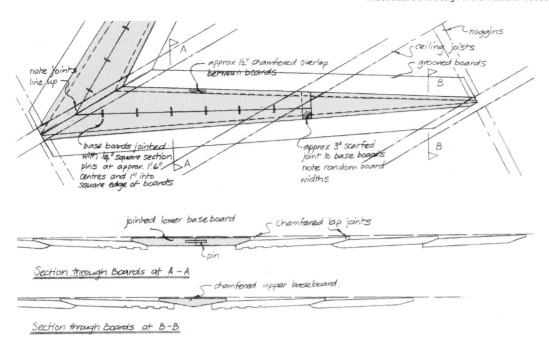

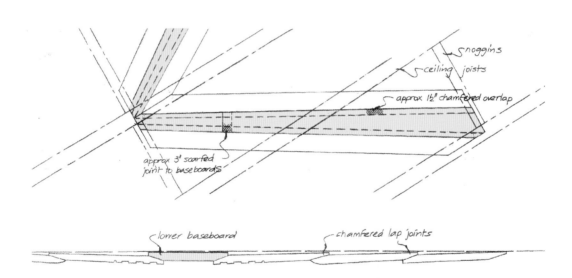

Fig 77 Typical baseboard layout and construction viewed from above, with sectional details (enlarged) (baseboards shaded; board nailing not shown): upper – in the horizontal section of the ceiling; lower – in the canted sides (not to scale) (drawn by Peter Ferguson)

intersect, one wonders why so much effort was made to achieve this result.

The border boards of the lozenges display various moulded edges – square, rounded or grooved – and the same sequence of mouldings was used for every lozenge (Fig 77; Fig 80; also Fig 100). Rounding board edges over enhances the painted border patterns by reducing the effect of those board edges. In addition, the boards making up the centre areas on which the figurative paintings were applied were particularly smoothed to make this whole space look flat and reduce the effect of the board edges to a minimum. The lower and upper board surfaces are chamfered where they overlap (Fig 77), so that adjacent boards fit exactly, and because they are laid clinker fashion, there are no gaps. It has

also been confirmed (below) that the upper surfaces of the boards were finished, though to a lower standard than the lower (painted) surface.

Quality of the carpentry

Generally, the quality of the joinery throughout the ceiling is very good; minor variation in overall quality of finished work was noticed, but this is hardly surprising in a structure of this exceptional size and complexity. The radially split boards are of high quality for evenness and thinness throughout their length. They exhibit a sophistication of edge detail and surface grooving, finely executed scarf joints, mitres and edge dowelling. Fig 81 shows a whole area of undisturbed original

Fig 78 Single baseboard scarfed to twin boards of unequal width (37/II, bay 1)

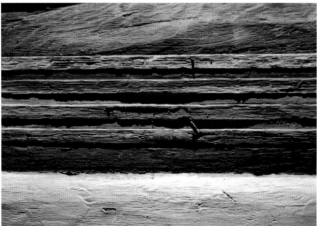

Fig 80 Triple-grooved boards: upper – triple-grooved boards at the junction of two panels (36/II, bay 1); lower – triple-grooved border board (14/III, bay 7)

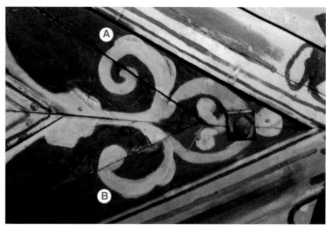

Fig 79 Matching adjoining boards (34/III, bay 2)

Fig 81 Undisturbed original work illustrating the high standard of workmanship in the original ceiling (9–10/II–III, bay 8)

work; the tight joints are remarkable and must be representative of the quality of the original joinery throughout the whole ceiling.

The techniques and standards of finish, however, could vary. In the course of examining the baseboards to determine their construction, a small area of hessian was lifted to understand what was happening above the ceiling. The board revealed happened to be in excellent condition (Fig 82) and it clearly shows the riven surface partly smoothed with a side axe with a nick in the blade. This is likely to be representative of the finish on the upper surface of all the boards. Very few marks of the finishing tools used to smooth the lower surface of the boards were seen. The exception is long parallel marks in the surface as though a draw blade has been used (Fig 83). Viewed against the consistent high standards of workmanship and materials, it therefore seems a trifle at odds that the original noggins exhibit such irregularity of section and that a small number of boards throughout the length of the ceiling display severe grain tearing, careless adzing or felling shakes and juddering in the planed grooves due to the scratch stock (a tool which is part scraper, part moulding plane) being set too coarsely (Fig 84). One can

Fig 82 The upper riven surface of a board revealed by lifting the hessian; the surface has been partly smoothed with a side axe with a nick in the blade (17/I, bay 6)

Fig 83 Long parallel marks in a board surface; note top where underpaint is visible (16/II, bay 6)

only surmise that the presence of these boards is indicative of a 'waste not, want not' guiding philosophy, and that in particular the noggin material available was somewhat substandard.

Incised marks, some deeper than others, have been noticed throughout the ceiling on the original boards. It is thought that they are from the original construction as many appear on boards which have original nails and do not appear to have been moved. These marks include two main types of probable assembly marks. One type consists of a cross roughly incised presumably to identify particular boards; some identification crosses are substantially hidden behind the overlap of the adjoining board. The second type is position marks, including circles and crescents, one/two/three incised marks across the joint and an incised line marking the overlap between two boards (Fig 85). Fig 86 shows the position for a dowel marked in the edge of the

baseboard. The preparatory work of dowelling two long boards to make a baseboard was probably done on the ground.

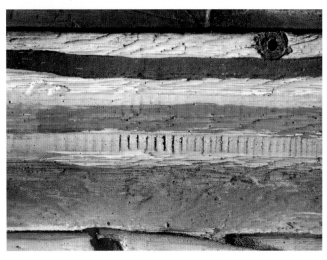

Fig 84 Examples of poorer techniques and standards of finish: upper right – severe grain tearing (19/IV, bay 6); lower left – careless adzing (face of Logic/Dialectic, 14/III, bay 7); lower right – scratch stock set too coarsely (9/II, bay 8)

Fig 86 Position for a dowel marked on the edge of a baseboard (20/III, bay 5)

Fig 85 Incised position marks (top to bottom): circular (34–35/II, bay 2); crescent (33/II–III, bay 2); across a joint (32–33/III, bay 2)

Fixing the boards

There is substantial evidence that the boards were painted before they were finally fixed (below, 4.3). As the patterned border boards are all different lengths yet require the patterns to intersect where they mitre, they either have to be painted *in situ* or set up temporarily, marked, and reset up accurately on the bench for painting. The lozenge centre boards require even greater accuracy of refitting. This would seem to explain why the position marks are required, but if

this degree of accuracy is needed, why are the marks not more frequent? In addition, why are only some boards marked with identification marks? Less than 5% of the boards have any of these marks on them and the same approximate percentage is found throughout the ceiling (below, 4.3).

The fixing of the lozenges had to start with the baseboards. Each board would be individually fitted to the previous one and then worked on a bench situated on a scaffold or down on the ground. In the original decorative scheme the baseboards were largely unpainted with only minimal decoration (a scroll design: cf Fig 100), while the border boards have only linear parts of the design and could easily have been painted on a scaffold bench. The central figures, each on a maximum of four boards, are more likely to have been set up and painted on a bench at ground level.

The method of attaching the boards to the noggins and joists was by nailing through pre-drilled holes using two types of nail, 'standard' with large domed heads and 'small-headed' where the head is often irregular and smaller than the standard. Both have long, fine tapered square shanks (Fig 87). Analysis of nail samples showed them to be made of iron of bloomery origin, consistent with ironwork of the 13th century (Gilmour 2003). Detailed recording of these nails established a pattern of usage for each type. Seven complete rows of panels were recorded producing an average of 117 standard and ten small-headed nails around the edge of panels. In the same area, there were an average of 34 standard nails and 33 small-headed nails securing the board edges per panel. In other words, the smaller nails are more often used to nail the board edges to each other than the boards to the ceiling structure.

Generally speaking, the boards were nailed to noggins with two nails at each end, and if they passed beneath a joist they were nailed to that with one or two nails. However, the narrow end of the baseboards was always nailed with a single nail. Nailing mid-span to intermediate noggins was haphazard throughout. Boards were nailed to each other along their lapped edges, nails being clenched over above.

original

20mm standard profiles   15mm small-headed ¾ profile

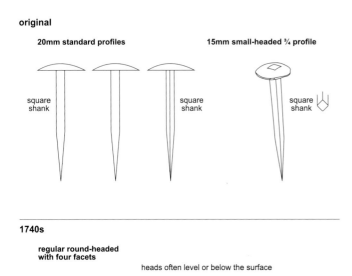

square shank   square shank   square shank

1740s

regular round-headed
with four facets

heads often level or below the surface

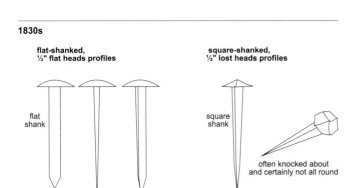

1830s

flat-shanked,
½" flat heads profiles   square-shanked,
½" lost heads profiles

flat shank   square shank

often knocked about
and certainly not all round

Fig 87 Types of nails used originally, and in the 1740s and 1830s

Fig 88 Detail of the lower side of the clinker-built ceiling at the east end of the nave

Spacing of nails was somewhat erratic, but an average approximation was *c* 18in (450mm) apart. All nailing was carried out from below and with great care, as no damage from hammer marks was found. Very occasionally a nail missed its target, so another was driven alongside, this time not in a pre-drilled hole. Unused nail holes occur regularly over the whole ceiling, almost entirely in the border boards. No reasons have been discovered for this. Where boards are scarf jointed they were normally nailed, although about 30% contained no nails at all. Nearly 50% of scarf joints had one nail, and 15% were nailed with two nails. One or two joints contained three nails. This somewhat irregular approach is consistent throughout most of the ceiling, except for the first few rows at the east end, where virtually every scarf was nailed with two nails.

Construction: discussion

The construction employed to realise the original nave lozenge design was extremely complex. Although looking as simple to construct as that in the transept, the nave lozenge design requires extraordinarily intensive attention to detail, partly because the narrow imported oak boards laid clinker fashion do not lie as flat as the much wider, English (?local) oak boards used in the transept (below, 4.2; above, 3.2) (Fig 88). Every board has to be mitred at both ends, not with one repetitive mitre, but with two of different length. The mitres are further complicated by being cut in boards that meet each other at an angle from the horizontal as they are clinker-built and do not lie flat in the plane of the ceiling. Where the ceiling changes angle, the mitres are even more complicated, being angled both ways. Furthermore, there are the three basic sizes of lozenge: the large horizontal central lozenges, and smaller and half-lozenges on the sloping sides. With every variation in length and particularly width of panels and lozenges, the lengths of all the boards are different, and so therefore would be the angle of the mitre. In addition to the general taper, all the boards have been chamfered and shaped to produce a tight joint with the adjoining board. This means that in practice every board has to be offered up, marked, cut on a bench, fitted to its neighbour, mitres cut and fitted, and then fixed in the ceiling.

The use of the clinker technique for laying the boards both in the transept and the nave is extremely rare. Shortly after its use at Peterborough, however, it was repeated in the timber vaulting of the nave of St Mary the Virgin, Warmington, Northamptonshire (Fig 89) (Pevsner and Cherry 1973 (445) suggest a date of *c* 1275). Local carpenters may have had experience of boat building, as suggested by the 1311 reference to Abbot Godfrey making a large ship, which he gave to the king (Sparke 1723, 164; King forthcoming). Clinker-built boats displayed in, for example, the Viking Ship Museum in Oslo (Norway) use planks of a similar width and thickness, jointed horizontally and vertically in a similar fashion (also Sørenson 2001). The fixing with wide-headed nails of the planks to the ribs of Viking vessels displayed there is similar to the work at Peterborough, and there is a moulded detail at the edge of the planks which is reflected at Peterborough (Fig 90). This edge groove is seen on joinery in Scandinavian stave churches, for example Torpo church, Hallingdal, Norway (Fig 91) (Hauglid 1970; Bergendahl Hohler 1999, i, 66–76). A groove is used extensively on the face of the Torpo timbers, as though to delineate the edge and it is further enhanced with polychrome. At Peterborough the board edge grooves would have been made with similar grooving planes.

Fig 89 The 13th-century clinker-built timber vaulting of the nave of St Mary the Virgin, Warmington, Northamptonshire (includes replacement boards)

Fig 90 Detail of moulded edge on the face of the boards of a Viking ship in the Viking Ship Museum, Oslo

Fig 91 (upper and lower) Flat and grooved edge mould details on the faces of timbers at Torpo church, Norway

4.3 THE PAINTED DESIGN AND ITS RELATION TO THE CEILING STRUCTURE

Richard Lithgow with Helen Howard, incorporating observations by Al Brewer and analysis by Jane Davies, Helen Howard and Ioanna Kakoulli

Introduction and sources for the investigation

The painted design follows the arrangement of the ceiling boards. It consists of three interlocking rows of lozenges, with a further row of half-lozenges on the north and south sides (Fig 69; Fig 70). The inner boards of each lozenge are decorated with a figurative subject or an entwined foliate motif. Investigations conducted throughout this project established that the 1740s and 1830s restorers in the main followed closely the original figurative subjects and foliate motifs on the lozenge centre boards, although the original lozenge border designs differ significantly from the present

scheme (below; Chapter 5). The figurative elements are small in scale relative to the surrounding decorative borders (Fig 68; Fig 94). The subjects include kings, archbishops, bishops, apostles, the Agnus Dei, a Janus head, demonic figures, images of vice, musicians and representations of the Liberal Arts; the relationship and significance of these subjects are discussed below (below, 4.5). Fig 94 omits the subjects of the figurative central portions but shows the background as red, blue or green, the justification being the likelihood of the 1740s restorers taking inspiration from, or matching, surviving traces of the original lozenge centre backgrounds.

Since there is little or no record of the original 13th-century paint scheme, and it is entirely covered by 1740s and 1830s repaint, evidence gathered during this project for the original scheme is based on close inspection of the ceiling boards, particularly under raking light, together with analysis of paint samples (below, 4.4; Chapter 6.7; Table 9) and art-historical analysis (below, 4.5).

In addition, there is one possible description of the ceiling decoration prior to the 1740s intervention in a letter

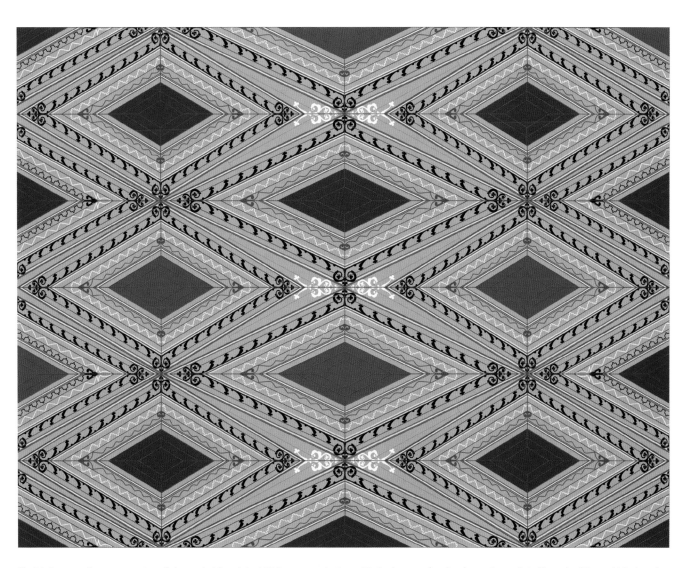

Fig 94 An overall reconstruction of the probable original 13th-century design with the lozenge border decoration painted in red, white and black and the background of the lozenge borders shown as unpainted oak; the figurative central portions are left blank here but coloured red, blue and green (east to top)

written by Governor Pownall to the Reverend Michael Lott in 1788 (Pownall 1789, 146). It is not stated whether Pownall is describing the painted decoration as it appeared before the 1740s restoration or after that work was complete. However, going by the findings of investigations and analyses carried out for the current project, the description is more likely of the original scheme.

The ceiling of the Cathedral of Peterborough is said to have been done at the time that the nave of the church was built, that is, at a period between 1177 and 1199. It is of wainscot formed into three compartments, running the whole length of the nave; a principal one along the middle, two lesser ones on each side. Each compartment is framed into panes and panels in the form of lozenges or half lozenges. The fillets, mouldings, and rosetts are gilt; a frett antique runs round the pannels as a bordure, and on the naked wood within this are the figures painted.

The reference to the gilded elements and the 'naked' wood are of particular interest. Although no evidence has been found to indicate the use of gold leaf in the original scheme, we are certain gold was not used in the 1740s restoration (Chapter 5.2, cf 5.3). Moreover, it is possible that in the original scheme some of the background to the lozenge border patterns and parts of the lozenge centre boards were unpainted (or at least painted in water-based 'distemper' and not in oil) (below and 4.4), which would fit the allusion to 'naked' wood, whereas the ceiling boards were entirely overpainted in the 1740s.

It is pertinent here to consider how the ceiling would have been prepared for the extensive repainting which took place in the 18th and 19th centuries. In order to ensure the adherence of new paint, the original surface is very likely to have been washed down and/or rubbed down quite vigorously and abraded to remove loose paint and dirt. Background areas may have been more harshly treated than the figurative areas in this respect. It may also be significant that distemper would have been more easily washed away and any areas so painted more readily abraded than those painted in oil. Documentary evidence regarding the 18th-

century repaint supports this: 'several of the figures were entirely encrusted with dirt, but that upon applying a sponge they became clear and bright', while 'parts came clear off from the wainscot' (Pownall 1789, 149; Chapter 5.2).

The sequence of painting and fixing

Prior to finding examples of original paint under original nails in lozenge centre boards, it was considered unlikely the figurative and floral elements on lozenge centre boards would have been painted before the boards were nailed in position, mainly due to the perceived difficulties in laying out the overlapping lozenge centre boards accurately in order to paint the detail (above, 4.1). There are instances of original alignment marks incised across the joints of original lozenge boards (above; Fig 85). These are deemed to be original because in many cases the boards have 13th-century nails in place and so have never been repositioned. If the incised lines served as reference marks to align the painted decoration though, one would expect to find examples on many more boards (above, 4.1).

The discovery, however, of original paint exposed from under missing original nail heads – including within lozenge centre boards – allowed a much better understanding of the original painting technique and sequence of painting and fixing (Fig 95). Analysis of samples and close examination of the exposed original paint established there was no uniform lead white ground for the figurative detail, but it was identified in a number of cases (below, 4.4). Most of the original paint was applied directly on to the wood. The wooden support would have been sealed (with a material such as size or oil) to prevent absorption of the binding media from the original paint layers.

Having established that all the boards were painted before being fixed in place, it becomes easier to explain why many of the incised lines that extend across two boards are slightly offset. The lines were incised when the boards were first offered up to the ceiling and cut to fit. They were then used to realign boards when they were laid out for painting. As soon as the paint was applied the incised lines became irrelevant and the painted decoration became the primary

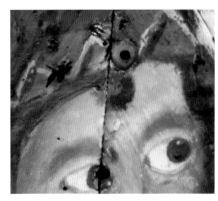

Fig 95 Examples of original paint under missing original nail heads on lozenge centre boards (left to right): 14/I–II, bay 7; king, 12–13/III, bay 7; 17/III–IV, bay 6

alignment indicator. Furthermore the significance of other incised lines serving to delineate the edge of the overlapping boards – particularly lozenge centre boards – became clear. With the extent of overlap marked and the individual boards cut to length, it was possible to accurately recreate the lozenge shape on a bench for painting, either at ground level or on a scaffold, without the need for cross-board reference marks (above, 4.1). This process would have been time-consuming, as we can see from the length of time taken solely to repaint the ceiling in the 1830s (Chapter 5.3).

There is only a little evidence surviving of preparatory or underdrawing of the complex design scheme or details (below, 4.4). There are, however, a number of incised 'setting out' lines following the paint scheme. For instance, some of the mandorlas framing subjects on lozenge centre boards are partially outlined in this manner. Fig 96 illustrates such a setting out mark for the mandorla of a bishop. It is not certain these are preliminary setting out lines for the original design, particularly as they are not more prevalent. However, on the St Peter lozenge a section of cusped mandorla has been incised where none has been painted; indeed there is no room for a mandorla around the St Peter figure. If the 1740s restorer copied exactly the St Peter figure he would not have thought to include a mandorla and it would follow that these incision lines must be original.

Finally, we must assume that nail heads interrupting painted detail were overpainted and any necessary adjustments to align the painted decoration made once the boards were finally attached to the ceiling.

Elements of the original 13th-century paint scheme visible in low relief

Some elements of the original scheme are visible in low relief (eg, Fig 97; Fig 98) beneath 1740s and 1830s paint. Detailed examination of board surfaces in raking light has been very instructive in this regard and, as part of the condition survey, all this shallow relief has been recorded on photographs and photogrammetric drawings of the present scheme. This

Fig 96 Setting out mark (arrowed) for a mandorla around a bishop (14–15/II–III, bay 7)

Fig 97 Shallow relief trefoil motif visible in raking light on an original board, overpainted with 1740s/1830s extended chevron pattern (34/III, bay 2)

Fig 98 A fox visible in shallow relief on the wyvern-like lizard or dragon lozenge (33/III, bay 2): left – the fox outlined in red; right – (detail) raking light defines the head and neck, and original underpaint can also be seen (grey)

detailed record demonstrates that, while there are significant differences between the original and present lozenge border patterns, the figurative and foliate elements generally have been little altered; an exception is the fox in bay 2 overpainted in the 1740s with a grotesque winged wyvern-like lizard or dragon (Fig 98) (Chapter 5.2).

Throughout the conservation project considerable efforts were made to explain the presence in low relief of original elements (further discussed in Chapter 6.6). Visual examination and sample analysis indicated the relief effect, first thought simply to be the result of impasto underpaint, was in most instances too pronounced for the thickness of surviving original paint to be wholly responsible. The shallow relief appears and fades along the boards with no trace of the jagged, stepped edges that would signify delamination and loss of a paint layer. That this relief decoration is so intermittent indicates it was not created by shallow carving. In addition, there are numerous instances where the shallow relief intersects and is level with prominent medullary rays suggesting the softer wood between the rays has receded through decay where it was not protected by a paint layer. It is inconceivable that a carver would have only carved the lower ground between the medullary rays.

Following his inspection of the ceiling during the phase 3 works, Al Brewer suggested that the relief of the trefoil designs was due to a masking effect of a painted surface: that is, the trefoils were painted, thus protecting them from a degrading factor such as weathering, while the surrounding was less protected, although not necessarily unpainted (Fig 97). The trefoils may simply have been painted with a more protective medium such as oil (as indeed indicated by the paint analysis, 4.4), while the surrounding may have been a water-based medium, such as a distemper; the latter may have entirely disappeared (Brewer 2000).

The findings of a survey recording the extent of weathering across border pattern boards do indicate at least some of the backgrounds were protected to some degree, although not to the extent provided by the oil-based paint used for the linear designs. However, no background paint was found beneath the original linear border designs; this strongly suggests that this linear decoration was painted directly on to the plain wooden background. The use of an oil medium for linear border decoration does not preclude the use of a water-based medium elsewhere.

The same close-ridged, receded surface occurs widely – but also somewhat unpredictably – around foliate and figurative detail on lozenge centre boards (Fig 98; Fig 130). Sample analysis has established the original oil-bound paint in various colours was applied directly over the timber surface or occasionally on what may be a preparatory drawing layer of carbon black.

Thus the 'weathering' of the wood surfaces not protected by oil paint indicates that on the lozenge centre boards the oil paint did not extend overall. Since it is likely the central compartment of each figurative lozenge was entirely painted,

the existence of low-relief detail implies the use of mixed media, with a water-based medium, such as distemper, also being used. Therefore it seems logical to suggest oil-based paints were used for flesh tones and other detailed features of the composition and distemper for the remainder. However, sample analysis established that oil paint was used on the background of at least some lozenge centre boards; original oil-based paint has been identified forming the plain red background to the Rhetoric figure (Fig 121).

Unfortunately, paint sample analysis (below, 4.4) found no definitive evidence for the use of distemper paint on the ceiling. Weathering has often occurred randomly not only within the backgrounds on lozenge centre boards but also within the figures. In addition, abrasion of the surfaces prior to repainting in the 18th and 19th centuries (above) may be responsible for patchy survival of original paint.

Lozenge border patterns

Detailed recording of the designs visible in low relief beneath the 1740s and 1830s paint and of paint exposed from under missing original nail heads (Fig 99) has established the

Fig 99 Original red paint exposed from under (missing) original nail heads: upper – on triple grooved border boards (15/I, bay 7); lower – within the outer groove of key pattern boards (8/I–II, bay 8)

original lozenge border designs differed significantly from their present appearance.

Starting from the outside with the baseboards, the original decorative pattern sequence was as follows (shown in Fig 100); individual paint samples are referenced by sample number/year taken (Table 9).

1) The baseboards had a white scroll design with trefoil ornament (established eventually by paint sample analysis as lead white with a few carbon black and iron oxide yellow pigment particles, 20/2000). The surface surrounding the scroll design in the majority of these boards is heavily weathered suggesting the background may have been unpainted.

2) A grooved board with the alternating red (red and white lead, 26/1999, 9/2001) and white (lead white, 6/2000) bands intersected at the corners by an elaborate black scroll with trefoil ornament (item (3), below). Black paint has been identified in one sample from a raised area between the grooves (7/2000) but this should be considered an aberration as, generally, the raised areas between grooves on these boards are excessively weathered, to the extent that the raised bands are often level or lower than the grooves. However, the inner half of these boards is predominantly smooth. These observations suggest that the inner half of the grooved boards may have been protected by a non-oil-based paint while the raised bands between the grooves were unpainted.

3) A series of regularly spaced black (carbon black, 27/1997, 16/1999; 39/1999, 17/2001, 13/–14/2001) trefoil motifs/trefoil-ended stalks springing from a black band along the inner edge of the board. At each corner an elaborate black scroll extends on to the outer coloured bands board (item (2), above). This pattern is mirrored in the opposite quarter of the lozenge so that the trefoil motifs spring out towards the extended corners forming

an impression of crocketed gables (Fig 94). The trefoil motifs vary considerably in shape – in some cases even along one board – and this suggests freehand painting rather than the use of stencils for repetitive motifs. The trefoil decoration is generally visible in relatively low relief as the background surfaces are only slightly recessed through weathering (Fig 97). The surface of this and of the other curved edged board in the series (item (6), wave pattern) appear recognisably different from the other boards, as if they were from a different batch of timber. It may be that they were simply less affected by the weathering process because an original, non-oil-based paint partially protected the background surfaces.

4) A grooved board with the alternating white and red bands (37/1999; 57/1999; 10/–11/2001). A notable finding in the weathering survey was that the raised areas either side of these grooves (on what have become grey chevron boards) are consistently less weathered than equivalent areas on the coloured bands boards (2) and (7). This finding would indicate that in the original scheme the raised areas between the grooves on this board were painted. However, there is no other visual evidence to corroborate this and it has not been substantiated by paint sample analysis.

5) A linear stepped chevron design in white (lead white, 23/2001; 25/2001). The original linear design is generally visible in prominent relief (Fig 101). While the background is generally receded either side of the linear design the (now) black areas (Fig 132) are consistently – and sometimes appreciably – more weathered than the white. This finding is significant as it suggests that the white areas on these boards may have been partially protected by a non-oil-based paint while the (now) black areas were unpainted.

6) A linear wave pattern in red (18/1999) with scrolled ends. The original design is only rarely visible, and then

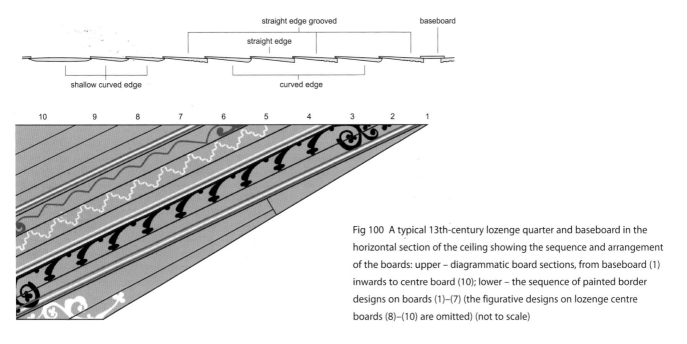

Fig 100 A typical 13th-century lozenge quarter and baseboard in the horizontal section of the ceiling showing the sequence and arrangement of the boards: upper – diagrammatic board sections, from baseboard (1) inwards to centre board (10); lower – the sequence of painted border designs on boards (1)–(7) (the figurative designs on lozenge centre boards (8)–(10) are omitted) (not to scale)

only in very low relief. In common with the other curved edged board in the border pattern series, the background surface is usually little affected by weathering; therefore it may have been covered by a non-oil-based paint.

7) A grooved board with the alternating red and white bands (examples exposed from under missing original nail heads but not sampled). As with the outer grooved board the inner half was recorded as being relatively unaffected by weathering while the raised areas between the grooves in the outer half are usually very weathered indeed. Therefore it is possible the inner half of the grooved boards may have been protected by a non-oil-based paint while the raised bands between the grooves were unpainted.

The lozenge border decoration varies for the smaller half-lozenges immediately over the ashlar boards. These boards have linear keyhole and dog-tooth patterns – both in black on off-white – in place of the stepped chevron and wave patterns (Fig 100, (5) and (6) respectively). The width and spacing of boards within the lower part of the canted panels varies considerably. As a result, the adjacent outer coloured band, keyhole and dog-tooth patterns (Fig 100, (7), (6) and (5) respectively; Fig 102) sometimes cover two rather than three boards. The linear keyhole is in black (charcoal black) (19/1999). In bay 5 an exposed area of seemingly original linear dog-tooth pattern in white was discovered on 22/IV/e (3/2000). The white tips of the original chevron/dog-tooth design is partially obscured by the displaced adjoining keyhole/'bun' pattern board. The original linear pattern extends on to bare wood that had been protected from subsequent repaint and weathering by the overlapping board. The visible original white paint aligns with the raised linear 'visible underpaint' of the dog-tooth pattern on this board. This visible evidence strengthens the hypothesis that the background to the linear border decoration was unpainted.

All these findings help to explain the curious shiplapped sequence of grooved, straight edged and curved edged boards (Fig 77; Fig 80; Fig 100). Each of the three grooved boards in the sequence was painted with alternating colours. The existence of the shallow grooves, which are certainly not visible from any distance, may be explained as a guide for the painting of these coloured closely spaced parallel lines or bands. The straight edges on the grooved and stepped chevron boards mark the division between tiers of decoration and help to create an illusion of depth. The shallow curved edges of the central boards minimise the impact of the shiplap construction on the figurative decoration. Similarly, the slightly steeper curved edges of the linear, stepped chevron and trefoil pattern boards act to reduce the appearance of a division between patterns on the same 'tier'.

Doubt remains, however, as to whether the backgrounds were originally unpainted or at least partially covered by a less durable, possibly water-based paint. On the one hand, no such paint has been identified by sample analysis nor has any been exposed under missing original nail heads or displaced overlapping boards. Conversely, there is the persuasive evidence of differential weathering of board surfaces either side of linear designs (eg, Fig 101; Fig 102) and anecdotal evidence from the man employed to repair the ceiling in the 1740s who said of the original scheme: 'the body of the painting (under what he supposed to be the coat of oil) was in distemper ...' (Chapter 5.2; Pownall 1789, 149).

The 1740s restorer's reference to distemper is clearly of interest and deserves some comment. The man would have been familiar with what is now called 'soft distemper' paint where the pigment is mixed with powdered chalk and bound with a glue-size (animal glue) medium; 'soft distemper' is eminently water-soluble and remains so over time. In the medieval period pigments were sometimes bound with skin-glue but they were not generally bulked out significantly

Fig 101 Lozenge border pattern: differential weathering either side of linear stepped chevron design on an original board (3/I, bay 10)

Fig 102 Lozenge border dog-tooth pattern, showing differential weathering either side of the linear design on this original board (3/I, bay 10)

with powdered chalk to form the soft chalky paint more commonly used in the 17th and 18th centuries.

The complete 13th-century lozenge border design in the central part of the ceiling is shown in Fig 94 and Fig 100 with the background shown as a plain, neutral colour. The location of scrolls on the ends of the lozenges, forming finials on a series of gable ends, cleverly combine in the centre of the ceiling with smaller scrolls on the centres of the lozenges to form foliage clusters which have an important influence on the overall design of the ceiling. The subtlety of the original design has been reduced by the 18th- and 19th-century overpaint which has emphasised the patterns of the lozenge boarding compared with the figurative centre compartments (cf Fig 133). The foliage finials and crockets originally could be expected to have the level of impact shown on the reconstruction graphic (Fig 94).

The original ashlar board paint scheme

In bay 5 there are two early oak boards (22/III/m and /o) that have a very different linear pattern visible in relief beneath the 1740s and 1830s repaint. The underpaint is a

Fig 103 Possible original decoration visible in low relief on a 13th-century ashlar board reused in the ceiling (22/III, bay 5)

foliate design unlike anything found to date on the ceiling. Both boards have a series of dowel holes with broken pegs along their exposed edge. The pegs alone indicate these boards did not originally form part of a ceiling panel. Only the original baseboards are pegged in this manner, but they have a different pattern visible as underpaint. It is possible these are original ashlar boards salvaged and reused as replacement ceiling boards when the entire frieze was replaced in the 1740s. The 'weathering' to the board surfaces is identical to that on many original ceiling boards. Alignment of tracings of the relief underpaint on these boards (Fig 103) indicates the foliate design would fit the space now filled by the 1830s ashlar boards (Fig 104). Sample analysis indicates the leaves were painted a bright red and the linking tendrils a dark red or purple (1/–2/2000; below, 4.4). Interestingly these colours were painted over an oil-based, lead white ground whereas the original lozenge border decoration, and indeed some of the original paint on the lozenge centre boards, has no such ground layer.

4.4 THE ORIGINAL DECORATIVE SCHEME REVEALED BY PAINT ANALYSIS

Richard Lithgow with Helen Howard, incorporating analysis by Jane Davies, Helen Howard and Ioanna Kakoulli

Introduction

A thorough technical examination of the original and added materials of the painted surfaces was considered a vital part of the conservation programme in order to determine the nature and extent of any original paint layers still remaining and to characterise designs and outlines showing in relief on boards with otherwise 'weathered' surfaces. From early in the project it became apparent that the original ceiling decoration differed in many respects from the present scheme (above, 4.3). Analysis indicated there is widespread survival of original paint, hidden beneath layers of 18th- and 19th-century repaint, with occasional traces of the original decoration exposed where nails were dislodged, especially

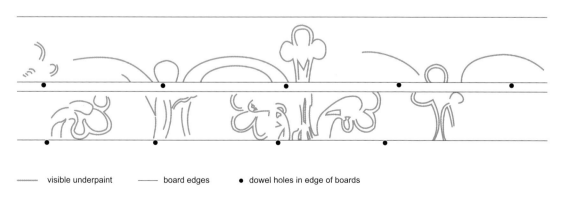

——— visible underpaint ——— board edges • dowel holes in edge of boards

Fig 104 Realigned tracings of the possible original ashlar decoration in bay 5: upper – board 22/III/o; lower – board 22/III/m

during the 1926 structural intervention above the ceiling. Examination of the numerous samples taken has contributed significantly to understanding the 13th-century scheme, in terms of both the nature and extent of surviving original paint layers and the design.

At the start of each phase of work, a sampling strategy was prepared and these strategies formed an important record of the developing understanding of the ceiling as the work progressed (Chapter 6.7). A total of 172 paint samples from the ceiling (referenced by sample number/year taken) were examined between 1997 and 2004 of which 134 were from original oak ceiling boards including the different border patterns and 64 samples from lozenge centre boards; samples were also taken from replacement boards together with three samples from the easternmost joist above the ceiling (Table 9 lists the paint samples referred to in this volume). Numerous examples of original paint under missing nails were identified within figurative subjects across bays 5 to 7 (eg, 1/–11/2003) (Fig 95). Various samples were taken from overpainted original nail heads in an unsuccessful attempt to find an original paint layer (added as part of final finishing); in fact, given the likelihood of paint loss resulting from corrosion prior to the 1740s intervention, it would be surprising if any original paint survived on the nails.

This large data set, combined with the circumstantial evidence of the condition survey carried out by conservators, has been interpreted and used to describe the original painting technique, and that of subsequent repaints (Chapter 5).

Preparation of the boards, grounds and underdrawing

Porous materials such as wood, and even stone, were commonly sealed to reduce the absorption of binding media from the ground and paint layers. For panels, this sealant was commonly animal glue (Bomford et al 1990, 17), and a glue sealant has been identified on an early 14th-century screen from Kingston Lacy (Tracy 1997, 28).

In north European panel painting generally, chalk (calcium carbonate, $CaCO_3$) grounds are most commonly employed, and indeed a chalk ground applied in three layers has been identified on the painted chamber ceiling panels of c 1263–6 from Westminster Palace (Lynn 1995, 499). Gypsum (calcium sulphate dihydrate, $CaSO_4 \cdot 2H_2O$) grounds have been identified on the early 13th-century Adisham reredos (Howard 2003b, 65–8) and on the most important surviving English medieval panel painting, the Westminster retable (c 1270) (Sauerberg et al 2009, 238), while a lead white ground was employed for the Kingston Lacy screen mentioned above (Tracy 1997, 28). On the Thornham Parva retable of c 1335, for example, the chalk ground is so thin in some places that it barely fills the wood grain, and over this chalk layer a lead white imprimatura has been applied (Bucklow 2003, 42). (For detailed evidence regarding original preparatory layers on early medieval English panels see Howard and Sauerberg 2009.)

The Peterborough sample analysis has shown that most of the original paint was applied directly over the wooden support. Traces of an interface layer between the wood and the paint, of gypsum mixed with animal glue, and in some cases with lead white, were found on 17 of the 134 paint samples obtained from original oak ceiling boards. Calcium sulphate dihydrate combined with a proteinaceous material – probably animal glue – for example, was identified by Fourier transform infra-red spectroscopy (FTIR) at the wood/paint interface in sample 7/1997. However, given the invasive conservation treatments sustained by the Peterborough ceiling – including the application of animal glue and hessian to the reverse of the boards in the 1920s (Chapter 5.5) – and the difficulty in identifying sealants which have often been almost completely absorbed by the porous support, it is not certain whether this represents an original or added material. Given the possibility of contamination from added materials, this is then insufficient evidence of a preparatory layer.

Traces of gypsum and a clay-rich material were also identified at the wood/paint interface in a number of other samples (7/1997, 8/1997, 23/1997 and 24/1997), and it is possible that these materials may have been employed to bulk out any sealant which was applied to the support. The calcium sulphate dihydrate here may have been employed as a material in its own right or may represent an alteration product of calcium carbonate. The degree of sulphation which occurs throughout the paint layers at Peterborough unfortunately makes certainty impossible as to whether calcium sulphate dihydrate or calcium carbonate was originally applied to bulk out the sealant; or indeed whether such a bulked-out sealant may actually be regarded as an initial ground layer.

In two samples where original paint layers are almost certainly present – 16/1997 and 23/1997 (Fig 107), where natural azurite is combined with yellow iron oxide – traces of a lead white ground are visible. This ground would have provided a compact and highly reflective surface to interact optically with the paint layers applied subsequently. In some samples (1/1997, 2/1997, 16/1997), calcium sulphate dihydrate was combined with the lead white in this preparatory layer, while in another sample (7/1997) a little carbon black was also incorporated to provide a slightly grey tone.

There is little evidence of preparatory drawing of the complex series of geometric elements and figurative details. Four samples taken from original lozenge centre boards, that is, from figurative subjects, have probable underdrawing: in three, it is a thin carbon black layer (2/1997, 24/1997, 16/2000); in the other, a red oxide/carbon black mix (2/1998).

With regard to elements of the original scheme visible as low relief beneath later repainting (discussed above, 4.3), analysis of numerous cross sections has shown that in most instances the relief effect is too pronounced for the thickness of surviving original paint to be wholly responsible. In many cases no original paint exists in the cross sections and where

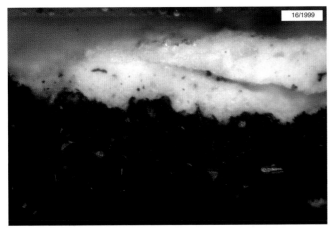

16/1999

Fig 105 Sample 16/1999 taken from a trefoil-ended stalk in shallow relief (28/I/p, bay 3) shows a thin yellowish layer over a white lead ground over a shiny charcoal black layer: upper – location of sample; lower – micrograph

it is present the layer/s are thin (3/1998, 5/1998, 16/1999, 18–20/1999, 15–22/2001). Sample 16/1999, for example, taken from a shallow relief trefoil-ended stalk visible in raking light on an original board, overpainted with 1740s/1830s extended chevron pattern, shows a thin yellowish layer over a lead white ground over a shiny charcoal black layer (Fig 105). It was these results and other circumstantial evidence that indicated the relief designs should be attributed to a masking effect of a painted surface.

Samples, however, do indicate the low-relief linear border designs were painted in oil-based paint directly on to the oak boards without an intervening preparatory layer. By implication this suggests the background to this linear scheme must have been unpainted: otherwise the finely painted border designs would overlay the previously applied background paint.

Original paint layers and their application

All the paint layers identified as original are in an oil-based medium. The pigments present in paint layers which appear to be original are as follows:

orpiment (As_2S_3) (yellow arsenic sulphide, lemon yellow/golden yellow);

carbon black (C) (black);

charcoal black (C) (charcoal made from willow, weak bluish black);

chalk ($CaCO_3$) (calcium carbonate, white);

basic verdigris ($Cu(C_2H_3O_2)_2 \cdot 2Cu(OH)_2$ but can vary) (copper acetate but can vary, bluish green);

natural azurite ($2CuCO_3 \cdot Cu[OH]_2$) (copper carbonate hydroxide, deep bright blue/greenish blue);

red iron oxide, also known as red ochre (Fe_2O_3) (red, with considerable variation);

yellow iron oxide, also known as yellow ochre ($Fe_2O_3 \cdot H_2O$) (yellow-orange, with considerable variation);

vermilion (HgS) (mercuric sulphide, brilliant red);

lead white ($2PbCO_3 \cdot Pb[OH]_2$) (lead carbonate hydroxide, dense white);

red lead (Pb_3O_4) (lead oxide, bright orange-red).

These pigments are consistent with those identified in other early English panel paintings (Howard 1997). For example, a similar palette was employed on the mid 13th-century painted chamber ceiling of Westminster Palace (with the addition of ultramarine blue and red lake), and on the early 14th-century screen from Kingston Lacy (with the addition of red lake) (Lynn 1995, 499; Tracy 1997, 28). Although only slight traces of paint survive on the early 13th-century Adisham reredos, vermilion, red lead, basic verdigris and lead white have been identified in its original polychromy (Howard 2003b, 65–8).

From the lozenge border patterns, a thin carbon black layer was found in two samples taken from the original crocket and finial-like foliage that is evident in low relief on many of the boards subsequently decorated with an extended chevron pattern (27/1997 and 39/1999). This thin black layer, which in many instances is visible with the naked eye through the white overpaint on these boards, is not an outline but covers the whole of the trefoil-ended stalks, indicating it is in fact the original decorative layer rather than underdrawing (Fig 106).

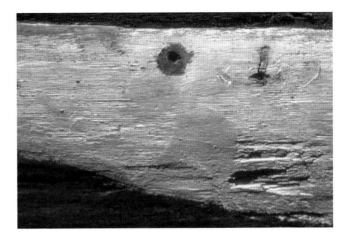

Fig 106 Thin black paint on a low-relief trefoil-ended stalk visible through the white overpaint on an extended chevron board (18/II/r)

Of real interest is the unusual use of an underpaint of natural azurite combined with a little yellow iron oxide and lead white to produce the effects of modelling in the flesh tones. Similarly, azurite – though combined with black and white pigments – was employed to outline the figures on the painted chamber ceiling of Westminster Palace, producing a bluish undertone in areas such as the chin of the prophet; a more complete pale blue underpaint is evident beneath the flesh tone of the prophet's hand (Lynn 1995, 499).

The flesh tones themselves were produced from varying combinations of vermilion and lead white (20/1997, 21/1997, 23/1997 from St Peter), and with the addition of a little yellow iron oxide and carbon black for the dulcimer player (7/1997). Sample 20/1997 from St Peter's head (Fig 107) shows the grey preparation applied to the wood support, over which the flesh tone of vermilion combined with lead white in an oil medium was applied. Sample 21/1997 (Fig 107) shows an underpainting in pale green was originally employed to model the flesh tones. This underpaint consists of a layer of natural azurite combined with yellow iron oxide and lead white, and was applied in a layer 60 microns thick. Over this was applied the flesh tone of vermilion combined with lead white. Similarly, sample 23/1997 (Fig 107) shows a layer of dark green underpainting produced by mixing natural azurite and some yellow iron oxide in a lead white matrix (cross section: lower) was employed to produce the tonal modelling for the flesh tones of vermilion combined with lead white (cross section: upper). A layer of repainting, consisting of lead white combined with a little carbon black, can also be seen on the surface of sample 23/1997 (Fig 107). The comprehensive later repainting of the flesh, undertaken

in lead white combined with red lead or carbon black – and with harsh outlines in black reinforcing linear details – effectively conceals any subtle effects of modelling which may have been intended by the medieval artist. Nevertheless, because it further implies a sophisticated technique, the finding that natural azurite was combined with yellow iron oxide and lead white to produce the effects of modelling in flesh tones is of great interest.

Natural azurite was also used in varying combinations of other pigments to form green paints. It is combined with a few particles of yellow iron oxide in a sample from St Paul's lobed mandorla (16/1997), and with lead white and a red/orange pigment, possibly iron oxide, in a sample from drapery within the Grammar lozenge (11/2003). A sample was taken from green paint on the drapery of the organistrum player, from beneath an original nail head now missing (5/2001; Fig 108). There is a single layer identified visually by Davies as containing a mixture of natural azurite with lead white, iron oxide yellow, chalk and orpiment. In dispersion (Fig 108, bottom) particles of yellow ochre, calcium carbonate and a blue copper pigment can be seen. In section (Fig 108, middle), the blue copper pigment looks like azurite and the red-brown particles of cuprite confirm this identification. In dispersion some particles do resemble azurite, but the majority have undergone change to other copper salts. Scanning electron microscopy with X-ray energy dispersive spectroscopy (SEM-EDXS) spot analyses certainly indicate the presence of orpiment in this sample. Iron oxide and chalk are also present.

The presence of orpiment in this scheme is worthy of particular note since there are relatively few examples of its

Fig 107 St Peter's head (30–31/II–III, bay 3): cross sections of paint samples 20/1997, 21/1997 and 23/1997

identifiable attribute, and no evidence has come to light for the presence of inscriptions on the ceiling. The kings and prelates are paired in peaceable dialogue, like figurines on a metalwork shrine. A biblical iconography of filiation such as the kings of Judah or a Jesse tree is ruled out by the bishops. A gallery of paired kings and high churchmen is much more likely to have been historical in nature: the later 13th-century pulpitum at Salisbury Cathedral is reputed to have had a gallery of kings, and there was a similar gallery of kings in Peterborough's own late 13th-century Lady chapel by 1295. Peterborough's number and selection of figures seems quite particular. The number of figures precludes a straightforward representation of the 'Kings of England since the Conquest'. Instead, it could indicate founder – or benefactor – iconography. Hugh Candidus describes the role in the foundation of the abbey and the establishment of its rights of King Oswald, Kings Oswy, Peada, Wulfere and Ethelred, their subject kings Sebbi and Sighere, and eventually King Edgar, from which a cast of a half-dozen figures is easy to establish (Mellows and Mellows 1941). The two archbishops could be Deusdedit and Theodore of Canterbury, and the bishops might be those cited in Candidus: Ithamar of Rochester, Wini of London, Jaruman of Mercia, Tuda of Lindisfarne and so on. Peterborough's kings and bishops are by this reading the figures involved in the early foundation and enrichment of the house, and in the defence of its privileges. This is a concept not unlike the huge array of sculpted figures, including charter-holding kings who

probably represent founders or benefactors, clustered on the contemporary west front of Wells Cathedral nearing completion in the 1240s (Sampson 1998). Later examples of monumental paintings arranged in a sequence of alternating kings and bishops or abbots include the interior entrance wall murals *c* 1290 of the chapter house of York Minster as recorded by John Carter (Norton 1996).

But a more obvious recent model suggests itself in the one building whose patronage was influencing most major Benedictine abbeys in south England in the generation after 1220, Canterbury. The Trinity chapel at Canterbury's east end finished by 1220 possessed a series of vault paintings representing standing and seated figures of saints, archbishops and kings old and new, some holding scrolls, with St Thomas of Canterbury, St Dunstan and Henry III among them (Caviness 1974; Fig 119). These pictures, probably executed around the time of translation of St Thomas in 1220 but only known through later sketches, would have complemented the Bible genealogy in the stained glass of the same structure. The Peterborough nave ceiling in contrast does not include an extensive local hagiography. St Peter is present with St Paul, but neither St Oswald (whose arm-relic was a treasure of the house) nor Kyneburga, Kyneswitha and Tibba nor St Andrew appear; nor (so far as we can tell) St Thomas who enjoyed a cult at Peterborough. Arguably, as at Canterbury, such subjects were painted on the lost medieval presbytery ceiling (replaced after *c* 1500: Tyers 2004).

Fig 119 Figures from the vanished vault paintings of the Trinity chapel, Canterbury Cathedral (left to right): St Peter; St Thomas (Becket of Canterbury); Henry III wielding a sceptre (Caviness 1974, pls XX c, XIX c, XXI a) (reproduced with permission from Canterbury Cathedral Archives)

The Liberal Arts, sun and moon (the west half of the ceiling)

The seven Liberal Arts in the form of the trivium and quadrivium are the only important English monumental instance of the topic (for this see Binski 2003, 50–2). The personifications accompany the kings and bishops in the west half of the ceiling, and fall into two triangular formations on the north and south perimeters of the ceiling (Fig 118; Fig 126). To the west, the quadrivium is disposed in a triangle with its base along the north side, with the trivium to the east. As an odd-numbered figure, the Arts are thus laid out lopsidedly. The cleaning of the images has not changed or cast doubt on their attributes and identification. From the quadrivium (Fig 120), Geometry and Music are immediately recognisable with their attributes, a pair of compasses and a set square, and an organistrum. Astronomy to the west is extensively repainted but appears to have held up an object, perhaps originally a sphere; Arithmetic has both arms raised, holding in her hands two attributes, of which one is probably an abacus. To the east, in the trivium (Fig 121), Rhetoric

with her tablets and stylus is conventional, as is Grammar with her disciplinary palmer and pupil. Very similar palmers or ferules for the chastisement of pupils and dating to the 14th century were found in the drain of a city school in Lübeck in 1866 (Warncke 1912). Logic or Dialectic makes a gesture of instruction to a tonsured clerk on a pedestal, who holds up to her a curious crocketted pyramidal object the nature of which has not been elucidated by cleaning.

As a 'proto-humanist' subject (ie, a subject preserving the classical Latin traditions of pedagogy before the 'true' Renaissance) the Arts were quite popular in the late 12th and early 13th centuries in north France (eg, Chartres, Déols, Sens, Laon, Auxerre), the Holy Roman Empire (eg, the Hortus Deliciarum) and Italy (eg, the Trivulzio candelabrum). Such themes were fashionable as a topic in Benedictine circles around 1200. By 1220 Christ Church Canterbury not only had vault paintings relevant to Peterborough, but also an ornate floor around the shrine of St Thomas, depicting the Psychomachia (battle of Virtues and Vices), the Labours of the Months, the Zodiac and monsters. Canterbury's shrine pavement almost certainly reflected prototypes in north

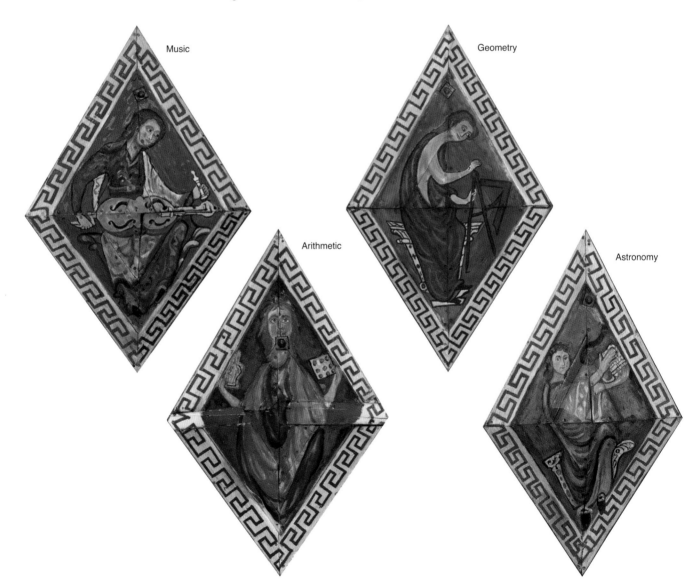

Fig 120 The quadrivium: Music, Geometry, Astronomy and Arithmetic (bays 7–9) (for location and context see Fig 118; Fig 126) (post-conservation)

Grammar   Rhetoric   Logic/Dialectic

Fig 121 The trivium: Grammar, Rhetoric and Logic or Dialectic (bays 6–7) (for location and context see Fig 118; Fig 126) (post-conservation)

France and Flanders such as that made *c* 1170 for the choir of the Benedictine abbey of St-Remi at Reims, originally including the Labours of the Months, the Zodiac, the Seasons, the Rivers of Paradise, Virtues, personifications of Terra, Mare and Orbis terrae, Old Testament narratives, evangelists, prophets and apostles, King David and the Liberal Arts. Possibly such topics circulated in model books in north France and south and east England in the early 13th century. Again we are reminded of the importance of studying pavements as well as ceilings.

The sun and moon (Fig 122) appear to the west of the

moon

sun

Fig 122 The sun and moon (bays 9–10)
(for location and context see Fig 118; Fig 126)
(post-conservation)

97

Arts, the sun on the south side falling opposite Astronomy (Fig 120). Though heavily repainted, both are in chariots that now lack their full complement of four horses and two oxen respectively. There is no reason to doubt the authenticity of their general appearance. They are festive pseudo-antique personifications that hint at a more distinguished ancestry. But we may suggest again that they emerged from within a consciously humanistic Benedictine visual culture in which repositories of Anglo-Saxon and Carolingian material at major monastic centres in the south and east of England played an important role.

St Peter-Agnus Dei and the east half of the ceiling

To the east of the trivium, and either side of the easternmost kings and bishops, are arranged four musicians including a cornet-blowing angel, also a fiddler and dulcimer player (Fig 123); these are certainly 'positive' musicians of the type found in the borders of *Beatus* pages in contemporary psalters like the Evesham Psalter, the angel being somewhat surprisingly the only concession to a Christian celestial imagery on the ceiling (Morgan 1988, fig 68 no. 111). St Paul (Fig 124) terminates this particular group, paired with the final, lamp-bearing, king. Next come the patron of the church, St Peter, and the Agnus Dei (Fig 124), hemmed in by a circle of demonic figures including much more obviously 'negative' musicians. The triangular arrangement of the Arts cedes to a quadriform arrangement for the positive musicians, and finally a circular arrangement for the demonic forces. Last to the east come Janus, and a medallion with four lions circling a fish.

The kernel of this end of the ceiling is the Agnus Dei-St

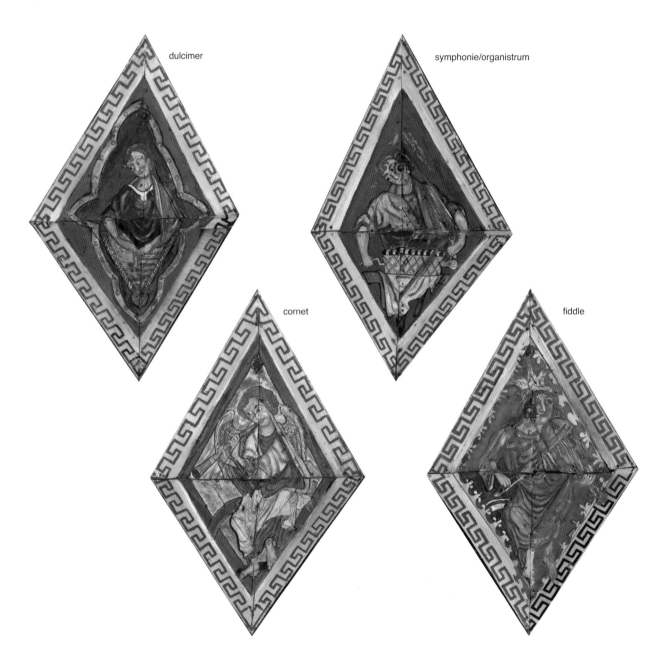

Fig 123 Four 'positive' musicians: dulcimer player, symphonie or organistrum player, fiddle player, angel blowing a cornet (bays 4–5) (for location and context see Fig 118; Fig 126) (post-conservation)

bay 7 | bay 6

Fig 126 b

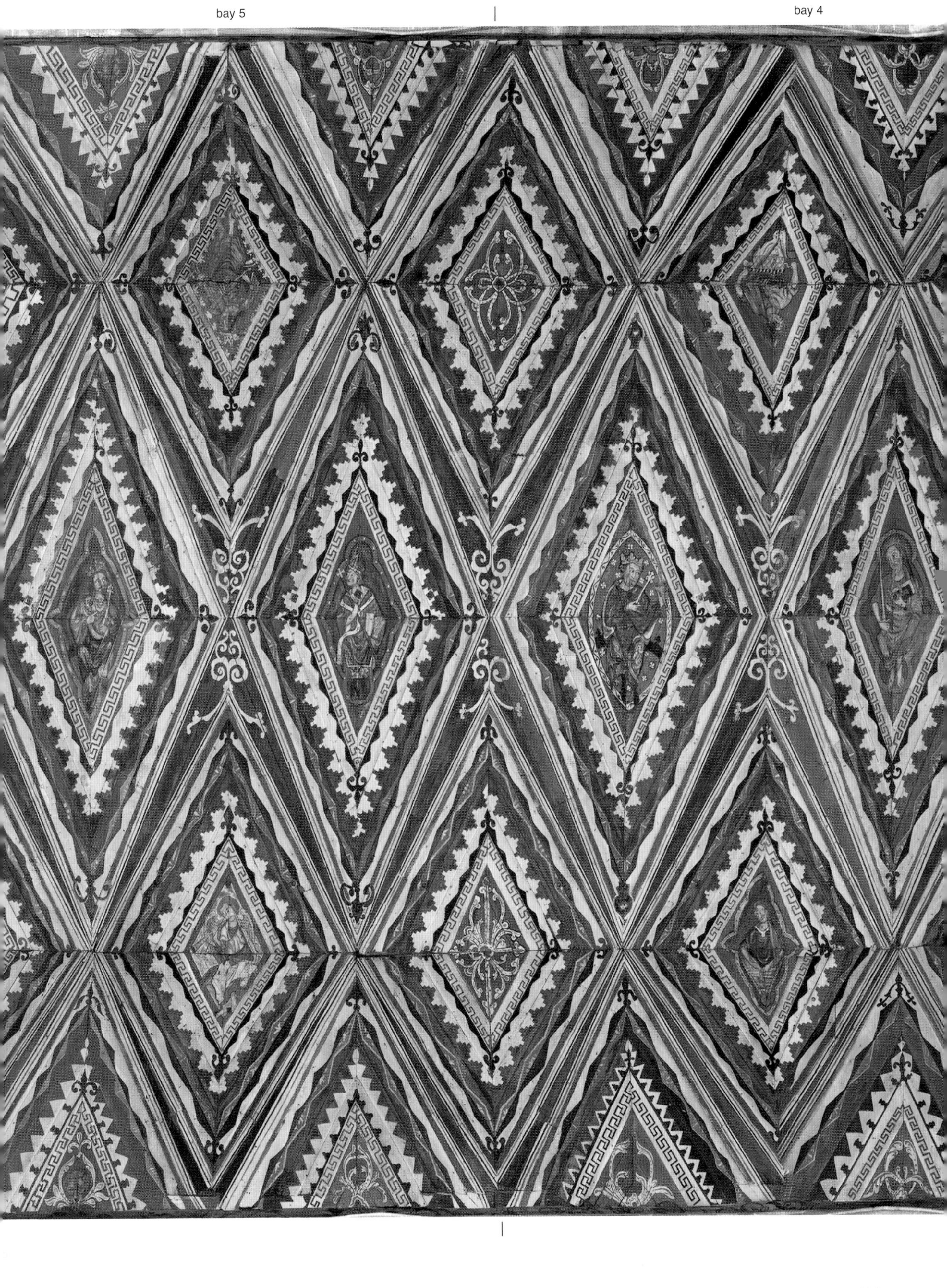
bay 5
bay 4

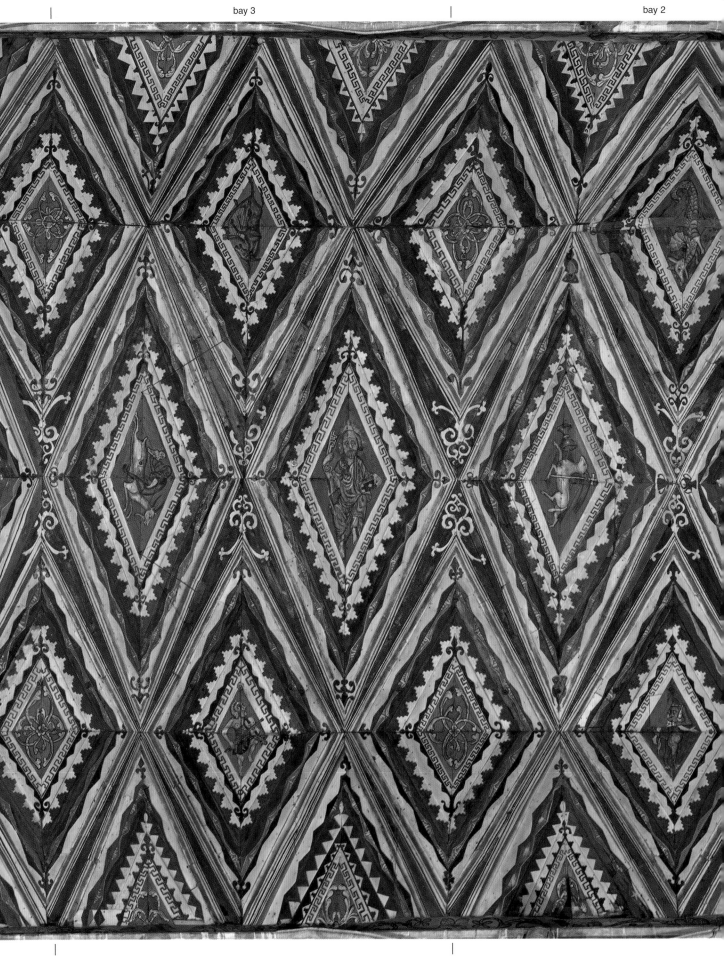

Fig 126 c

n

106

east

5 POST-MEDIEVAL REPAIRS AND RENEWAL

Following the Benedictine abbey's surrender in 1539, the abbey church became the cathedral church of the new see of Peterborough, founded in 1541 and consisting of a bishop, dean and six prebendaries, with the diocese comprising the counties of Northampton and Rutland (*VCH* 1906, 83–95). This chapter summarises the post-medieval history of the structures described in Chapters 2, 3 and 4. Here the focus is on findings from the conservation work and tree-ring analysis relating to the programmes of repairs and rebuilding of the later 17th, mid 18th and 19th centuries, and of the 1920s, and how these works affected in particular the nave roof, the transept roofs and ceilings, and nave ceiling. In addition, documentary sources illustrate the significant expense and time required by both the structural repairs and repaintings.

5.1 THE 17th CENTURY

Documentary evidence

Jackie Hall, Tim Halliday and Donald Mackreth

The post-medieval history of the building begins with the evidence in the acts and audit books of the post-Dissolution cathedral. Many of these records, however, are unspecific, such as the 1629 payment of 5s 4d for one day 'sodering on the roof of the church' (CUL, PDC MS 52, ann 1629, fo 29v). In 1640, the significant sum of £20 was spent 'mending the roofe of the South Ile', including eight man-days sawing timber, but it is not clear if an aisle is meant (either nave or presbytery) or the south transept, also generally referred to as the 'south ile' (CUL, PDC MS 52, ann 1640, fos 3–3v). A slater was also involved.

The destruction caused by Cromwell's forces in the Civil War is well known, especially of tombs, glass, screens and other images – muskets were even fired at the image of Christ enthroned in the presbytery ceiling (Gunton 1990, 334–5). Clearly, the nave ceiling, covered in images, only survived because it was so difficult to reach. In a contemporary account, Francis Standish records the sad story of the son of a Parliament officer who, rifling jackdaw nests in the roof of the nave, fell through some rotten ceiling boards on to the organ loft and died (ibid, 338). Although the cathedral church was allowed to continue in use as a parish church during the Commonwealth, major repairs – and record keeping – did not begin again until the

Restoration of Charles II in 1660 and reinstatement of the dean and canons. The consequent programme of repairs and rebuilding throughout the church and precincts stretched well into the 18th century.

Frequently, work cannot be identified from payments alone, but the 'South Ile' and the 'North Ile', perhaps the transept arms, are mentioned in the accounts of 1664–5 (CUL, PDC MS 52, ann 1664–5, fos 1 and 4); the 'lanthorne tower' was also subject to major works post-Restoration. The 'roofe of the North Ile' is specifically mentioned three times, including 'putting in new spares [spars] and supporters the timber being broken'. Further work is recorded in the 'South Ile' in November 1668 (CUL, PDC MS 52, ann 1668–9, fo 6). This was substantial, since it cost over £16, included a new beam and work on the ceiling, required scaffolding and used many hundreds of nails. Without question, this must document the only 17th-century work still physically present in the nave and transept roofs and ceilings, recorded further below and actually dated 1668 on the tie beam at the south end of the south transept (below). A small proportion of the replacement ceiling boards of this date also survive.

The next account that may refer to the ceilings in question is a payment of £25 in 1671 to John Lovin (or Loving) 'for whiting the upper part of the minster', with a further payment to him of £8 for 'mending all the seeling of the church' (CUL, PDC MS 52, ann 1670–1, fo 4v). There are several more payments, including for 'mending the great beams', but for all of these the precise work and its location is not clear. There is no physical evidence that the ceiling paint was restored during the 1668 intervention (below) and it is possible that the 'whiting' refers to the west transept vault. Major releading of the 'south isle' in 1672 could refer to the south transept, since later records show that it was covered in lead before 1761 (below). It, and references to carpentry and ironwork in the 'south isle' in 1674, might refer to many areas – the south transept, the nave south aisle or the presbytery south aisle (CUL, PDC MS 53, ann 1672, fo 3v; ann 1674–5, fo 3). The ceiling of the 'north isle' is mentioned in 1676, at the same time as the ceiling over the altar (although it is not clear which altar is meant; CUL, PDC MS 53, ann 1676–7, fo 3); work continues into 1677, including 'securing the north isle in the body of the church' (ibid). In 1678, significant work takes place not just in the north 'isle' but 'in the roof of the body of the church', before returning to the 'south side of the body of the church', presumably the nave south aisle (CUL, PDC MS 53, ann 1677–8, fos 2v and 4v). Also in 1678, the south transept ('isle') roof was fixed with timber and iron to the crossing tower (CUL, PDC MS 53, ann 1678, fo 3v). None of this work is now clearly visible in the surviving structures, however, and so it is to the 1668 work in the south transept that we now turn.

17th-century repairs to the transept ceilings

Hugh Harrison, Richard Lithgow, Cathy Tyers and Ian Tyers

In the absence of evidence in the building, it seems that the medieval transept ceilings remained substantially unaltered until after the Restoration in 1660 when substantial repair work was undertaken.

Major structural repair was carried out to the south transept ceiling when the southernmost tie beam (no. 14) was replaced, together with substantial amounts of boarding. The quality of timber and finish on beam 14 is not as good as the medieval work; it may have been made in two pieces due to the unavailability of larger prime timber. Scarfing the beam at the centre led to the decision to insert support brackets at each side; these are visible from the underside, have been given decorative moulded ends and are dated (1668) and initialled, possibly by the carpenter Thomas Brown who billed for ceiling work and 'placing a new beam in the South Ile' in November 1668 (Fig 127) (CUL, PDC MS 52, ann 1688–9, fo 4v). From the pattern of surviving original and replacement boards intermediate between the original medieval boards and the 19th-century replacement boarding, it would appear that all the boarding to the ten panels in southernmost row N was replaced at this time, together with localised areas of boarding to most (nine rows: D–G, J–N) of the other rows (Fig 63). The intermediate oak boards are exceptionally wobbly grained, full of knots and fairly fast grown. They tend to have pit sawing marks on the backs and they show more evidence of splitting and

fragmenting than the earlier boards. Boards measured were generally 9mm thick and of variable width up to about 300mm. Two boards that were measured each featured one edge chamfered at about 45°, though the precise reason for this is not clear; their widths were almost identical at about 265mm.

An excellent set of tree-ring results was obtained from boards identified as 'intermediate' boards; these boards were found only in the south transept and were retained as part of Pearson's 1880s ceiling (below, 5.4). Of the 55 intermediate boards, seven were selected. All of these form a sequence dated AD 1482–1656 inclusive (Fig 128). Three of these series include sapwood rings. The heartwood/sapwood (h/s) boundaries of these three samples are at AD 1640, AD 1644, and AD 1647, the first of these also has sapwood rings out to AD 1658 (the last two rings are unmeasured). Combining these provides a felling date range for this material of AD 1658–86. Samples 8, 9 and 11 from two different adjacent lozenges may be derived from a single tree. These boards are English and probably sourced locally. The seven dated intermediate boards are therefore a coherent group all of which, on tree-ring evidence, are likely to have been felled in the third quarter of the 17th century (or a few years later). The felling date range corresponds nicely to the recorded date of 1668 on the tie beam support bracket. (The tie beam could not be tree-ring dated and the brackets were unsuitable for analysis as they had too few rings.)

No evidence was found to show definitively that the ceiling paint was restored at the time of the 1660s intervention, but given the replacement of boards in the south transept it is likely that at least part of this ceiling was painted (below, 5.2).

Reused washers identified on the underside of the ceilings – 12 in the south transept and 27 in the north transept – bear a close physical resemblance to the 17th-century washers used for the scarf bolts on tie beam 14 and are of equal dimensions at 75mm diameter and 2–3mm in thickness. The washers, which would thus appear to belong to the 17th century, have a function more decorative than

Fig 127 Bracket supporting beam 14 on the west side of the south wall of the south transept, inscribed 'TB 1668'

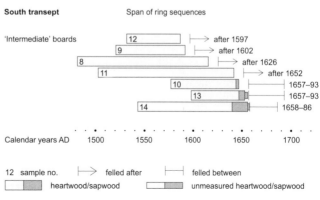

Fig 128 Bar diagram showing the chronological positions of the dated material from the 'intermediate' boards in the south transept (sequence PCF2); the felling period is also shown

structural and are all placed at the central point of each lozenge (eg, Fig 60). Examination of the original board ends where these washers are missing or misplaced shows no evidence of the washers' imprint in the paint shadow which suggests that they are a later addition. Two samples of paint surviving on a washer's surface have been analysed and were found to be very similar to the paint used on the nave ceiling in the 1740s (below, 5.2; Fig 130). A 17th-century date does not, however, explain the preponderance of washers in the north transept where there are no surviving intermediate boards and the only common link is that all the washers occur under Pearson's replacement beams and had evidently been reused.

5.2 THE 18th CENTURY

Documentary evidence

Jackie Hall, Tim Halliday and Donald Mackreth

By contrast with the immediate post-Restoration repairs, the 18th century is rather more poorly documented, with few payments clearly identified with any particular building or part of building. The repainting of the nave ceiling in the 1740s is well known, however, from the 1788 letter of Governor Pownall who, having applied to the bishop of Peterborough for information, discovered that in 1773 the then bishop had met the restorer. The bishop had heard

> … that the man, who about thirty years ago was employed to repair the ceiling, was still living. He sent for him, and learnt from him that the whole was repainted in oil. He told his lordship that several of the figures were intirely encrusted with dirt, but that upon applying a sponge they became clear and bright, whence he concludes that the last coat was of oil. He was altogether of the same opinion with what I had suggested, that the body of the painting (under what he supposed to be the coat of oil) was in distemper: parts came clear off from the wainscot. He assured his Lordship that he only retraced the figures, except in one instance the third or fourth compartment from the West door, where the whole figure peeled off: in this single instance he followed his own fancy having nothing else to trust to, and even here he endeavoured to imitate the style of the rest … . (Pownall 1789, 149)

Some confirmation for this date comes from William Stukeley's diary under 17 August 1747:

> I went to Peterborough. They are new whitewashing, or rather dawbing the cathedral, and new painting the roof in ridiculous filigree work, party-coloured, that has no meaning in it; and above all they have, for greater ornament, as they fancy, painted the ceiling over the high altar in imitation of marble. (Stukeley 1887, 70)

This certainly suggests that the cathedral was, in summer 1747, some way through a programme of redecoration, probably of the transept and presbytery ceilings. Only the conservation programme tells us that this also included replacing many of the nave ceiling boards and, probably, the entirety of the ashlar boards. Any structural work that may have taken place on the roof at this time will have been lost to the wholesale removal of timbers in the early 19th century (below, 5.3).

Shortly after this, the south transept roof was again in trouble (cf above, 5.1), since in 1761 a survey found that its south end was ruinous and should be taken down and replaced (PCL, PDC MS 54, fo 115). The new roof was to be covered with Westmorland slates, perhaps putting Peterborough Cathedral in the vanguard of using this material at such a distance from the quarries (two years later Westmorland slate was also chosen for the choir: PCL, PDC MS 54, fo 118v). The expense was to be met partly by selling whatever lead came off and the remainder by taking out a loan; the total costs were £286 9s 4½d of which the cathedral received back £240 16s 6¾d from sale of the lead (NRO, PDC Box X5157, ann 1761; NRO, ML 869, 1762–3). Only six years later, 'part of the roof of the south isle … has latterly fallen in' but it is not clear if this refers to a different section of the south transept or to a different part of the building (PCL, PDC MS 54, fo 124v). Examination showed that the transept ceilings, as well as that of the nave, were repainted (below). It is possible that further searching in the many unindexed boxes of vouchers would provide documentary evidence of further works.

1740s repair and repainting of the nave ceiling

Hugh Harrison and Richard Lithgow, incorporating analysis by Jane Davies, Helen Howard and Ioanna Kakoulli

It is not known if there were significant interventions to the painted decoration of the nave ceiling prior to the 1740s; however, it would be remarkable had nothing at all been done to the scheme during the intervening 500 years. Some structural alterations certainly would have been made to the east end of the nave ceiling when the tower arch was rebuilt in the 14th century (Chapter 4.3, 4.4). Nonetheless, the earliest repair and repaint for which we have firm evidence is that of the 1740s, and there is no surviving evidence for structural repairs to the nave roof at this time (Fig 129).

There were very few reliable features visible from the scaffolding to distinguish 1740s softwood replacement boards from later, 1830s, softwood replacements. In the absence of conclusive evidence, such as obvious underpaint, identification of 1740s replacement boards involved an assessment of numerous physical and contextual factors including dimensions and manufacture of the board, properties of adjacent boards, nails, nail holes, shot holes, thickness of the paint, etc.

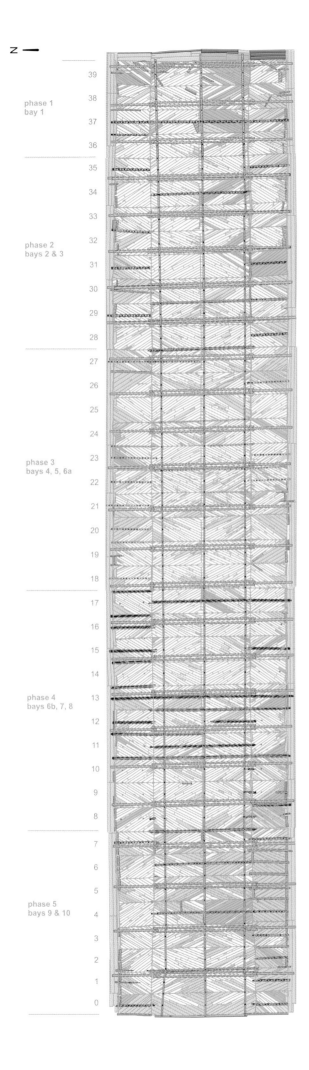

phase 1
bay 1

phase 2
bays 2 & 3

phase 3
bays 4, 5, 6a

phase 4
bays 6b, 7, 8

phase 5
bays 9 & 10

Ashlar and ceiling boards renewal

The original oak ashlar boards were apparently replaced entirely during this intervention; at least two original oak ashlar boards were salvaged and reused as replacement ceiling boards. The new softwood ashlar boards were painted with a new design. In turn, the 1740s ashlar boards were entirely replaced in the 1830s at which point a number of 1740s boards were salvaged and reused as replacement ceiling boards. Within the east half of the ceiling (rows 21–39) during the survey 23 softwood replacement boards were identified as being 1740s ashlar boards salvaged in the 1830s. There is nothing to indicate what filled the space between the west end of the ceiling and the stonework over the west arch (now occupied by 1830s tongue and groove softwood boards aligned vertically).

A number of original oak ceiling boards were replaced with softwood boards. A total of 258 replacement ceiling boards have been identified (including 60 reused original boards), more or less evenly spaced over the whole ceiling, but with almost double the average used at the east end of the ceiling (Fig 129). It is interesting to note that the bottom edges of the replacement 1740s boards in the canted side panels line up with the original board ends which are frequently short of the present ashlar panelling, suggesting the 1740s ashlar was on the same line as the medieval ashlar. With the discovery of whole panels of undisturbed 1740s ceiling boards, it is axiomatic that their nails are coeval. These have faceted heads rising to a point in the middle, and are irregular in size and shape (Fig 87).

At both the east and west ends of the ceiling (bays 1 and 10) original boards had been sawn through partially or completely replaced, indicated by 1740s boards on one or both sides of a cut. In other places there are 1830s boards on one side of a saw cut and 1740s boards on the other.

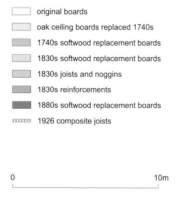

☐ original boards
☐ oak ceiling boards replaced 1740s
▨ 1740s softwood replacement boards
▨ 1830s softwood replacement boards
▨ 1830s joists and noggins
▨ 1830s reinforcements
▨ 1880s softwood replacement boards
▥ 1926 composite joists

0   10m

Fig 129 The extent of surviving 18th-, 19th- and 20th-century work recorded for the nave ceiling during conservation phases 1–5 (reflected view of boards) (scale 1:250)

The nave ceiling conifer boards and noggins: identification and potential for tree-ring analysis

Cathy Tyers

The initial work in bay 1 focused on the original oak boards and only once this had proven successful was it decided to attempt to extend the tree-ring analysis to the later replacement conifer boards, using boards from bays 2–6 (phases 2 and 3 of the site work). The reasons behind this were two-fold: the conifer boards were considered a potentially valuable source of data for the ongoing English-Heritage-funded research project investigating the viability of tree-ring analysis of conifer timbers imported into England (Groves 2000a); if successful, it would potentially aid the classification of conifer boards, being undertaken during the conservation programme, as belonging to either the AD 1740s or AD 1830s interventions.

A general assessment was carried out by inspection of the underside of the boards. However, more detailed investigation of individual boards was carried out from above, where the boards in rows I and IV extended beyond the ashlar boards, allowing access to a cross-sectional surface, and also following the lifting of some small sections of protective hessian from the upper surfaces of the ceiling boards. Exposed conifer backing noggins were also assessed. The criteria used during assessment to determine the potential for tree-ring dating of the conifer boards accessible during phase 2 of the site work were the same as those applicable to oak, though, whereas oak can be reliably identified from ordinary visual inspection of its cross-sectional surface, with conifers it is necessary to undertake microscopic analysis of the transverse, tangential and radial planes. Consequently, in order to identify the type of conifer used, it was necessary to remove a small section of wood, which comprised either a *c* 5–10mm cube cut from the exposed edge of ceiling boards extending beyond the ashlar boards or a short core obtained by a 9mm diameter plug cutter, drilled from above.

Wood identification of samples from 20 boards (including seven with a frieze underpaint layer: below), all thought to date from the 1740s intervention, indicates that the 1740s restorers used a single wood type (assigned type A here, from the red pine group of the genus *Pinus* which includes various individual species of pine which are native to either Europe or North America). A further 40 boards were thought to derive from the 1830s intervention and these comprised at least two wood types: 20 type A and 20 type B (type B being most likely *Picea* spp but possibly *Larix* spp, spruce or larch, both of which have individual species also native to either Europe or North America). The results of the wood type identification did not, however, appear to aid the differentiation between the 1740s and 1830s replacements, although the identification of a wood type B board would, assuming those analysed had been correctly assigned, support the conclusion that it is one of

the later replacements. The 18th-century refurbishment occurred at a time when Scandinavian imports dominated the timber trade, whilst by the early to mid 19th century North America had apparently become a major supplier, though the Baltic and Scandinavian regions were still of importance, particularly for quality or specialist timber (eg, Dollinger 1970; Lower 1973; Fedorowicz 1980). The differentiation between European and North American species purely on wood anatomical grounds is not possible. Successful tree-ring analysis would, however, have allowed the provenance of the timber to be identified, and hence the species.

The assessment of the conifer boards ascertained that they were suitable wood types and that many contained sufficient numbers of rings for dating purposes. However, extracting these ring sequences proved to be the stumbling block. The cross-sectional surfaces of the conifer boards generally abutted the adjoining panel boards, leaving no access to the cross-sectional surface on the vast majority of boards from below the ceiling. The cross-sectional surface was accessible from above on at least some of the boards that extended beyond the ashlar boards, although many were covered by additional sections of timber or hessian and they were often cut at an acute angle. It was not possible to employ the FIMO technique used for the oak boards because of basic anatomical differences between oaks and conifers (Schweingruber 1990). However, it is possible to obtain ring width measurements from the grain showing on radial sections rather than cross sections of conifers (Topham 1998). In such instances the grain is highlighted on highly polished and varnished surfaces. Unfortunately, at Peterborough, where small sections of protective hessian had been lifted, the rougher and unpolished upper surfaces were considered unsuitable. The removal of thin cross-sectional slices from ceiling boards overhanging the ashlar boards was also considered but the acute angle that those accessible were cut at was again problematical. Following consultation with the conservation team, the overall conclusion was that the necessary intervention to obtain samples suitable for tree-ring analysis (viz removing and cutting boards) was too great. This, combined with the fact that the results from identification of wood type proved incapable of providing information useful in separating different phases of conifer repair, led to the abandonment of any further work on the conifer boards in the nave ceiling.

To conclude, it has not been possible to provide any independent dating evidence for the conifer boards used in the 1740s and 1830s interventions, either through tree-ring analysis or species identification. Analysis of the wood types of the conifer replacement boards indicated the presence of at least two types, whose distribution does not reflect the refurbishment phases to which they had been assigned. This material has potential for tree-ring analysis, but it proved impossible to recover reliable ring series from this material using a low intervention method in accordance with the conservation programme. Their analysis may have provided dating evidence and information relating to variation in provenance of different conifer types through time, as some of the previous analyses of conifer timbers have demonstrated (Groves 2000a). In addition, it may have allowed independent verification of their assignment to specific refurbishment programmes on the basis of their paint and other factors.

The 1740s decorative scheme and paint layers

THE CEILING LOZENGES

The entire ceiling was overpainted in the 1740s. Observations from the scaffolding combined with evidence from paint sample analysis have established that the 1740s (and 1830s) restorers in the main followed closely the original, 13th-century, figurative subjects and foliate motifs on the central boards of the lozenges, although the original lozenge border designs differ significantly from the present scheme. Even at the west end of the nave ceiling, where there is a significantly higher proportion of softwood replacement boards, it should be assumed that the 1740s and 1830s restorers studied the surviving paint prior to the replacement of deteriorated boards and that they made every effort to recreate the original subject matter.

The figurative and foliate lozenge centre boards were entirely repainted in oil-based paints. A detailed study of incision lines on lozenge centre boards and of original detail visible in low relief as a result of the weathering process does not quite corroborate the restorer's statement that he 'only retraced the figures, except in one instance the third or fourth compartment from the West door' (Pownall 1789, 149); rather, there is evidence to suggest the subjects of not just one but possibly at least two figurative lozenges have been entirely created by the 1740s restorers and not based on the original subject.

The grotesque winged wyvern-like lizard or dragon lozenge in bay 2 has been identified as a 1740s invention. Underpaint visible in raking light indicates the original scheme had a 'renard' occupying only one quarter of the lozenge (Fig 98; cf below; Fig 131). Not enough low-relief underpaint survives within the other three-quarters of this lozenge to indicate in itself the original subject; Binski suggests that the fox may be connected with Aesop's fables (Chapter 4.5).

The eagle lozenge in bay 10 has significant traces of a lobed mandorla visible in low relief on two of the original boards (Fig 130). There is nothing to indicate whether the mandorla originally framed a smaller eagle or another subject. A sixth bishop, continuing the series of alternating kings and bishops, would seem more likely. However, a small area of 1740s paint, exposed from under a temporarily removed 1830s ceiling bolt and washer – as well as impasto underpaint on a 1740s replacement board – suggests that even the 1740s scheme within the eagle lozenge may have been very different from the 1830s one we see now.

Fig 130 The eagle lozenge centre boards (2–3/II–III, bay 10); the red drawing outlines a shallow relief mandorla

Pigments identified in paint belonging to the 1740s ceiling scheme are as follows: carbon black (C); basic verdigris ($Cu(C_2H_3O_2)_2 \cdot 2Cu(OH)_2$); red iron oxide ($Fe_2O_3$); yellow iron oxide ($Fe_2O_3 \cdot H_2O$); vermilion (HgS); red lead (Pb_3O_4); and lead white ($2PbCO_3 \cdot Pb(OH)_2$). A lead white ground was used to prepare softwood replacement boards and was applied over a considerable percentage, but not all, of the original scheme. Sample analysis has established that the 1740s restorer did not apply a preparatory ground over all the figurative and foliate panels prior to repainting and some dark elements of the border patterns (below) do not have an underlying ground layer. Much of the 1740s decoration is directly over the original paint layer. Where a plain lead white layer underlies the 1740s paint it is not always clear whether it is original or a 1740s ground. The olive green (basic verdigris mixed with yellow iron oxide) and red (red iron oxide with red lead) background paints of the figurative elements have a characteristic granular texture. The black outlines are painted with a distinctive brown/black paint, also used for much of the border decoration (below): a mix of carbon black, lead white, iron oxide and hydroxide particles (34/1999).

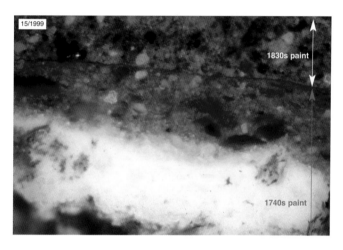

Fig 131 The wyvern-like lizard or dragon (over fox) lozenge centre boards (33–34/III–IV, bay 2) (upper) and (lower) cross section of sample 15/1999 from the blue/green background near the wing, showing, from top, 1830s Prussian blue, 1740s basic verdigris pigment mixed with yellow iron oxide particles, white lead ground

A sample (15/1999) from the blue/green background of the grotesque winged wyvern-like lizard or dragon lozenge (Fig 131; also Fig 98) shows clearly the 1740s basic verdigris pigment mixed with yellow iron oxide particles over a lead white ground; the whole is covered by 1830s Prussian blue paint. Two samples of flesh tones from the head of the angel with cornet (Fig 123) included apparent 1740s paint: white coloured with both iron red and vermilion (13/–14/2000). The red background paint has been identified as red iron oxide with red lead inclusions (eg, 55/1999). The olive green background paint is basic verdigris pigment mixed with yellow iron oxide particles (eg, 3/1997, 15/1999, 19/1999).

The original linear lozenge border pattern (Fig 100) was significantly changed by the 1740s restorers. Thereafter, the 1830s restorers did not significantly alter the design but simply repainted many elements. The altered border ornamentation of this (the existing) scheme is similar for most of the lozenge compartments (Fig 132). Starting from the outside, the 1740s decorative pattern sequence was as follows (paint sample numbers in parentheses):

1) the baseboards filling the spaces between the diamond-shaped compartments as before have a white scroll design with trefoil ornament (20/2000) on a black background, created by the very characteristic brown/black paint (a mix of carbon black, lead white, iron oxide and hydroxide particles) over an off-white (lead white) ground (17/1999);

2) the outer half of the next board is black- and red-coloured bands (charcoal black and red lead) (35/–36/1999) over a lead white ground (previously red and white bands); the inner half of the board is painted with a grey/brown thinly applied wash (not sampled); no attempt was made to keep the coloured bands within the grooves on this board;

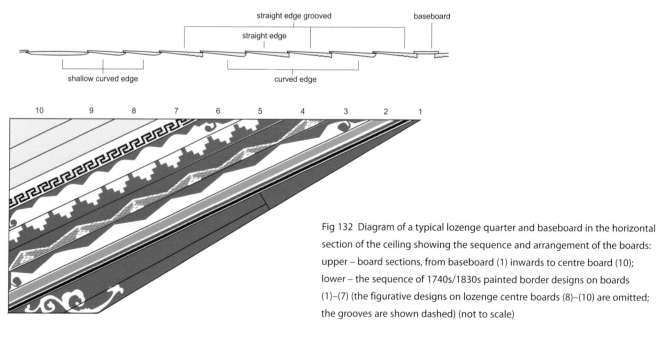

Fig 132 Diagram of a typical lozenge quarter and baseboard in the horizontal section of the ceiling showing the sequence and arrangement of the boards: upper – board sections, from baseboard (1) inwards to centre board (10); lower – the sequence of 1740s/1830s painted border designs on boards (1)–(7) (the figurative designs on lozenge centre boards (8)–(10) are omitted; the grooves are shown dashed) (not to scale)

doublers and stiffeners (subsequently removed in the 1920s). As Blore cut back some of the collars at least 1ft (300mm) each side short of their joints, often several in a row, the boards of the sloping sides must have played a significant part in propping up the edges of the horizontal ceiling.

In addition, the Dean and Chapter Audit Accounts show that Blore installed a central walkway, the doors from the roof space to the parapets, and the west wall panelling. Perhaps the most complete surviving aspect of Blore's intervention is the additional west wall panelling and the rebuilding of the ashlar, both consisting of ¾in-thick tongue and groove boards nailed to posts. The boarding at the west gable end was renewed or inserted to close what had previously been an opening into the roof over the west transept crossing. All of the ashlar boards were renewed on the present line at this time; the ashlar panelling is made up of two or three boards of random width; panels generally span four rows (approximately 21ft 0in or 6.4m).

The 1830s campaign was far more intrusive as regards the ceiling than that in the 1740s with the removal of many original ceiling boards and their replacement with softwood. It also included the repositioning of original boards and 1740s ashlar boards. Fragile areas above the ceiling were patched over with oak boards. Many of the, presumably loose, original ceiling boards were additionally nailed (with square-headed or dome-/flat-headed nails) (Fig 87), both at their ends into noggins and joists above, and along their edges, from board to board. There were also minor repairs to some boards.

Blore replaced an average of 148 boards per bay, which included an average of seven reused original oak boards, 31 reused 1740s softwood boards, and 110 new softwood boards. This left a significantly larger number of 1740s boards at the east end than over the rest of the ceiling. It is also of note that significantly more boards than the average have been replaced at each end of the ceiling. As regards disposition, 43% of boards renewed were on the north side and 57% on the south, probably a reflection of the prevailing south-westerly wind's effect on the building as a whole (Chapter 6.4). It is notable that at the west end very few original boards survive at the bottom of the south sloping panels.

Generally the replacement 1830s softwood boards have a uniform finish, but a few were found to have had little preparation, thus leaving exposed the sawn surface, the regular indentations indicating that the board was cut mechanically. The softwood boards used in the 1740s were *Pinus* spp (red pine group), while the 1830s boarding is a mixture of *Pinus* spp (red pine group) and *Picea* spp or *Larix* spp (above, 5.2).

Repainting the nave ceiling

THE CEILING LOZENGES

The 1830s restorers – with few exceptions – followed very closely the 1740s scheme (above, 5.2); generally they simply repainted many elements with oil-based paints. Nevertheless,

the repainting was extensive and time-consuming. The 1835 Layton receipt itemised the labour as '4 Men 117 days each' and '1 Labourer 46 days' (below and Table 6). Assuming six-day working and the work was continuous, it would have been completed by the four restorers in approximately five months, and they were assisted by a 'labourer' for almost half of that time. This, together with the quantities of each material used (eg, over 8cwt of lead white, 56lb of Brunswick green, 48lb red lead, 28gals of linseed oil), serves to put into context the scale of the 1830s restoration.

Areas of 1740s paint on the lozenge centre boards, revealed during the conservation project by the temporary removal of 1830s ceiling bolts and washers, illustrate how closely the 1830s restorers followed the earlier scheme, as for example the fiddle player lozenge, where two areas of 1740s paint (outlined in yellow) were covered in the 1830s by softwood patches and so escaped the overpaint (Fig 138).

Whereas nearly all the figurative detail was overpainted during this intervention, a considerable proportion of the 1740s olive green and red background paints were left uncovered. The olive green paint is very distinct from the 1830s blue/green repaint; the 1740s red is darker and more matt than the 1830s version. However, it appears the 1830s restorers made significant changes to the 1740s scheme in two central figurative lozenges. The 1740s red background paint to the Astronomy lozenge was changed to black in the 1830s (Fig 139). The 1740s scheme within the eagle lozenge may have been very different from the 1830s (above, 5.2). A less significant but more obvious change was made to the archbishop (2) figure (Fig 118) where the inscription 'COBLEY 1834' is painted on the pages of an open book, and 'R^D LAYTON 1834 SEXTON' is on the lower border of the archbishop's robe (Fig 140).

Pigments identified by analysis as present in the 1830s

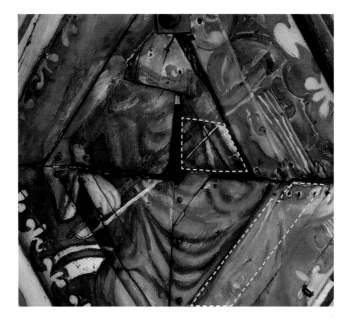

Fig 138 Detail of the fiddle player lozenge restored in the 1830s (taken during conservation work), showing two areas of 1740s paint (outlined in yellow) (21–22/III–IV, bay 5)

Fig 139 Background of the Astronomy lozenge altered from red to black in the 1830s (5–6/II, bay 9)

Fig 140 1834 inscriptions on the archbishop (2) lozenge (18–19/II–III, bay 6) (post-conservation)

scheme overall are as follows: carbon black (C); red iron oxide (Fe_2O_3); yellow iron oxide ($Fe_2O_3 \cdot H_2O$); Prussian blue ($Fe_4[FE(CN)_6]_3$); vermilion (HgS); red lead (Pb_3O_4); and lead white ($2PbCO_3 \cdot Pb[OH]_2$). In samples of white paint, lead white has been found with and without barium sulphate ($BaSO_4$). Barium sulphate was highly likely to be present in the pigment as purchased as it was used generally as an extender. Lead white is also present in varying degrees in most of the 1830s pigment mixes. Only on 1830s softwood boards is there an initial ground of lead white in oil, in some cases with the addition of barium sulphate (probably as an extender). The painters generally used no ground on original boards, the paint being applied over the 1740s scheme following the same pattern.

For most of the project it was thought that the inclusion

of barium sulphate as a component of some paints provided a useful *terminus post quem* of the end of the 18th century and therefore, in the absence of any evidence to suggest more than two significant interventions to the paint layer (the 1740s being the first), paints containing barium sulphate must belong to the 1830s. The identification of barium sulphate in original green paint from under a missing nail head within the background of Grammar (7/2001) caused us to question this assumption, but the conclusion of the analysis is that this is a contaminant (Fig 110; Chapter 4.4). Having reviewed all other instances from the ceiling where the presence of barium sulphate in a sample had identified the paint layer as from the 1830s intervention, in no case was there contrary evidence to recommend an earlier date for that paint layer.

On the lozenge centre boards 1830s paints and their components identified by sample analysis include: a brownish matrix of charcoal black, dispersed red iron oxides, yellow iron hydroxides, lead white (including barium sulphate) (34/ and 55/1999); a porous red paint consisting of red lead, iron oxide, lead white and barium white (22/1999); the same red without barium white (55/1999); a pink paint of red iron oxide (red ochre) and lead white (44/1999); a blue-green paint of pure Prussian blue (15/1999); and a matrix of Prussian blue and lead white (with barium sulphate) over a lead white layer (41/1999). Sample 14/1999 from lozenge centre board 29/III/b (ass with harp lozenge) shows paint from all three schemes: the upper orange red layer is an 1830s red lead and iron oxide particles; three layers of 1740s paint – charcoal black over lead white over a yellowish lead layer; the original is a thin charcoal black over a haematite-rich red ochre layer (Fig 141).

The 1740s lozenge border pattern scheme (above, 5.2) was not altered, rather 'refreshed' with a repainting. Starting from the outside of the decorative pattern sequence (Fig 132; Fig 133), the method of repainting and the pigment mixtures were as follows:

1) on the baseboards, the 1740s brown/black paint was 'strengthened' but not entirely overpainted with a black pigment consisting of a mixture of lead white, barium white, iron oxides and hydroxides, and charcoal black (17/1999); the scroll design with trefoil ornament was overpainted in lead white (20/2000);

2) the outer half of the next board with two coloured bands – black (charcoal) (35/1999) and red (red lead mixed with lead white) (36/1999) over a lead white ground – was overpainted in white and then the red and black lines replaced; a grey/brown thinly applied wash – usually over a lead white ground but occasionally directly on the wood support – covers the inner half of this board;

3) the 1740s extended chevron pattern was entirely overpainted throughout the ceiling in the 1830s with a lead white ground and charcoal black with lead white and barium sulphate inclusions (10/1999);

4) the 1740s grey extended chevron pattern, separated from a brown/black background with a white line, was

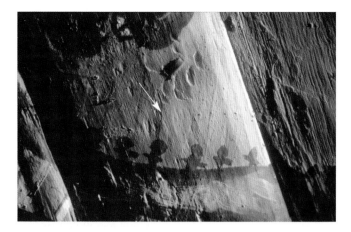

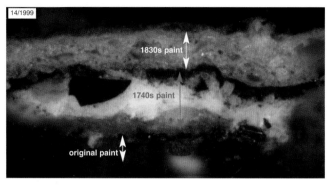

Fig 141 Paint from the three major schemes visible in sample 14/1999 (29/III/b, bay 3): 1830s red lead and iron oxide particles; 1740s charcoal black over lead white over a yellowish lead layer; original (13th-century) thin charcoal black over a haematite-rich red ochre layer

untouched by the 1830s restoration from rows 39 to 32 (bays 1–2) except for some strengthening of the brown/black paint, as happened with the baseboards (item 1); from row 31 (bay 3) westwards, the grey chevrons' white edging and V-shaped 'leaf' motif were entirely overpainted and replaced with a lighter grey chevron (carbon black/lead white with some red, yellow and brown oxide particles) (28/1997), usually with white edging and a white motif of graduated brush strokes;

5) the 1740s white ground on the stepped chevron pattern board was overpainted with lead white paint (31/1999); the brown/black stepped chevron pattern was strengthened with a brownish matrix of brown and yellow iron oxide particles combined with brilliant yellow and black (17/1997, 52/1999);

6) the wave pattern boards were treated inconsistently by the 1830s restorers: in the east part of the ceiling they did not entirely overpaint the 1740s black and white decoration, particularly not the matt black areas; elsewhere, some boards have been entirely overpainted with white before the resinous black paint was applied, on the remainder the black and white paints were simply strengthened;

7) the white background to the 1740s Greek key pattern decoration was entirely overpainted and the brown/black key pattern has for the most part been strengthened with

a lustrous black layer with red and yellow inclusions (25/1997, 13/1999).

The strategy for repainting the lozenge border patterns was, it appears, to carry out the work as quickly and as efficiently as possible. For instance, rather than trace around the 1740s Greek key pattern (7) with white paint it was quicker, and did not involve too much extra paint, to cover the linear pattern and then recreate it. Generally the 1830s restorers made an effort to retain or simulate the brown/black colour of the 1740s scheme on the baseboards (1), grey chevron (4), stepped chevron (5) and key pattern (7) boards. Thus the brown/black stepped chevron boards were not entirely overpainted with white but the chevron edges were carelessly overlapped with the white paint and then redefined in a resinous brown/black (Fig 142). Only instances of paint loss and discoloration were repainted in the main body of the stepped chevrons. Fig 143 shows a detail of an original stepped chevron board under raking light: the area outlined in red includes 1740s paint loss retouched with 1830s brown/black paint that is indistinguishable in appearance from the 1740s composite brown/black. On certain boards then the 1830s restorers took care to match closely the underlying paint, yet on other boards (eg, Fig 144) they made no effort at all. Most of the grey chevrons and white embellishments were also repainted but not usually the brown/black backgrounds. The much larger area of brown/black background on the baseboards was generally repainted, probably because the surface discoloration was more distracting in these plain areas.

A different approach was adopted for the extended chevron (3) and wave (6) pattern boards, both of which had the 1740s matt black paint rather than the characteristic brown/black. The majority of these boards were entirely covered with lead white paint in the 1830s and then the patterns repainted in a resinous black. However, for some reason at the east end of the ceiling many of these boards have little or no 1830s overpaint. As the survey for this project began at the east end, this led us to believe the single layer of decoration was 1830s and that the original trefoil and

Fig 142 In ultraviolet light the 1830s white paint appears as a brown wash over the earlier white layer on this stepped chevron board (23/III, bay 5)

Fig 143 Detail of an original stepped chevron board under raking light where the area outlined in red includes 1740s paint loss retouched with indistinguishable 1830s paint (22/II, bay 5)

Fig 144 Detail of a stepped chevron board where the 1830s restorers did not bother to match the underlying paint (17/II, bay 6)

linear wave patterns were not overpainted in the 1740s. It also led us to the mistaken conclusion at the start that all matt black was from the 1830s and all brown/black paint

from the 1740s. In fact, the 1740s scheme included both the matt black and the brown/black and the 1830s restorers made some effort to copy them, although the result was inconsistent. Analysis identified four categories of 1830s black paint: a composite black; a pure black; a charcoal black mixed with lead white; and a resinous black. Perceived variations within these categories result from slight differences in the pigment mix, the ratio of medium to pigment, the application of one black paint over another and the thickness of the layer.

THE ASHLAR FRIEZE AND WEST END

The ashlar boards on the north and south sides were entirely replaced during the 1830s intervention and the 1830s frieze decoration was painted *in situ*. The majority of the ashlar tongue and groove boards are covered by a single paint scheme. Detailed examination and paint sample analysis has confirmed that the existing ashlar boards and painted decoration date from the 1830s restoration. Eight samples of the frieze decoration were analysed and compared with samples from 1830s softwood replacement ceiling boards; the results confirmed the painting technique and materials were identical.

The decorative frieze pattern runs the length of the nave over the top of the north and south walls and comprises a scrolling design of stylised tendrils – in black, red, green and off-white – with recognisable flowers depicted in every downward loop alternating with stylised four-petal flowers (Fig 145). Apart from the rose, the flowers are difficult to identify, but look similar to common garden plants, such as mallow and cranesbill. The 1740s paint scheme (above, 5.2) was similar to this, the existing scheme, whereas the 13th-century scheme was different (Chapter 4.3, 4.4).

On the north and south ashlar boards, within rows 39 to 34 (bays 1–2), there is complex scrollwork underpaint that is significantly different from the overlying scheme. The name and date, 'W·Stallard' and '1835', are just visible through the overlying white background paint. This inscription – which is also on a ceiling board (Fig 146) – and paint sample analysis indicate the scrollwork decoration (Fig 147) was applied in the 1830s as a trial scheme; that trial must have been abandoned in favour of the present scheme. There are three other painted inscriptions from the 1830s on the ashlar boards: the names

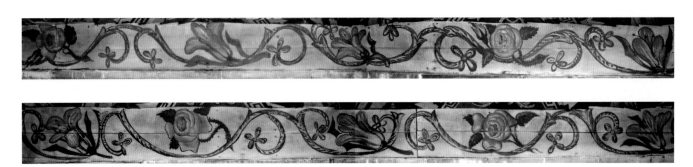

Fig 145 The existing, 1830s, decorative frieze pattern on two sections of north ashlar boards: upper – adjacent to panels 10–13/I, bays 8–7; lower – adjacent to panels 2–5/I, bays 10–9

(reusing 3.2% of the original material in the north transept and 25.8% of the original and 17th-century material in the south), together with all the noggins to both ceilings. He inserted perimeter traps in both. He also replaced four tie beams (1, 3, 8, 14) in the north transept, presumably because they were no longer structurally sound, and seven tie beams (1, 3, 5, 7, 9, 11, 13) in the south transept. In the case of the north transept, these replacements were hung off Blore's 1820s longitudinal beams hung from the roof tie beams, but for the south transept Pearson devised an upper and lower tie beam system connected by posts and braces which was worked in alongside the earlier roof. This is shown on J T Irvine's drawings (PCL, Irvine Papers, ix, fo 74; ix(a), fo 19; Fig 46) and on Fig 150. Pearson's new tie beams were substantially of the same dimensions as, and alternated with, the retained originals suggesting that his reason for replacing them was not the specific condition of each individual beam but the need to provide an overall new support system to a generally weakened structure without removing all of it.

Some of the main tie beams carry brand marks on their ends together with cargo marks and hauling hook marks (Fig 151). The brand marks have all been hammered into the grain and are about 25mm in height. The most commonly occurring is 'H2P'; others noted were 'ME' and 'A1V'. A few

beams had contemporary ferrous S-shaped reinforcement cramps driven in across radial splitting occurring from the heartwood. The timber has been mechanically cut and shows characteristic band saw marks on each surface; some show distinctive scored lines on their sides, which would appear to be caused by a fault in the saw milling process. Different docks or ports used different cargo marks to indicate from where the timber came and/or where it was going to. Tree-ring analysis (below) suggests that the new oak used for both transept arms is from a common source.

Pearson's clerk of works, J T Irvine, was known to have been sympathetic to retaining as much of the medieval fabric as possible and it is probably due to him that many of the medieval and 17th-century replacement boards were reused. Access to the underside of both transept ceilings, afforded by scaffolding in 2002, made it possible to establish for the first time that the boards retained in the 1880s were marginally realigned at that time; and that the decision to remove the paint scheme (the 1740s scheme repainted in the 1820s) was made after the ceiling was reinstated. Smeared residues of this paint scheme survived on some 1880s and earlier retained boards from when dissolved paint was wiped from earlier boards and smeared on to adjacent machine-cut 1880s boards. The smeared residues would suggest the paint

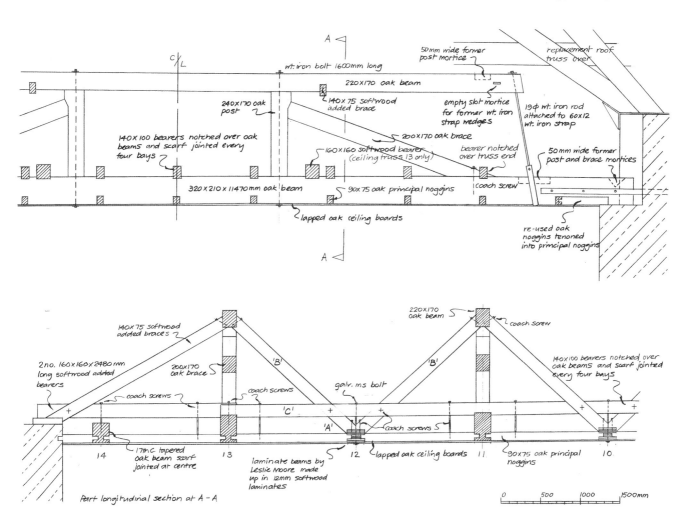

Fig 150 Typical form of the relict trusses (truss nos 3, 5, 7, 9, 11, 13) of the south transept together with the ceiling boards and noggins (upper shows east wall, lower the south wall) (drawn by Peter Ferguson)

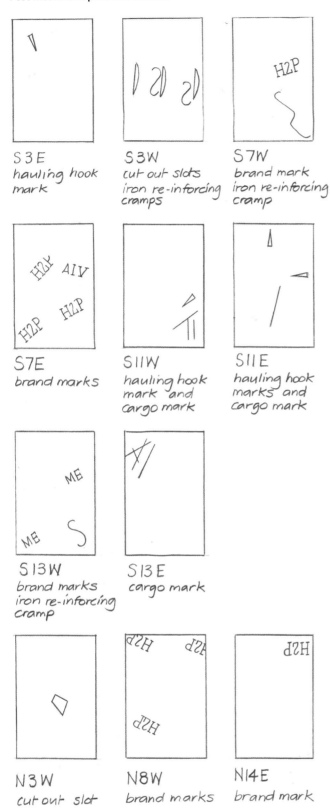

S 3 E
hauling hook
mark

S 3 W
cut out slots
iron re-inforcing
cramps

S 7 W
brand mark
iron re-inforcing
cramp

S 7 E
brand marks

S 11 W
hauling hook
mark and
cargo mark

S 11 E
hauling hook
marks and
cargo mark

S 13 W
brand marks
iron re-inforcing
cramp

S 13 E
cargo mark

N 3 W
cut out slot

N 8 W
brand marks

N 14 E
brand mark

Fig 151 Examples of marks on 1880s transept tie beams (not to scale)
(drawn by Peter Ferguson)

stripping process was solvent-based. Residual decorative paint on retained 17th-century metal washers was overpainted in black.

There is no appreciable difference in quality or finish on either ceiling. While there is some considerable variation in both thickness (13–17mm) and board width (120–450mm), all without taper, there are however very few extreme boards, the majority falling within the 150–250mm width band. The oak boards then are of a generally uniform width, but they are a mixture of radial and tangential conversions presumably from quarter sawing through largish trees; they are moderately even grained, with few knots. They are circular sawn on the backs and some are on the front, with the rest planed, possibly finished by machine planers; they have little or no sapwood present, and they have a distinctive bevelling and edge fillet in profile.

The overall board layout, while conforming to the original shiplap fixing sequence throughout (Fig 54), shows considerable variation in terms of the number of boards used in each panel due to the apparent random selection and perhaps supply of board sizes. Thus we find in the north transept combinations of nine, ten, 11, 12 and 13 boards used; this compares with from four up to eight boards per panel where original boards have survived complete.

An important difference distinguishes Pearson's board arrangements for the north transept from those of the south transept, apart from the far fewer number of original boards reused in the north transept (Fig 152). In the north transept, the setting-out detail of the nave ceiling (Fig 77) is consciously picked up, with the creation of a tapered space/face between each lozenge (approximately 200mm wide diminishing to 100mm). Each baseboard is centred over the diagonal line of the panel with the rest of the boards clinker-built. In the south transept, where there are many more original boards reused, the new boarding, with only one or two exceptions, is not set out to produce this tapering space/face to the baseboard. It does not appear to have been a feature of the original board layout and Pearson has not introduced it here even where panels have been completely reboarded; furthermore, in most instances the baseboards are not centred on the diagonal line of the panel and neither are the original panels.

Pearson's arrangement of the centre boarding to the lozenges differs in the main from the original layout, which used either small or large boards but always in fours. Pearson uses four in the south transept in association with the reused original boards, but where he completely reboards the two rows of panels adjacent to the crossing tower he uses, with one exception, two boards only (Fig 152). This practice of two boards is extended over the greater part of the north transept, the centre lozenge varying considerably in size. There are, however, exceptions which occur randomly, where a very small single board is sometimes used and in other cases four small boards, which all adds up to the careful use of the board offcuts presumably to save time and materials.

Pearson fixed his new boarding using broad dome-headed nails with a long flat shank, without apparently pre-drilling the board edges. Nailing conformed approximately to two per board end, three in the case of the widest boards, with edge nailing at approximately 300mm centres and about 19–25mm from the edge. Where Pearson used wrought iron

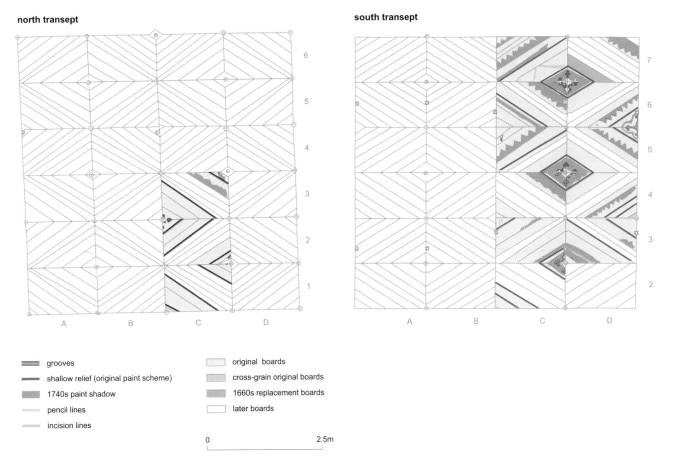

north transept

south transept

grooves

shallow relief (original paint scheme)

1740s paint shadow

pencil lines

incision lines

original boards

cross-grain original boards

1660s replacement boards

later boards

0   2.5m

Fig 152 Detail of Pearson's board arrangements in (left) the north transept and (right) the south transept (reflected view of boards) (scale 1:80)

bolts and straps (in lieu of wooden pins) in association with his timber jointing to support the structural timber above, boarding was cut round these obstructions and additionally nailed as necessary; the cutting around was noticeably crudely carried out in many instances. Pearson reused older washers at the centre of the board lozenges in association with new nails, up to 20mm in diameter across the domed head. Curiously, this mainly decorative use of ironwork is not carried through at every board lozenge and there is no evidence to suggest that where missing they have been subsequently removed. As no new washers are used, it would seem as if this is another example of Irvine's conservation practice where he simply kept what remained of these earlier washers rather than discard them.

Tree-ring dating of the later 19th-century transept roofs and ceilings, and timber sources

Ian Tyers

The majority of the boards in both transept ceilings are termed 'modern' (Chapter 3.1) and are taken to be 1880s boards from Pearson's restoration. The 'modern' boards that were analysed were chosen from the perimeter hatches in both transept arms (Tyers 2004; Table 4). Eight out of nine

from the south transept and five out of eight from the north transept form part of two undated, mutually exclusive, sequences, PCF3 and PCF4. This demonstrates that these two groups are derived from a common, though possibly mixed sourced, stock of planks.

Cores were taken from transept structural timbers. Four south transept cores form part of the sequence PCF5 which is dated AD 1716 to AD 1882 inclusive (Fig 153). These four cores are entirely heartwood although the latest ring present (sample 208) is dated to AD 1867 and this was cored from the heartwood/sapwood boundary on the timber from which it is derived. This sequence matches modern data from Poland and south Lithuania and it is thus likely that this material is derived from this area of Europe. Applying appropriate sapwood estimates to the material (T Wazny, pers comm) indicates it is derived from trees felled between AD 1875 and AD 1891. These four timbers within PCF5 are from the relict roof trusses in the south transept which still suspend the ceiling although they have otherwise been replaced by later softwood roof trusses. The other two timbers within PCF5 are from the documented 1880s Pearson repairs to the tower roof. The linkage of the four timbers to the crossing tower vault material makes it most likely that the present south transept structures were constructed for Pearson in the later 19th century. Two other

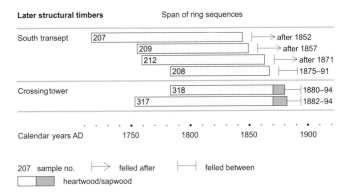

Later structural timbers   Span of ring sequences

Fig 153 Bar diagram showing the chronological positions of the dated material from the later structural timbers in the south transept roof and crossing tower of Peterborough Cathedral (sequence PCF5); the felling period is also shown

cores from the south transept structures (samples 205 and 206) are from two sections of a single tie beam formed by scarfing two quartered timbers together. These were found to be derived from a single somewhat distorted tree ($t = 6.33$) which has not proven datable.

The later 'Pearson' timbers both in the crossing tower and the south transept exhibit a common set of distinctive mechanical sawing marks. An unusually large number of the other cored 'modern' structural timbers in both areas do not match the PCF5 sequence. The PCF5 sequence also does not match the two PCF3 and PCF4 sequences even though it seems likely that they are all Pearson's work. The present evidence suggests, therefore, that the later 19th-century work at Peterborough may be based on a very mixed collection of oak sourced from a number of distinct locations. The PCF3/PCF4 distinction may indicate that for the reboarding of the transept ceilings Pearson sourced the rather fine, straight-grained oak from a number of locations. Much of the sampled material from the south transept thus unfortunately fails to provide any useful information. This relatively poor success rate may be due to a combination of the presence of material from many different periods or sources in the south transept roof and ceiling structures, along with the relatively short sequences derived from many of the noggins.

The successful dating and sourcing of late 19th-century imports at Peterborough was, however, a tree-ring first for the UK. The highest correlation values are with those from modern east Poland in the area of the Białowieża forest (T Wazny, pers comm); this is an area formerly Lithuanian, although at the time this material was exported it was under Russian control. Russian companies were certainly involved in exporting timber out through the Baltic at this period; for example, Schama (1995, 27–36) discusses his ancestors as timber cutters rafting logs down to the sawmills. The tree-ring confirmation of material such as this being used at Peterborough in the 1880s is interesting, but it may only represent a temporary preference for such timber, as at around this time the 'Arts and Crafts' movement was promoting the use of local timber by denigrating the quality

of the imported timber compared to the supposed quality of contemporary English product (H Harrison, pers comm). Peterborough's requirements could probably not be met by local sources anyway since the transept required a large number of 12m tie beams, and the associated rafters would also have been unusually long; the tower repairs also needed some timbers of significant length.

5.5 THE 1920s

Documentary evidence

Jackie Hall, Tim Halliday and Donald Mackreth

On the one hand, the work of the 1920s needs little introduction: it is the last major work on the roofs; can still be seen today; and did not form part of the conservation project. Nonetheless, it forms part of the mass of works which make it so difficult to see through to the medieval structures today – or even to the 18th- and 19th-century ones, so a summary is useful. The work was undertaken by the then cathedral architect Leslie Moore and started in 1924 (Fig 154). Here we are helped by a paper he wrote for *The Architects' Journal* in 1925. For the nave roof, Moore's main concern was beetle attack, lack of ventilation and lack of light; as to the nave ceiling, he felt that many of the medieval timbers holding the canted sides (the old scissor braces: Chapter 2.2; Chapter 4.1) were in a parlous state and required strengthening. He also thought that the transept ceilings were medieval, although we have seen how far from true that was, given previous phases of repair.

Regarding the south transept roof, Moore deplored 'the conservative spirit of the restorers' in retaining any of the old timbers as leaving food for the beetle, but more seriously he also discovered dry rot (Moore 1925, 262–3). As with the nave, he recommended treatment with preservative, better

Fig 154 The 1920s work on the roofs, from the south (from the *Peterborough Advertiser*, 12 November 1926: PCL)

work in detail had commenced.

Decisions not to pursue wholesale hessian removal were taken because of the damage removal would do physically to the timber. Further decisions to remove surface grime using a very delicate dry mechanical process in the main were confirmed and the chosen material, Wishab™ sponge, was tested and analysed for any harmful residues, which were not found. The level to which grime should be removed to achieve a unified effect was agreed over several assessment visits by the whole team.

Loss replacement – both of timber boarding and of painted decoration – was discussed at length. In the first phases all was left as found. However, for later stages and after the 2001 fire, certain larger losses when viewed from ground level were deemed too intrusive to be left as blank gaps and minor timber inserts were applied, as described by the conservators (below, 6.6 and 6.7).

By 1998 environmental monitoring and assessment was fully in place. Paint analysis and dendrochronology were producing definitive results and the three-dimenional grid survey had begun. In the same year the assessment of condition and dating of bolts, screws and fixings gathered pace, alongside confirmation that the boards were 13th century of probably north German origin, whilst the joists (formerly the medieval roof) were of English oak (Chapter 2.2, 2.3). Options for screw removal, for dealing with surface stains and for checking and protecting the metal bolts were determined at this time. Also the boards were further protected from abrasion by the new steel fixings by fibre washers between. Just as the recording system was extended and expanded to accommodate new findings, such as within the early roof structure, the craftsmanship and significance of the skilful timber construction at Peterborough from this early period could be better recognised as the work progressed. The project was multidisciplinary, highly inclusive and consultative.

The sudden impact of the 2001 fire had a profound effect on the whole cathedral building. For the conservation of the ceiling it provided a further stage of reappraisal. Certain tentative steps taken in the earliest phases could now be adjusted with the experience of work on the later phases. Areas of insecure paint could be revisited and perhaps be refixed if needed. Above all, integration of the continuous whole of the painted area could be achieved with the benefit of seeing it as a whole from ground level. And, indeed, treatment and assessment of the presbytery, crossing and the transept ceilings came to follow, and with this even better understanding of the building sequences of those ceilings within the cathedral. Surface cleaning and securing of all these areas was done by a team of people who really knew what they were tackling. Such continuity had an immense benefit for the final result and is very clear throughout the cathedral today; Fig 157 illustrates the conservation process in the context of the complex construction of a lozenge centre.

The records made of the structural and painted elements,

and of their condition and treatment, are the baseline for any and all future work. Future conservators and architects can also be helped by knowing the outcomes of further monitoring and whether adjustments or activities are called for which may affect the ceiling condition in the coming decades. Conservation processes being carried out, with technical descriptions during execution, were recorded as part of the considerable high-quality video footage of the ceiling, together with much detail of the structure and of the painted decoration. This footage is a significant part of the long-term record of this intervention and a potential resource which could be used for further promotion of conservation needs of the cathedral.

6.2 DOCUMENTATION AND ARCHIVING

Tobit Curteis

Because of the nature and scale of the project, it was clear that a great deal of documentation would be produced, and that the medium of the documentation would vary considerably, including not only paper reports, but also photographic material, digital records and even videotape (above, 6.1; below, 6.3, 6.5). An archiving and access system was developed, employing Microsoft Access (a standard and widely used database) and Access 97 was used throughout the project. Records were separated into two subsections, 'documents' and 'graphics'. The level of documentation produced relating to the conservation work, and the associated research and administration, did indeed prove to be extremely large, but the use of a standard software application allowed easy distribution among the project partners.

Although the primary intention of the database was to be a document management system, rather than an archive of the data itself, the advantages of including certain digital records soon became apparent to the project and the ongoing work. Where report authors were agreeable and copyright allowed, PDFs were included on the database. In order to limit the size of the database, most graphic material was restricted to screen resolution.

As part of the conservation record, a detailed survey of the condition of the structure and paint layers on each board was conducted by the conservators. Although this board-by-board survey was initially stored on an Excel spreadsheet, once the database was developed it became apparent that it would be useful to include it in the same system. A secondary database was developed within the main system to accommodate this information.

Because of the multiple copies of many of the documents which were produced, it was important to identify one complete set of documents which would form the archive material. Only this set of documents, which was stored at a single location, was labelled with adhesive accession numbers. During the course of the work, this was in the

Fig 157 A figurative lozenge centre – the king in bay 9 – painted on boards from four panels (4–5/II–III) (clockwise from top left): pre-conservation; photographed in ultraviolet (UV) light (to produce ultraviolet-induced visible fluorescence); post-conservation

cathedral architect's office. Following the completion of the project, the set of records was transferred to the cathedral office and then to the archive (Chapter 1.3).

6.3 METRIC SURVEY

Paul Bryan

Metric survey – the process of measuring a site, building or feature using known, repeatable survey methods which lead to the presentation of the recorded information in a scalable form and which minimise subjectivity – was a key part of the nave ceiling conservation project. Back in 1994, the photogrammetric unit of English Heritage (EH) was approached for advice on the survey requirement within the proposed project. This advice focused on the potential use of photogrammetric survey techniques to provide a base metric survey of the ceiling in order to enable both the architect and conservators to plan and record the required treatments. Initial discussions centred on the production of a suitable specification to enable a traditional photogrammetric outline

form), the question remains as to why there is relatively little apparent damage to the paint layer. The answer appeared to lie in the compressive as opposed to the tensile strength of the paint layer. Although a paint film such as this has a relatively low tensile strength (ie, it will break if it is stretched), the compressive strength is relatively high. In other words, if the paint layer was slightly compressed (as would be the case if the ceiling boards distorted in the way described above), it would be able to recover to its original alignment without cracking. Were the distortion of the boards to be of the same level but the other way around (convex on the lower side of the board) it is possible that the tensile strength of the paint would be too low, allowing the film to crack. Of course, the compressive strength of the paint layer is separate from the strength of adhesion to the ground layer and board and, if the concave distortion were too great, the paint layer might delaminate causing areas of 'tenting'.

Macroclimatic context

Peterborough is situated in a low-lying area of East Anglia, south-west of the Wash, where the average height above sea level is less than 6m. The cathedral, which is at *c* 8m above sea level, is one of the highest points in the vicinity and is relatively exposed. As with the rest of the country, the predominant wind direction is from the south-west, although in spring more northerly winds are experienced. The average wind levels throughout the year are relatively high for the south of England. Nevertheless, the mean annual temperature in the area is between 9°C and 10.5°C, well within the national average.

East Anglia is one of the driest areas of the country, with an annual rainfall of approximately 600mm, including the Peterborough area itself (Meteorological Office nd, data for 1961–90). During the period 1961–90, an annual average relative humidity of 82–85% was recorded for the region as a whole. However, during the period of monitoring the annual average outside the cathedral roof was only 75%. As may be expected, the diurnal fluctuations of relative humidity and ambient temperature vary considerably between the summer and winter months (Jenkins et al 2008).

Artificial influences on the microclimate

Heating

Prior to the mid 19th century there was no significant heating in the cathedral. In the late 1860s, following the introduction of gas lighting, a set of coke boilers was installed; these were replaced in the 1950s by four coke-fired Gurney stoves in the nave, two in the transept and two in the chancel (Fig 158). In 1963, these were upgraded to run on oil and in 1993 they were converted for use with gas (Fig 160). During the 1993 alterations, thermal insulation blocks were added to the stoves in order to increase their long-term heat

Fig 160 A stove in the south aisle

retention, effectively causing them to act as storage heaters. Anecdotal evidence suggests that the efficiency of the stoves has been increased since the introduction of the gas. However, there is also anecdotal evidence that the boilers used to glow red hot in the 19th century, so it is in fact possible that the heating was more extreme in the past.

The stoves in the nave are situated at the east and west ends of the nave in the north and south aisles (Fig 158). Smoke stains can be seen directly above them on the aisle vaults and also on the inner walls of the gallery and clerestory above, giving a clear illustration of the passage of hot air and combustion products; it is presumed that most of the smoke occurred when the stoves were coke- and oil-fired.

At the time of the conservation project, the stoves were in use from approximately mid November until mid March or April, as they are now (N Drewett, then head verger, and J Limentani, pers comm). During the period that the stoves were active, they were run for 24 hours per day usually at the full setting, although the half setting was occasionally used. The north-east nave stove was not usually used, unless a particularly cold period occurred. Of the seven remaining units, all were usually used during the winter, although if the weather was milder some were occasionally turned off.

The stoves are fitted with water trays which can be used

141

to increase the level of water vapour in the internal environment, through evaporation. Although these have not been regularly used in recent years, a test was carried out between December 1995 and January 1996. The trays of each of the three active stoves in the nave were filled with eight gallons of water each day at 7am. These were found to have completely evaporated by 3pm. During the period that the trays were used, the relative humidity in the nave was reported to have remained higher than would otherwise have been the case (English Heritage 1996). However, calculations based on the weight of water to the approximate volume of the nave suggest that, even with no air exchange, and assuming the most benign conditions, the AH could not have been increased by more than approximately $0.5g/m^3$ per hour.

Ventilation

Although some of the windows in the clerestory are fitted with hinged lights, these were at the time of the project kept permanently closed and in most cases the operating cords had been removed. Small levels of ventilation through minor irregularities in the building fabric aside, the main ventilation to the body of the cathedral therefore is provided by the south and west doors. In both cases, twin door systems are employed so that direct air exchange is limited, unless both doors are fixed open at the same time. Although this is avoided for most of the year, for occasional large services and other events it is necessary that the doors (particularly those at the west end) remain fixed open for significant periods. From approximately June until August, the west doors were fixed open during the day; on fine days both the inner and outer doors were opened, while in bad weather the outer (glass doors) were kept closed (N Drewett, pers comm). Spot tests were carried out in order to assess the general impact that the opening of the doors would have on the internal environmental conditions. These showed that, in the centre of the nave at 1.5m, the level of air transfer was both swift and significant, with the internal temperature dropping by 3°C and the relative and absolute humidities increasing by up to 21% and $1.1g/m^3$ respectively, within three minutes (external conditions at the time of the test (13:50, 14/01/2000) were 84% RH and 5.5°C). Although the doors were open for approximately four minutes no significant change in conditions was recorded at the east end of the ceiling where the monitoring probes are located (the doors were open at 13:50 and a reading was logged at approximately 13:57). This suggests that, in order to have a significant effect on the internal environment at ceiling height, the doors would need to be open for a considerable length of time.

The principal sources of ventilation within the roof void from the exterior are the vents above and below the glass panels in the north and south sides (Fig 161), as well as those at the apex of the roof. Irregularities in the roof structure and the loosely fitting doors to the parapets would also provide

Fig 161 Exterior view of the south side of the nave roof: installed in the 1920s, vents above and below the glass panels provide ventilation to the roof space but the glass panels when not covered allowed sunlight to fall on the upper surface of the canted boards

minor sources of ventilation. Air exchange with the body of the cathedral can occur when the east access door is open and through irregularities and damage to the ceiling structure. However, air exchange from these sources is very limited in comparison to the external sources.

Building use

The use of the building by worshippers and other visitors has both an indirect and a direct influence on the interior microclimate. The indirect effect is achieved through the requirement for heating while people are in the building as well as the need to use access points, which, in turn, allow ventilation. The direct influence is caused by the introduction of moisture to the environment as a result of breathing and perspiring, and the introduction of wet clothing. A single person may be expected to expire 50g/h water vapour (Camuffo et al 1999, 211).

In general, in an air space as big as that in the cathedral (approximately $56,500m^3$), the influence of people will be marginal. However, for certain large services, such as on Christmas Eve when a congregation of more than 1500 may be present, the influence should be taken into account.

Glass roof panels

During the 1920s restoration, glass panels were installed at the base of the roof on the north and south sides, in the mistaken belief that these would disrupt the life cycle of death watch beetle (Chapter 5.5; Fig 154; Fig 161). This has since been shown not to be the case, but, as a result of the location of the panels, sunlight fell directly on to the back of the lower tier of ceiling panels (ie, the canted boards), causing extreme fluctuations in the conditions.

Monitoring results

Overview

The recorded conditions showed mild variations from year to year, depending on specific weather patterns, but were generally similar. (Detailed results of the monitoring programme can be found in the archived reports (Curteis 2000; 2001; 2002; 2003).) On the lower side of the ceiling the annual average values for RH and AT were approximately 57% and 17°C (in the shade). The extremes for RH were 82% and 33% while those for AT were 11°C and 29°C (excluding 2001 fire conditions; below). Summer averages were 61% and 21°C with diurnal fluctuations (based on visual estimates) of 8% and 3°C. Winter averages were 53% and 15°C with diurnal fluctuations of 4% and 2°C. The equivalent annual conditions in the roof space were 65% and 14°C. Extremes for RH were 91% and 32% while those for AT were 32°C and 3.5°C. Summer averages were 59% and 21°C with diurnal fluctuations of 18% and 6°C. Winter averages were 66% and 11°C with diurnal fluctuations of 9% and 3°C.

At no point did dew point temperature rise above surface temperature on either side of the ceiling. However, on the upper side of the ceiling, dew point temperature was approached on a number of occasions during the spring and autumn, usually as a result of a sudden increase in external relative humidity, indicating that condensation may have taken place.

Heating and ventilation

The data showed that there was a significant variation between the conditions in the roof space and those on the underside of the ceiling (Fig 162). The divergence is particularly extreme in the winter. In the roof space, the high level of ventilation, and low level of thermal insulation, meant that the microclimate fluctuated in accordance with the external conditions. Some level of buffering occurred, but it was limited, and the AH in particular followed the external conditions very closely. Diurnal conditions were most unstable in the summer months, but in the winter the fluctuations were less extreme.

The conditions on the underside of the ceiling were far more stable due to the low level of ventilation and the high degree of thermal buffering offered by the building structure. In the summer, the primary factor destabilising the microclimate was the minor fluctuation in temperature, caused by the effect of the external conditions, and the resulting destabilisation of the RH. In the winter, the internal AT was dominated by the high level of artificial heating, with an average AT between 15°C and 20°C, and therefore the conditions were generally extremely stable (although the RH below the ceiling was very low compared to that in the roof

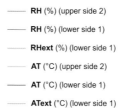

—— RH (%) (upper side 2)
—— RH (%) (lower side 1)
—— RHext (%) (lower side 1)
—— AT (°C) (upper side 2)
—— AT (°C) (lower side 1)
—— AText (°C) (lower side 1)

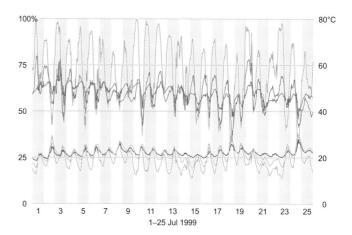

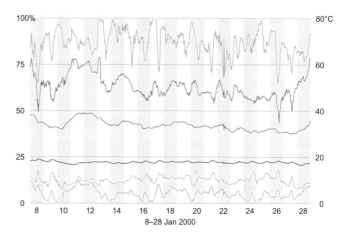

Fig 162 Charts showing the variations in the pattern of internal relative humidity (RH in %) and ambient temperature (AT in °C) at probe 1 (below the ceiling) and probe 2 (above the ceiling) during July 1999 (upper) and January 2000 (lower); external RH (RHext) and AT (AText) are also shown

space).

During the winter, opening the doors caused sudden air exchange with the exterior, resulting in sharp fluctuations in the internal microclimate; this occurs when one set of doors is open, but the effect is exacerbated when two sets of doors are open allowing cross-ventilation. In the summer, the contrast between internal and external conditions was less significant and therefore sudden changes were smaller. Irregularities such as this were short-lived, and the AT and RH returned to their previous levels within one or two hours of the incident. Interestingly, the events recorded in the cathedral diary when the doors were open did not always show in the data. Experience in other cathedrals demonstrates that wind direction has a significant effect on the level of air exchange, as well as periods when more than one door is open at the same time allowing cross-ventilation.

Sunlight

The effects of direct sunlight on the upper side of the panels was dramatic, with a sharp increase in ST and AT with consequent falls in RH (Fig 163). During the periods of greatest solar heating, surface temperatures of up to 38°C were reached in the roof space with a diurnal fluctuation of up to 22°C. In these periods the RH dropped to as low as 25% with a diurnal fluctuation of up to 50%.

As the glass roof panels were found to serve no practical purpose, it was decided that they should be covered with wooden boards in order to prevent solar radiation striking the upper side of the ceiling. This was undertaken in two phases with rows 8–39 being covered in July 2002 and rows 1–7 covered in October 2003. The results were extremely successful, with the spikes in the ST being almost completely eliminated (Fig 163). However, although the ST on the boards was no longer affected, the AT in the immediate vicinity still showed a significant influence of solar radiation, with an effect on the RH as would be the case with an increase in AT from any other source. The fluctuation of the AT is not solely associated with the heating of the boards. The solar radiation on the tiled roof also caused a significant increase in the internal AT due to the low level of thermal insulation.

Movement

The boards showed little measurable movement in response to short-term environmental fluctuations. However, longer-term fluctuations in the microclimate were clearly reflected in the expansion and contraction of the wood. The precise response time was difficult to determine due to the relatively crude system of measurement. However, any significant changes in microclimate which lasted over approximately five days appeared to have an effect.

The recorded movement appeared to be proportional and opposite to the change in RH (Fig 164). In other words, when the RH decreased, the lower sides of the boards expanded, and when the RH increased they contracted. While the RH above and below the ceiling varies in level and short-term patterns, the longer-term patterns are similar. So, it appears that the dimensional change that was observed at this resolution is a response to the overall change in RH on both sides of the boards, rather than the result of differing conditions on either side. However, as the upper, unpainted, sides of the boards, with hessian and glue facing, are more porous and hygroscopic than the lower painted sides, it is possible that an increase in RH has a disproportionate effect, causing a greater level of expansion as the RH increases, resulting in concave deformation on the lower sides. This may also be exacerbated by the methods of fixing from above.

The level of movement at probes 1 and 2 (mounted on a

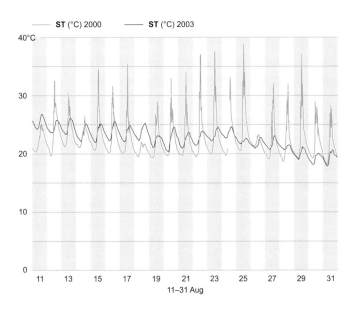

Fig 163 Surface temperature (ST in °C) at probe 3 (below the ceiling) in August 2000 (shown in red); and in August 2003 (shown in blue) after the insertion of wooden boards inside the roof space in front of the glass panels

softwood and an oak board, respectively) was found to be very similar, with a movement range of <300μm. Although the pattern of movement for probe 3 (mounted on an oak board) was similar, the range was far higher at <1000μm. No obvious difference between the two oak boards was observed and so it appears probable that the variation in movement levels is associated with the methods with which the boards are fixed.

Light

The initial light monitoring programme was complicated by the presence of the scaffolding and the lighting used for the conservation work which had a considerable influence on the data. Although this made the correlation of specific light sources with lux and UV levels difficult, it was clear from the data that the level of light was relatively low. It is interesting to note that the sharp increases in lux levels, thought to be associated with the lighting for the conservation work, had little impact on the UV data, as the low-power compact fluorescent lamps have a lower proportion of UV than halogen lamps, and a far lower proportion than daylight.

Following the completion of the conservation work, the probe was moved to a location over the choir at the east end of the nave where it was not in shadow. A clear pattern emerged, with a distinct variation between the summer and winter months. In the summer, when the ceiling was exposed to indirect daylight, lux levels of up to 140lux occurred on a regular basis during the day, with lower levels on dull days. The proportion of UV was relatively high at up to 200μW/lm and approximately 20mW/m². In the winter, when the lighting was predominantly artificial, the lux levels tended to be slightly higher at up to 160lux, but with UV levels

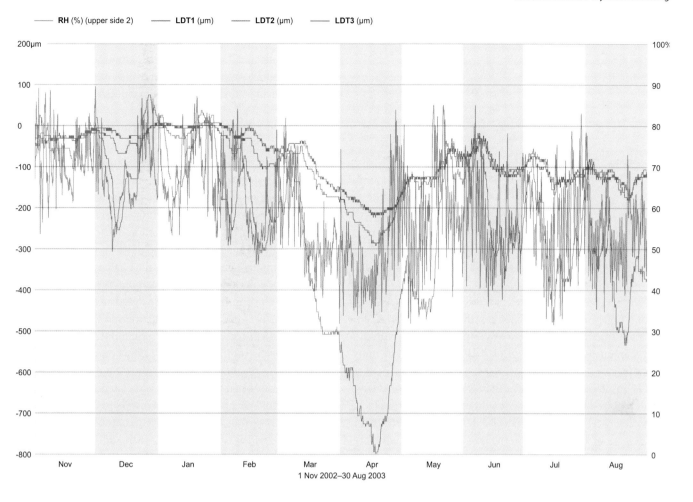

Fig 164 Movement in the boards, recorded by linear displacement transducers (LDT) 1–3, plotted against the relative humidity (RH in %) in the roof space at probe 2, November 2002 to August 2003: a decrease in relative humidity can be seen to induce expansion in the boards (NB movement data are displayed on the chart in reverse so that the correlation can be clearly seen, therefore a decrease in dimension on the chart in fact represents an increase in actual dimension)

averaging approximately 60µW/lm and 3mW/m².

The upward-facing lights at clerestory level are understood to be 1000w tungsten halogen lamps. This type of lamp is known to produce 49–127µW/lm of UV radiation (Cassar 1995). The suppression characteristics (if any) of the cover glass is not known. Daylight, even through standard glass, contains a far higher proportion of UV radiation and this was evident from the data (Thomson 1986, 29–32).

Therefore, while lux levels are usually within the recommended band of up to 200lux, UV levels are often above the recommended level for photosensitive materials, generally considered to be 75µW/lm. However, the paint analysis suggests that the painting is generally fairly robust in this regard (Chapter 4.4), and these levels of radiation should have only a very limited deleterious effect.

The 2001 fire

Environmental monitoring equipment, installed at ceiling level during phases 1 and 2 of the conservation project, was within the east part of the ceiling, that nearest to the 2001 fire (which occurred at the east end of the north aisle), albeit on the south side. The sensors recorded air and surface temperature and also relative and absolute humidity both above and below the ceiling at half-hourly intervals. Therefore the conditions before, during and after the fire were recorded (Curteis 2002).

For a brief period air temperature below the ceiling rose from a norm of 17°C to 55°C and surface temperature from 15°C to 48°C (the temperatures experienced by the sensor are towards the limits of their range and, therefore, a margin of error should be anticipated when considering the data) (Fig 165). Above the ceiling in the same period air temperature rose from 13°C to 19°C and surface temperature from 14°C to 22°C. Relative humidity below the ceiling decreased quickly but briefly from 53% to 9% and above the ceiling rose from 51% to 70%. These temperatures are considerably below what might result in blistering of the paint or physical alteration of pigments (Rickerby 1991). The RH fluctuations are likely to have caused damage only if they had lasted over a longer period. Water from fire hoses caused a brief rise in absolute humidity (AH) and consequently RH to c 56% for about an hour after the fire was put out, but RH then reduced to pre-fire levels. However, the speed with

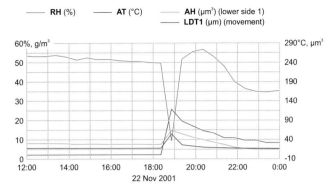

Fig 165 The recorded conditions on the evening of 22 November 2001 during the fire: note the increase in absolute humidity (AH in g/m3) as a response to the increase in temperature (AT); LDT1, situated some distance to the west, also shows a considerable level of movement

which temperatures soared illustrates the fire officer's statement that the destruction of the wooden ceiling would have been unstoppable if detection had been delayed by only 15 minutes.

The more gentle decrease in the AT (compared to AH), which followed the fire being brought under control, was immediately reflected in an increase in RH which, because of the increase in AH, rose above the level where it stood before the fire began. Following the reduction of the AT to its normal level, the RH decreased in accordance with the prevailing AH (the accuracy of the Humitter probe may have varied by up to an additional 1.5% at 55°C). At the height of the fire, the LDTs, which were located approximately 45m from the source of the fire, recorded an increase of up to 120μm. However, it is possible that the change in dimensions was caused by the effect of the heat on the mountings rather than on the board itself.

Results of soot analysis following the fire indicate pH levels of 8.1 to 8.5 at clerestory level; furthermore, the chloride concentrations of the soot deposits were low (3μg cm-2) (Hawkins and Associates, pers comm 2001; Bodycote Materials Testing Healthcare, pers comm 2001). These results, and further component analysis to identify other components, indicated the nature of the soot deposits was relatively non-aggressive. However, the potentially corrosive nature of soot in conditions of high humidity and where there was risk of condensation remained a concern; at the very least, if the surface deposits were to become damp and then allowed to dry they would become considerably more difficult to remove. The soot was deposited on top of the hessian especially thickly adjacent to joints in the boards. This could demonstrate very strong upward currents of air through the joints between the boards – strong enough to carry the soot through both joints and hessian whose weave is clogged with glue. There was a particular concern that in the uncontrolled environment of the roof space excess moisture in the form of condensation might activate any aggressive agent effect in the soot; therefore, its removal was considered a priority (below, 6.7).

Discussion and conclusions

The data collected throughout the programme demonstrated that there is an extreme variation in conditions that regularly occurs above and below the painted ceiling boards, particularly during the winter months. This is largely due to the low ventilation, high level of thermal buffering and high heating level in the body of the cathedral, in comparison to the level of ventilation and low level of thermal buffering in the roof space. As a result, the hygrothermal gradient across the boards is often extremely high. However, despite these conditions, there appears to have been little associated deterioration of the paint layer.

Although the measurement system was relatively crude, it clearly demonstrated that, when the relative humidity increases for a period of more than about five days, there is a consequent contraction in the painted surface of the boards. This is a significantly shorter period than was thought to be the case. Conversely, when the relative humidity decreases the lower side of the board expands. Although this reaction is, in many ways, counter-intuitive, it appears possible that the reason is associated with the fact that the lower side of the board is covered in oil paint and therefore less porous and responsive than the upper surface of the board which is covered in hessian and hygroscopic animal glue. In addition, the RH in the roof space is generally higher than that on the lower side. Therefore, as the RH increases, the upper side of the board expands more than the lower side, causing a mild concave curve on the painted side.

Maximum movement is in the order of 200μm over a five-day period, and an annual expansion contraction range of up to 1mm, across an average-sized board. (The sensors were mounted across only a section of a board so the full movement would have been a multiple of the movement measured.) However, most movement is far less than this. The only explanation as to why this does not cause the paint layer to delaminate is that it retains enough compressive strength to absorb this level of movement. It is possible that over the long term, as cross-linking of the medium increases, the paint layer may become more brittle and prone to crack or delaminate. However, the paint is already over a century old and so it seems unlikely that significant change will occur. (In order to confirm this hypothesis, a more sensitive method of measurement would be necessary on both sides of the ceiling.)

During the period of measurement, the effect of sunlight from the glass panels on the south side of the roof was to cause sudden fluctuations in temperature, sometimes up to 38°C, with consequent fluctuations in the relative humidity. The wooden panels inserted across the windows to prevent this have effectively eliminated these sharp fluctuations, creating a microclimate which is almost identical to areas of the ceiling which have always been in shade. The ventilation grilles were not covered, so the hygrothermal buffering between internal and external conditions remains low and, as a consequence, the background microclimate in the roof space remains unstable.

Despite the fact that the initial light monitoring was complicated by the necessity of moving the scaffolding, useful data were recorded. The lux levels, resulting from indirect daylight, tungsten halogen lamps and fluorescent working lamps, were fairly low and generally within the recommended levels in museums for photosensitive materials. UV levels were higher than recommended, but the paint in the 1740s and 1830s schemes is not particularly photosensitive; of the pigments identified by analytical microscopy in these paint layers, lead white, vermilion and Prussian blue could be described as photosensitive (R Lithgow, pers comm). Since the measurements were taken, the lighting scheme has been replaced with a new system which has UV filters on the lamps; regular monitoring of this new system, and of the microclimate as a whole, is needed.

6.5 RECORDING THE HISTORY AND CONDITION OF THE NAVE AND TRANSEPT ROOFS AND CEILINGS

Hugh Harrison and Richard Lithgow

Objectives

The specified aims at the beginning of the conservation project on the nave ceiling were to:
  investigate the ceiling support structure (the original medieval roof);
  investigate the ceiling boards and ascertain their age;
  investigate the boards' present condition;
  record any previous work and intervention;
  investigate how much paint is left on the boards and ascertain its condition;
  carry out analysis of the paint;
  remove the grime and soot on both sides of the boards;
  make sure the timbers are secure and sound and that there are no loose nails;
  document the conditions and work carried out on the nave and transept ceilings.
In particular, great emphasis was placed on the need for a thorough technical examination of the original and added materials of the painted surfaces. The objectives were to:
  determine the nature and extent of any original paint layers still remaining;
  characterise designs and outlines showing in relief on boards with otherwise 'weathered' surfaces;
  characterise the various phases of later repainting;
  assess the implications these results might have for the conservation of the ceiling;
  address queries arising from the ongoing condition survey

and treatment works.

These broad objectives were also applied to the work on the transept following the 2001 fire. Consistency of recording formats and treatment methods was of course considered very important but, as the main phases progressed and our knowledge increased, there was a need to modify the categories of information recorded as part of the condition survey.

The emphasis was on the collection rather than the display of information; over 80 categories of ceiling data were recorded. A considerable amount of data is now available in written and graphic formats, only a small selection of which is presented in this report; all additional data are archived as source material.

Graphic record

The photogrammetric drawings (above, 6.3) provided a base for the graphic illustration of the technical survey and treatment record. Categories of damage, deterioration, surface residues and previous interventions were plotted on to the graphics. This hand-plotted information was scanned into the computer and redrawn as multi-layered vector graphics using Corel Draw software. In this form, categories of information were superimposed on to the photogrammetry and could be printed out in any combination, scale or format.

For the condition survey of both the structure and the painted decoration categories of damage and deterioration were plotted on to photogrammetric plans of individual transept panels at 1:15 scale and in the nave of individual panels, vertical ashlar boards and west end vertical boards at either 1:10 or 1:15 scale. For the treatment record all interventions made during this phase were similarly plotted and identified. All this information was transferred on to overall plans of the transept ceilings and reproduced at 1:55 scale and on to overall plans of the nave ceiling bays and reproduced at either 1:50 or 1:35 scale in the respective condition survey/conservation record reports (each of the five phases of the nave ceiling project includes a set of 13 graphics at 1:35 or 1:50 scale covering the area treated in that phase).

The graphic record was digitised so that any combination of categories could be generated in any format on overall plans of the transept or nave ceilings or on plans of the individual panels. To supplement the digitised graphic record created by the Perry Lithgow Partnership, Peter Ferguson of Hugh Harrison Conservation produced numerous hand-drawn diagrams and sections illustrating aspects of the transept and nave ceiling structures (see, eg, Figs 20, 26, 47, 54, 55, 72, 75, 77, 150, 151).

Written record

To complement the graphic record, many aspects of the construction and condition of the nave ceiling boards were recorded on a spreadsheet for each ceiling panel. Information relating to the structure includes wood type, measurements and shape, joints, displacement, interventions, forms of insect damage and decay. Similarly a board-by-board condition survey of the paint was compiled. This records the decoration on each board, visible underpaint, surface residues and alterations to the paint surface as well as descriptions of damage and deterioration. These board-by-board surveys of the ceiling structure and painted decoration were recorded as tabulated data using the Microsoft Excel spreadsheet programme (above, 6.2).

A tabulated written record was compiled describing the condition of all 13th-century and 17th-century boards remaining on the north and south transept ceilings, and the 1880s boards in the north transept. The original, hand-written tabulated sheets also were converted into electronic format.

To ensure the documentation remained consistent throughout the project we developed a glossary of categories, terms and definitions relating to all elements of the structure and condition of the ceiling. Copies of the glossary and other statements defining the recording process were given to all members of the Perry Lithgow Partnership/Hugh Harrison Conservation team and appended to the phase reports (Harrison and Lithgow nd a–e). The team members collaborated throughout the recording process to ensure consistency.

Photographic record

The nave photographic record includes identical sets of colour transparencies and prints. In an effort to keep the number of record photographs for this phase within manageable proportions the following strategy was adopted. All areas were photographed from the scaffolding, both before and after treatment using moderately angled flashlight. The larger, horizontal panels (/II and /III) are covered by three photographs each, the canted panels (/I and /IV) by two. In addition, the figurative lozenges – each painted on boards from four panels – were photographed as individual objects (eg, Fig 157).

Examples of deterioration and phenomena categorised in the graphic and written records were photographed repeatedly in different lighting conditions before, during and after treatment. The area covered by each photograph and the lighting conditions employed were recorded on reference sheets. In addition, plate reference sheets (based on the photogrammetric drawings) locate the area of ceiling covered by each photograph.

The transept photographic record consists of colour prints. Each transept ceiling panel (130 per ceiling) was photographed following treatment using moderately angled flashlight. In addition, examples of deterioration and phenomena categorised in the graphic and written records were photographed before, during and after treatment.

6.6 CONSERVING THE TIMBER STRUCTURES

Hugh Harrison

The nave ceiling: condition

The ceiling support structure

The horizontal and sloping original roof timbers (the original medieval scissor truss roof structure, truncated and used as ceiling joists: Chapter 2.2) show little sign of any past infestation (and certainly none presently active) from either death watch beetle or common furniture beetle except in localised areas. Detailed surveys were carried out on joist numbers 1–9 at the east end and 48–65 at the west end to record the actual condition of the joists and to try to explain the extent of Blore's stiffening in the 1830s and Moore's subsequent, 1920s, replacement of so many original joists.

The recording revealed areas of death watch beetle infestation along board edges and at the bottom ends of the sloping joists where higher levels of damp might be expected. There are isolated but extensive areas of common furniture beetle infestation but there seems to be no apparent significance to these instances. As proof of the generally excellent condition of the original joists, it is worth noting that the heavy trafficking over the top surface of the joists during conservation work has not caused damage. Had extensive tunnelling been present under the surface, even allowing for the care taken by operatives, there is no doubt that surface breakdown would have resulted. The extent of infestation and decay was found to be minimal and therefore it seems extraordinary that joists adjacent to those still in excellent condition were found to be so weakened by Blore and Moore that they had to be renewed or reinforced. There was little correlation between the number of adjacent, replaced and surviving, heavily infested boards and decayed joists. As a corollary, neither was there any increased infestation or decay in the joists in proximity to areas of replaced boards. One surmises that some joists were locally weakened, explaining Blore's reinforcing, and Moore's replacement must be due to over-concern at that time with low-level death watch beetle infestation. (No evidence of infestation was found in any of the 1920s softwood noggins, joists, binders or patches where they were revealed.)

The fixings above the ceiling in good or satisfactory condition are: the hanging bolts and nuts inserted in the 1830s (except for light surface corrosion); the cast iron shoes, well painted as recommended by Moore in his programme of works in 1924; the steel hangers used by Moore for his binders over the sloping ceiling and the 1830s ironwork, all painted with a red iron oxide-type paint by Moore; the visible heads of coach screws/bolts through the binders into the lower sections of the scissor braces (Blore's sloping ceiling joists) and those used in the construction of the laminated joists which seem to have a zinc or galvanised coating; the shanks of the screws within the timber used to fasten the laminations forming the noggins (except the heads and projecting ends which had started to corrode); steel nails used in the laminations and the triangular side pieces on the joists.

The boards

A board-by-board survey of the lower surfaces was carried out over the entire ceiling and the condition of each board recorded for nine categories of damage for both original and replacement boards: splits, wood losses, intended wood losses, infestation by common furniture beetle and death watch beetle, wet rot, lead shot, surface degradation, impact damage/scratch marks, subsequent interventions. Some boards remain in excellent condition. The condition of the hessian on the upper surface of the ceiling boards is satisfactory, although splits have occurred where hessian bridges overlapping boards, etc.

It is suggested that the majority of the splitting of original boards has occurred relatively recently and is shrinkage splitting since the building has been extensively heated in the winter (above, 6.4; Fig 166, upper). Pre-drilling the nail holes would substantially reduce the incidence of splitting at the time of first fixing, which explains the comparative lack of splits between the nails and the ends of the boards. Splits were also created when the nails were driven from above and clenched over during Blore's restoration works (Fig 166, lower). These boards would have become comparatively brittle by the 1830s, so they would split easily if the nail were driven through a spot where the timber was vulnerable. Replacement boards also show splitting from both initial fixing and subsequent shrinkage.

Most wood losses on original boards can be attributed to acute infestation that has so weakened the timber that it has freckled away, or detached by contact or through handling during previous restorations (Fig 167, upper). The most common loss is that seen along board edges and this is found frequently throughout the ceiling (Fig 167, lower). This has the appearance of infestation on a sap edge, though the tree-ring analysis showed these edges as being the boundary layer just below the heartwood/sapwood junction. Other losses have occurred when boards were cut back and moved around when the replacement boards were inserted. There are few wood losses in the replacement boards which have not been touched since they were first fitted.

Infestation in the original boards by common furniture beetle is widespread, and more so by death watch beetle, as

Fig 166 Splitting in oak boards: upper – shrinkage splitting (36/III, bay 1); lower – splitting caused by Blore's 1830s restoration works (9/III, bay 8)

Fig 167 Wood loss: upper – to original board (38/II, bay 1); lower – along board edge (1/I, bay 10)

one would expect in oak; neither is active (the upper surface of the boards was treated with Silvertown Solution in the 1920s, as specified by Moore) (Fig 168). It occurs either as a general outbreak throughout the whole of a board, or is confined in a certain area. Where the infestation has been intense, so much of the wood has been consumed that the remainder has crumbled away completely, and the adjacent areas that have survived are very fragile and vulnerable to damage.

Surface decay was found, noticeable as a general softening of the surface and as miniature cross-checking. Surprisingly little sign of wet rot was found in the original boards. The small areas that do occur appear as surface cross-checking and this rot is entirely confined to board edges, where there has also been infestation. This may be associated with the fact that the edge of the board is exposed to the air on two adjoining sides and is likely to have a higher moisture content than other parts of the board.

A pattern of carefully drilled holes in original oak boards was revealed, consisting of sets of three holes in line across the centre of the ceiling and spaced approximately two panels apart down the length of the ceiling. Four complete sets were found, and many that were incomplete, with far more holes found in the centre and north sides than in the south side which is almost entirely made up of replacement boards. It seems likely that these holes indicate the position of a lighting system while extra holes recorded in the centre of the ceiling may reveal another earlier (or later) single light system. With the three-light system, none of the holes are particularly close to a joist, so the lights must have been suspended from noggins placed across the joists. It is notable that little sign of wear was seen on the edges of these holes, suggesting that the lights were fixed low enough to the floor to be easily accessed.

Throughout the ceiling patches of lead shot were found embedded in the boarding (Fig 169). A comparison (Wilson nd) of samples of the shot with modern shot used for game bird shooting puts the shot in this ceiling as nearly buck shot size! Analysis of the type of board containing shot, and whether the shot holes are overpainted, seems to reveal the periods when pigeon shooting was most popular. The high level of shot in 1740s boards indicates that this is an 18th-/early 19th-century pursuit, there being fewer shots recorded in the 1830s replacement boards. Vouchers in the NRO show that the Dean and Chapter bought powder and shot in 1809–10 (amongst many items from 'R. T. Farside', presumably an ironmonger) and again in 1814–15 (NRO, PDC Box X5051, ann 1810 and 1815) and also 1829–30 (NRO, PDC Box X5052, ann 1829–31), while the Dean and Chapter accounts show purchases in 1824 (Mesrs Farside and White, £1 3s 8½d), 1825 (11s 4d), 1826 (Thomas White jr £1 3s 8d), 1827 (Thomas White jr £1 13s 2d) and 1832 (an unspecified amount in a much larger sum to William Johnson Frost) (NRO, ML 872, ann 1824 and 1825; ML 874, ann 1826, 1827 and 1832). Examination of the angle of entry of the shot suggests that many shots were fired from the floor

Fig 168 Infestation in original boards by death watch beetle ('A') and common furniture beetle ('B') (3/III, bay 10)

Fig 169 Lead shot embedded in boards (9/III, bay 8)

at birds roosting or perching on the projecting stone wall head mould, directly in front of the ashlar boards. Another theory to explain inconsistencies in the placing of shot is that much shooting occurred whilst the roof was open in the 1830s whilst it was being renewed, affording easy access and comfortable roosting for the birds.

Surface degradation is an interesting feature of the boards. A phenomenon was noticed throughout the whole ceiling on original oak boards where original painted schemes are revealed in very low relief which is not formed from the survival of multi-layered earlier overpaint (eg, Fig 97; Fig 98). In the same manner, medullary rays and to a lesser extent the late growth in annual rings have great prominence due to the loss of the early growth of the annual rings. It was also noticed that where the surface has been protected by nail heads and board overlaps, the low relief effect is either non-existent or less prominent.

Fig 175 Insertion of stainless steel screws: top – no. 8 stainless steel screw with washer (37–38/III, bay 1); middle and bottom – stainless steel fixings touched in with acrylic colour (3–4/II and 4/II, bays 10–9)

Fig 174 Insertion of 3mm threaded rod: top and middle – bent over to form an angle and then fixed above the ceiling with nuts and washers (37/II, bay 1); bottom – bent a second time to form a hoop (the second leg was either cut off above the angle or returned above the ceiling and secured with a second nut and washer) (37/III–IV, bay 1)

Windows cut in the hessian, either for samples sent for testing or to find screws beneath, were made good with sailcloth (code no. 00169/23A manufactured by Richard Hayward & Co.) and attached with Beva™ 371 (a heat seal adhesive developed by G A Berger in 1970: an ethylene vinyl acetate co-polymer). The sailcloth, coated with four coats of Beva™ 371, was cut into patches to fix over the windows in the hessian and heat adhered. Prior to fixing, the area to be covered was given a coat of Beva™ 371 and allowed to dry. The position of all new sailcloth patches was recorded. To obscure shafts of light (originating from the 1920s glass panels: Fig 161) penetrating through holes in the boards and hessian behind (probably caused by insertion of marker sticks to aid location of screws above and below the ceiling), pads of Plastazote™ LD45 were glued with Plextol™ B500 to the upper side of the hessian.

To prevent further wood loss from small areas of boarding that were unstable due to decay or infestation, exposed wood was consolidated with infusions of Paraloid B72™ (10% in xylene). Only in the first phase was a board found to be so fragile that Paraloid B72™ could not provide sufficient strength to hold the fragment at the end of a board that was vulnerable to vibrations from movement above the ceiling (37/II/u, bay 1). In this case, the upper surface was consolidated with Bencon™ 19 epoxy resin.

As an added precaution against loss of both wood and overlying paint, following consolidation treatment with Paraloid B72™, a filler was inserted where necessary to secure vulnerable edges (Fig 176). The filler consisted of 1 part Polyfilla™, 1.5 parts fine oak dust, 1 part Plextol™ B500 (10% solution). The filler was touched in afterwards by the paint conservators. Splits were injected with Plextol™ B500 by hypodermic syringe and in phase 1 stainless steel fastenings were inserted to hold the joint together. After the first phase this was modified and the fastenings omitted. Where the fragment to be glued was loose, wedges were temporarily driven to hold the joint together as the glue cured (Fig 177).

It was felt that some lacunae in the boards would be sufficiently visible and distracting from the floor that they should be made good either with a new timber insert or by inpainting. No attempt would be made to disguise the timber inserts, but equally the reintegration would not be made artificially visible. In addition a number of added softwood repairs were considered disproportionately distracting that their removal was thoroughly investigated. Having agreed the criteria for using a timber insert or removing a distracting softwood addition, the ceiling was inspected at each phase (by J Limentani, G Lewis, R Lithgow and H Harrison), and a list of softwood removals and inserts, as well as inpainting of backgrounds, was agreed.

The figurative central section of each lozenge was

considered to be a focal point and therefore lacunae would be particularly noticeable. Fig 178 shows the infill of such a central section of a lozenge. Fig 179 shows a large softwood cover strip over a joint in the Logic/Dialectic lozenge where such an intrusion would be considered particularly noticeable. In Fig 179 (middle) it can be seen that once the softwood repair was removed, the damage revealed is seen to be very minor. All the repair required was the making up of one board end, which was a minor intervention compared

Fig 176 Consolidated and filled wood loss (white) on board edges prior to reintegration (retouching) (15/II, bay 7)

Fig 177 A split (top), being repaired with a wedge and glue (middle) and post-treatment (bottom) (11/III, bay 8)

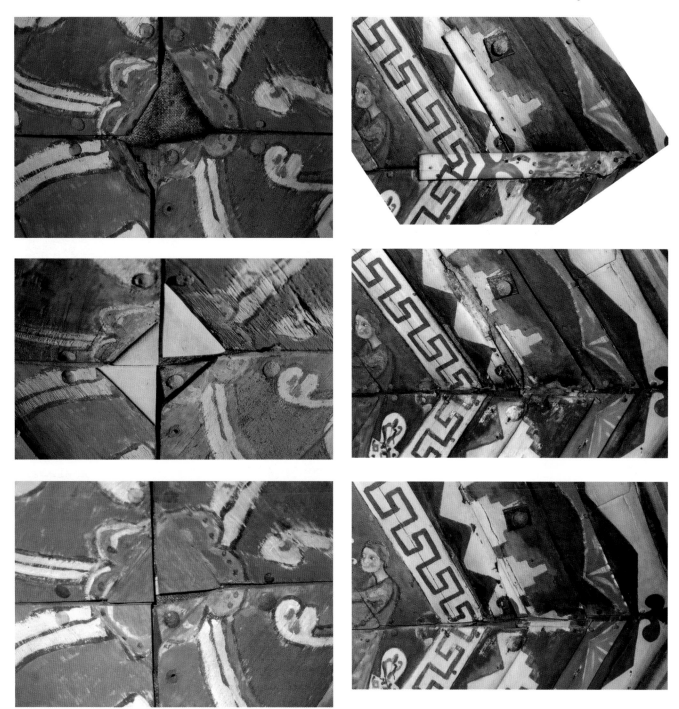

Fig 178 Before (top) and after fitting and painting (middle and bottom) timber inserts in a foliage lozenge centre (11–12/I–II, bays 8–7)

Fig 179 The Logic/Dialectic lozenge: top – with softwood cover strip; middle – strip removed; bottom – area after repair (13–14/III–IV, bay 7)

with the major benefit of removing the repair. The stepped chevron board edge was also repaired, but this would have been made good with a timber insert anyway.

The repairs shown in Fig 180 and Fig 181 were considered to be obvious candidates for treatment. The foliage lozenge illustrated in Fig 180 fulfilled all the criteria: the centre of a lozenge was involved and a distracting softwood repair had been inserted. An example of a repair to a figurative lozenge, the anthropophagus lozenge, is discussed below (below, 6.7; Fig 200; Fig 201). Fig 181 is included as a typical example of repairs to border boards.

The transept

The ceiling support structure

No treatment was required to any of the structural timber in the roof spaces except for reinstatement of noggin ends removed for tree-ring analysis (Chapter 3.2). An initial vacuum cleaning of all exposed surfaces in the roof space was undertaken. No evidence was found of active fungal decay and insect infestation, splitting or loose joints. The ceiling support structure to both transept ceilings is in very good order. There has been some minor deflection of

Fig 180 A lozenge centre with a softwood repair (clockwise from top left): before treatment; with the repair removed; the same area with two new timber inserts, as yet unpainted; with these inserts painted (15–16/III–IV, bays 7–6)

Fig 181 A new insert of oak in a border board, (above) pre- and (right) post-repair (3/IV, bay 10)

Pearson's upper tie beams in the south transept due to Moore's later intervention (Chapter 5.4, 5.5).

Preliminary tests were made on a few randomly picked support structure fixing bolts dating from Moore's

interventions. The bolts, when withdrawn, showed some minor corrosion, sufficient to warrant extracting all bolts in this category for examination and treatment in both transept arms; the number of bolts scheduled for removal in the north transept totalled 104 and in the south transept 54; the number in the south transept was considerably lower on account of the greater number of Pearson tie beams present where the use of bolts was minimal compared to Moore's structural system which relied heavily on their use. The bolts removed, which were all about 500mm in length, were those from which Moore's laminated beams are suspended from the softwood bearers in the south transept and the cambered composite beams in the north transept. Those in the south transept were sheradised and painted in red iron oxide whilst galvanising protects those in the north transept.

Bolts were treated as per the strategy previously agreed for the nave (above). In the north transept, 76 bolts were removed and checked from a total of 104 identified (the remaining 28 could not be withdrawn, being obstructed from above by other structural components). However, all nuts were loosened and the bolts lowered sufficiently to enable Plastazote™ LD45 pads to be fitted. The same operation and specification was carried out in the south transept where all 54 bolts that had been identified were taken out and serviced, none being obstructed from above due to the structural support system being of a different design to that of the north transept. As a precaution against possible movement damage, an Acro prop was temporarily inserted beforehand adjacent to each bolt to be taken out (Fig 182).

The boarded ceilings

Tree-ring analysis of original (13th-century), 'intermediate' (17th-century) and modern (Pearson, 1880s) boards (Table 8) required their removal. Extreme care was exercised. The nails, which are all 19th-century, were removed and saved. At the start of the operation it was decided that the boards would be very carefully freed from the hessian leaving the latter in position and intact. This technique was subsequently abandoned when it was realised that an unacceptable proportion of the fragile wood surface was detaching and remaining fixed to the hessian. The hessian thereafter was cut to release the boards and left on the back.

After analysis, boards were replaced using stainless steel wood screws and washers, the heads being painted in acrylic colour to match the wood. In the majority of cases this

Fig 182 A conservator removing ceiling bolts for condition inspection, greasing and insertion of Plastazote™ LD45 pads, with Acro prop in position to support the ceiling panels (south transept)

operation was relatively straightforward, but there were a number of places where the overlap between board edges was very minimal and the board edges themselves very thin. In these instances an oak strengthening batten was introduced over the hessian above the board edges which were then screwed to it. Where the hessian had been cut, this was sealed from above using strips of sailcloth heat-applied using Beva 371 wax adhesive (Fig 183) (as in the nave, above).

A board-by-board survey of all the 13th- and 17th-century boards was carried out in both transept arms and, in general, all of the boards retained by Pearson are sound with little evidence of previous repair. There were no loose boards that required fixing, only a number of small loose fragments that were secured by the conservators. A board-by-board survey was carried out in the north transept, but not in the south transept, of the 19th-century boarding, all of which is still in very good condition and securely fixed with only one or two minor exceptions. On original, intermediate and Pearson boards there were some signs of earlier wet rot along edges, and thus some minor timber loss, and earlier common furniture beetle and death watch beetle attack (no longer active) was noted intermittently over many of the boards, but less so on the 19th-century boards. A small number of original boards exhibited heavy weathering on the face. Splitting, due to shrinkage and nailing (boards not pre-drilled), is commonplace on 19th-century boards, with a number of the longer splits extending to the full length of the board, but confined to board ends on earlier boards. All boarding, new and reused, was fitted or refixed by Pearson using new nails which are still in excellent condition and tight. All nail heads on the underside of the boards were treated by the paint conservators. Screws were inserted from above during Moore's 1920s restoration and, when they

Table 8 Transept ceilings: categories of board

Board category	South transept	North transept
Original (13th-century) boards	243	42
Original (13th-century) grooved boards	105	25
Original (13th-century) cross-grained boards	20	1
Intermediate (1660s) boards	56	0
Pearson (1880s) boards	914	1467

Fig 183 The upper side of the south transept ceiling showing reinstatement repairs following removal of (intermediate) boards for tree-ring analysis, with a new oak noggin inserted in the centre of the panel to support the boards after refitting, and strips of sail cloth covering the positions where the hessian had been cut (panel K/8)

emerged through the underside of the ceiling boards, some splintered the surface. Such splintering was recorded but very few splinters were unstable and required treatment. A number of boards display surface damage by gunshot and the angle of entry shows that most shots seem to have been fired from almost directly below (above, 'The nave ceiling: condition').

The upper walls of both transept arms were to a limited extent cleaned (eg, glue and water stains) and repointed.

6.7 CONSERVING THE PAINTED DECORATION

Richard Lithgow

The nave ceiling

Condition

Damage, surface residues and other phenomena recorded in graphic form (above, 6.5) can be itemised as follows.

PAINT LOSS AND DISCOLORATION
The primary cause of delaminating paint on the nave ceiling was long-term water infiltration leading to deterioration of the wood support and subsequent loss of adhesion. Other influences were the materials, technique and the extent of each historic intervention; these factors have had a direct bearing on the pattern of delaminating paint across the ceiling. A study of the graphic record reveals that the lead white background to the lozenge border patterns is generally stable, as are the paints which overlie this layer. The paints susceptible to delamination were the characteristic thick brown/black 1740s paint and the thin velvety black 1740s paint of the wave pattern decoration within the east part of

the ceiling and also on some outline drawing of the figurative and foliate lozenges, where these 1740s paints did not overlie lead white ground but lay directly on the wood support (Fig 184). Any moisture in the boards resulting from water infiltration was unable to escape through the resistant lead white paint but was able to do so by disrupting the black paint layers.

Within the figurative lozenges, the 1740s granular, olive green background paint (Fig 184) and the black line drawing were particularly prone to delaminating; and the red less so.

Fig 184 Examples of 1740s delaminating paint: top – thick brown/black 1740s paint (39/IV, bay 1); middle – thin velvety black 1740s paint (39/III, bay 1); bottom – 1740s granular, olive-green background paint within a figurative lozenge (king (1), 24/III, bay 4)

Fig 185 Delaminating paint on the head of St Peter (upper, left and right) and (lower) detail of St Peter's head following reattachment of paint flakes (30–31/II–III, bay 3) (1997 emergency treatment phase)

The detached green paint did not tend to lift and curl as much as the red or black. The extent of this delamination varied considerably across the ceiling, with no obvious variation in technique to account for this. Past environmental factors, such as the position of heating stoves, may have contributed (above, 6.4). Particularly severe delamination on the face, hands and feet of St Peter was considered to be the result of localised water infiltration (Fig 185). Delaminating paint was also caused by the contraction of overlying glue deposits (below).

Many of the metal fixings visible on the underside of the

ceiling have corroded to some degree and caused the overlying paint to flake. Nearly all nail heads and ceiling bolts covered by the 1740s brown/black paint without an intervening lead white ground were corroded to the extent that little or none of the covering paint survives; the brown/black paint evidently offered very little protection to the metal (Fig 186).

1740s and 1830s paint on softwood replacement boards throughout the ceiling was generally stable. Powdering paint was found on only one panel of the east end infill boards. Generally, the 1740s and 1830s oil-based paints were adequately bound. All significant instances of paint loss since the 1830s repaint are recorded in the tabulated board-by-board paint survey. Small losses as a result of delaminating paint, impact damage and the insertion of nails and screws during previous interventions were generally too small to be recorded on the graphics.

The extent of surface discoloration since the 1830s restoration was indicated by the condition of 1740s paint exposed under temporarily removed 1830s ceiling bolts and washers which had been protected from later overpaint and surface residues (Fig 187). The yellowed surface discoloration over all the ceiling is likely to have resulted from products of combustion emanating from coke-fired

Fig 186 Corroded nail heads (upper) and applying the Paraloid B72™ adhesive solution to a nail head (lower) (9–10/II–III, bay 8)

Fig 187 Examples of temporarily exposed 1740s paint that has been protected from subsequent overpaint and surface residues by 1830s ceiling bolts and washers (from top: 10/III, bay 8; 30/III and 30/II, bay 3)

stoves. These deposits were not entirely removed by surface cleaning with Wishab™ sponges.

Paint sample analysis identified some evidence of pigment alterations in both the original and later phases of painting (Howard 1997). This includes the transformation of natural azurite to copper oxalate (sample 23/1997) which indicates deterioration of the original painting and which may be partly due to an episode of high humidity at some time in the past. The alteration of verdigris to form a copper chloride (samples 3/, 4/ and 8/1997) was not apparently caused by the use in the later 19th century of the pigment Brunswick green since the overpaint found on the surface of the affected paint layers in these samples contains only Prussian blue, lead white, yellow earth or carbon black or mixtures of these pigments; the application of Silvertown in 1926 as an insecticide may be implicated in this alteration, since it would have provided a ready source of chlorides. There is no evidence of paint alteration within the visible 1740s scheme.

GLUE, SURFACE STAINING AND RESIDUES

Liquid (animal) glue used in the 1920s as an adhesive for the hessian backing material has in places penetrated between the boards, dried on the painted surface and caused the paint to delaminate. Ultraviolet light was particularly helpful when

checking for glue residue (Fig 188). On the horizontal central panels the glue tended to travel vertically down the edge of a board and drip on to the floor below, often leaving thick, raised droplets over the paint on the edge of a board (Fig 189, upper left). Many of these thick droplets have contracted in the dry environment and detached from the surface pulling away the underlying paint. On the canted side panels and ashlar boards the glue residue was more extensive (Fig 189, lower left and upper right). On penetrating the boards the glue travelled in rivulets across the canted surface before drying. In general, the glue has caused paint delamination only where it has collected in thick droplets or runs. The white background paint was less liable to flake as a result of

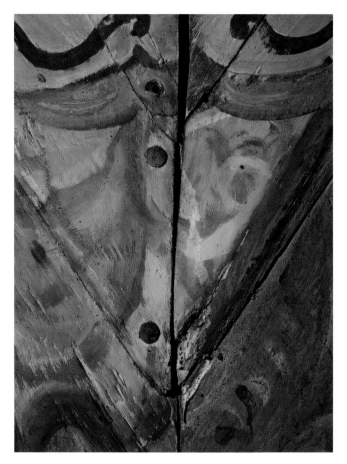

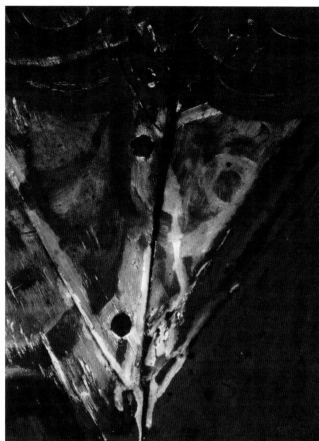

Fig 188 Thin rivulets of glue on the surface of the organistrum (symphonie) lozenge shown in (left) incidental and (right) UV light (13–14/I)

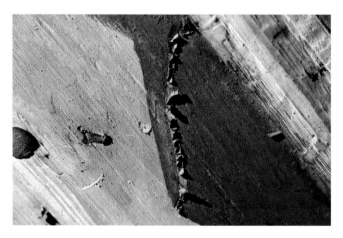

Fig 189 Examples of glue: on (upper and lower left) horizontal, canted and (upper right) ashlar boards (39/II, bay 1; 19/II, bay 6; ashlar boards on south side adjacent to 9–10/IV, bay 8)

surface glue deposits.

All stains on the surface of the painted decoration resulted from liquid material penetrating down between the boards or through cracks in deteriorated boards. Stains fell into four categories:

water stains where water had run across the paint surface leaving distinctive trails of lighter paint and brown surface deposits; these occurred more on the ashlar boards than on the ceiling panels;

chemical stains resulting from treatment to the ceiling structure above, viz:

a) mostly dark brown in colour (FTIR analysis of a sample

163

from bay 1 (11/1998) indicated the presence of shellac; a sample obtained during the emergency phase from unstained grey paint on a grey chevron board (28/1997) also indicated the presence of shellac in the upper portion of the paint layer, but the shellac may be from an applied coating or an accidental accretion)

b) a small number of 'clear' stains which saturate the paint surface without causing undue discoloration (not analysed)

c) light brown drips frequently found on the edge of ceiling boards or around holes and splits in the boards (analysis of a sample indicated the substance is organic but the results were otherwise inconclusive);

resin exuded through the paint layer from knots in the softwood replacement boards;

bat excreta on the north side ashlar boards (at the junction of rows 19–20, staining and surface residues were consistent with bat urine and degraded faeces).

Surface residues fell into seven categories: white efflorescence; patchy white deposits; brown/white spots and blotches; surface bloom; 'tendril' deposits; purple grains; surface dirt.

At the east end of the ceiling most efflorescence took the form of a white chalk line. This was only found on boards decorated with the wave border pattern (Fig 190, upper). The chalk line follows the shape of the decoration and occurs on the lead white background paint, although it was always associated with micro-delamination of adjacent, deep matt black, wave pattern paint. XRD analysis of a sample obtained from bay 1 (9/1998) provided a clear and strong pattern for ammonium lead sulphate and a little sodium sulphate. In bays 4–10 there were very few instances of micro-

delamination of the black wave pattern since there are generally two layers of black paint on those boards. As a result there was no chalkline efflorescence associated with the wave pattern; instead there was efflorescence very similar in appearance to 'chalkline', but occurring on other boards particularly around the edges of splits (Fig 190, lower). The paint surface on the west end vertical boards was partially obscured by a white efflorescence which was largely removed during the cleaning process.

Patchy white residues associated with the thick resinous 1830s black paint/coating remain unidentified (Fig 191). Initially considered to be some form of microbiological growth (MBG), analysis by B Ridout (pers comm 1999) indicates they are accumulations of irregularly shaped, translucent plate-like crystals. Sugar of lead (lead acetate) was used by the 1830s restorers despite contemporary reservations that it could result in a white efflorescence (Chapter 5.3). As it is, we remain uncertain whether these patchy white residues are the result of seepage from the paint layer or a reaction caused by adverse environmental conditions.

Similarly, the 'brown/white spots' and blotches which were widespread across the ceiling may be linked to the use of sugar of lead in the 1830s paint (Chapter 5.3; Fig 149, right). Ridout describes these as irregularly shaped, translucent granules. Observations from the scaffolding suggest the blotches have a fuzzy edge; under x15

Fig 190 Chalkline efflorescence outlining the matt black wave pattern (upper) and similar efflorescence on board edges (lower) (38/I, bay 1, and 8–9/I, bay 8)

Fig 191 Examples of patchy white residues (upper, 21/II, bay 5; lower, 32/IV, bay 2)

magnification the paint surface does not appear disrupted, but a fine white dust was noticeable within the paint texture. The spots were generally brown and at the centre there appears to be a dark brown particle, like a grain of sand; around it was a lighter brown or off-white halo with a fuzzy edge. Field (1835, 56) warned against the use of sugar of lead 'without grinding or solution, which … will ultimately effloresce on the surface of the work, and throw off the colour in sandy spots'.

The paint on some obviously 1830s softwood boards has a characteristic milky or silvery surface sheen; analysis characterised it only as a thin pale coating (Fig 192). This sheen was significant over a considerable number of boards but this surface bloom did not respond to surface cleaning with Wishab™ sponges.

Tendril deposits, resembling miniature spiderweb, joining larger elements together, were relatively rare across the ceiling (Fig 193, upper). Ridout suggests (pers comm 1999) they have originated through microbiological action as some collapsed strand material was found in samples analysed. Purple grains – a suspected MBG residue – found in bay 1 were not present in bays 2 to 10 (Fig 193, lower).

The layer of surface dirt over all the painted decoration was conspicuously thicker and more discoloured within the west ceiling bays, possibly due to their proximity to the west doors which act as the main entrance to the building. In addition, within the west half of the ceiling it was noticeable that less surface dirt had accumulated where the ceiling boards are backed by structural elements. As a result, before surface cleaning, it was just possible to discern the position of some ceiling joists from below. Bays 9 and 10 were the only bays not treated prior to the 2001 fire in the building and, consequently, within the phase 5 area the soot was mingled with and largely indistinguishable from the surface dirt layer.

GRAFFITI AND INSCRIPTIONS

All pencilled graffiti and painted inscriptions are listed in the phase 5 archive report (Harrison and Lithgow nd e) and briefly described above (Chapter 5.4); most date to the 19th century and some record the names of painters involved in the 1834–5 intervention (Fig 140; Fig 146). By intention, pencilled graffiti were not removed during surface cleaning.

Treatment

As part of the feasibility study superficial cleaning trials using solvent solutions were carried out but proved invasive (Hirst Conservation 1995). These were followed in 1997 by an extensive series of tests carried out by the Perry Lithgow Partnership as part of the emergency conservation treatment phase to determine appropriate techniques, materials and methods of application for the reattachment of delaminating paint, the removal of glue film and surface cleaning. Those tests, the subsequent emergency treatment and sample analysis in 1997–8 indicated the paint was profoundly sensitive to

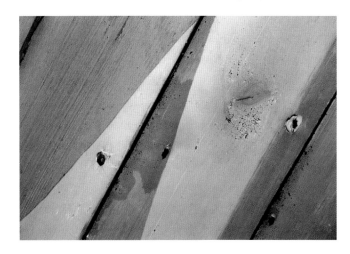

Fig 192 Detail of 1830s boards with the silvery surface sheen; note also a stain from a clear liquid that has penetrated the replacement board and staining of the paint over a knot in the wood (this was sometimes accompanied by resin drips from the knot) (35/IV, bay 2)

Fig 193 Tendril deposits (upper) and purple grains (lower) (39/IV, bay 1; 37/III, bay 1)

moisture. Traces of calcium sulphate dihydrate were identified at the wood/paint interface and also at varying concentrations throughout the paint layers. In addition, some 19th-century paint layers were found to contain high concentrations of both calcium sulphate dihydrate and clay-rich minerals. The clay-based materials swell readily in the presence of moisture, as was demonstrated by the severe blanching of some of the 19th-century paint colours following even brief contact with water (Fig 194). This discovery was highly significant and affected all aspects of treatment.

Phase 1 treatment was preceded by visual examination of the painted decoration in the easternmost bay and analysis of paint samples from that area confirmed the same original and added materials were present as from the emergency phase. The methods and materials identified as appropriate for the emergency phase were retested and a representative panel was treated to a finished level and approved by members of the project team. No new treatment materials were used during subsequent phases. With the benefit of increasing experience some methods of application and techniques were modified slightly, as described in the treatment method statements.

PAINT SAMPLE ANALYSIS

Paint samples taken from the easternmost bay in 1995 were examined (Hirst Conservation 1995). In 1996, Gillian Lewis obtained a number of paint samples during the inspection of the entire nave ceiling from a mechanical hoist; these were examined and analysed by Lewis and Helen Howard (reported in Howard 1997). From 1997 onwards the technical investigation and documentation of paint samples

was undertaken initially by Helen Howard and then by Ioanna Kakoulli, both then of the Conservation of Wall Paintings Department, Courtauld Institute of Art. Their findings are documented in three reports (Howard 1997; Howard 1998; Kakoulli 1999). Due to other commitments, the Courtauld was unable to carry out further research; therefore Jane Davies, an independent paint sample analyst, was commissioned to examine paint samples gathered during the succeeding phases of conservation. Her findings are set out in four reports (Davies 2001; 2002; 2003b; 2004).

At the start of each phase of work on the nave ceiling, the Perry Lithgow Partnership prepared a sampling strategy listing outstanding queries and including proposals for sampling and appropriate sample locations. Howard, Kakoulli and Davies each visited the site to discuss the strategy and obtain samples, although during the final two phases the paint samples were obtained by the Perry Lithgow Partnership and sent to Davies with all necessary supporting information. A tabulated inventory of the samples including basic stratigraphy, pigment identification and the analyst's comments was drawn up to facilitate the interpretation of findings from all seven paint analysis reports. The samples are grouped according to the boards from which they were

Fig 194 Cleaning and glue removal tests using water during the emergency treatment phase resulted in blanching of the paint surface of the St Paul lozenge in bay 4 (27/III (left) and 27/II)

obtained: the eight different border patterns, lozenge centre boards and replacement boards; with the three samples from the easternmost joist above the ceiling listed finally (Chapter 4.4; Chapter 5). The complete inventory is appended to the phase 5 condition survey and treatment record (Harrison and Lithgow nd e). Individual samples are referenced there and in this volume thus: (sample number/year taken). A total of 172 paint samples from the ceiling have been examined since 1997: 134 are from original ceiling boards of which 64 are from lozenge centre boards. Samples referred to in this text are summarised in Table 9 appended to this chapter.

Samples were taken following a detailed inspection of the ceiling in normal, raking and ultraviolet (UV) fluorescence illumination, and at low magnification. The three analysts employed very similar techniques and equipment for sample preparation and laboratory micro-analysis. In general these were: binocular microscopy (BM); polarised light microscopy (PLM); microchemical tests (MCT); scanning electron microscopy with X-ray energy dispersive spectroscopy (SEM-EDXS) for elemental analysis; Fourier transform infra-red spectroscopy (FTIR) for identification of organic materials and additional confirmation of inorganic components. Specific details of the methodology used in each phase are listed in the individual analyst's reports.

Consideration was given to investigating oil binding medium residues in the wood as a means of differentiating between original oil on raised linear design and later oil from 1740s work on receded background. To that end advice was sought from Raymond White of the National Gallery, who had occasionally met this problem of vestigial early layers thoroughly coated in later material which is all-pervasive. Consequently he thought this problem did not sound to be at all an easy one. It would be particularly difficult if the original paint is very thin and fragmentary (as at Peterborough). If already fragmented, it will have acted like a sponge to the later upper layers and is likely to be heavily contaminated by them (as found by Howard). In such a situation it is almost impossible to sort out the contents of the sample. The only hope might be to pick out original fragments using a micro-manipulator under binocular microscopy; a combined cross section infrared examination (perhaps embedded in silver chloride) might be carried out. If the differences were sufficiently marked, one might assemble a corpus of partial fragments, but then another group of corroborative samples would still be needed to confirm any findings. Such procedures would be very labour-intensive, quite complex and the end results probably would not justify the time and expense involved. Previously Howard had expressed similar reservations so the project team decided not to pursue this line of investigation.

DELAMINATING PAINT AND PAINT CONSOLIDATION

All the delaminating paint on the ceiling was reattached. Where possible the flakes were treated individually; although areas of micro-delamination and some interconnected larger flakes had to be relaid in groups. The two aspects critical to

the success of this process were paint relaxation and the adhesive.

Distorted, thicker paint flakes had to be relaxed to a point where they could be eased back into place without fracturing (Fig 195). This degree of flexibility was achieved by applying

Fig 195 Paint reattachment tests during the emergency treatment phase (from top): paint relaxation using the Preservation Pencil®; injecting the adhesive; applying pressure to the flake (head of St Peter, bay 3)

a delicate jet of warm dry air from a Preservation Pencil®, using the largest nozzle, set at 40°C and to minimum moisture output; any moisture emitted by the pencil at this temperature setting evaporated without affecting the paint surface. The nozzle was held close to the surface for 3–5 minutes, depending on the thickness of the paint and the level of distortion; immediately following, undiluted industrial methylated spirits (IMS) was injected behind the flake to pre-wet the void. IMS applied in this way did not cause surface blanching or adversely affect the adhesive. Preliminary relaxation with the heat source was not always necessary for the less distorted or thinner paint flakes, particularly the 1830s black paint on the wave pattern boards.

Trials were conducted using three fixatives, Plextol™ B500, Paraloid B72™ and Isinglass, each known to have good ageing properties and an ability to withstand some variation in environmental conditions. Plextol B500 was identified as the most suitable material for readhering paint flakes in this instance. (Plextol B500, a product of Röhm and widely used as a paint fixative on both wall paintings and panel paintings, is an acrylic dispersion of a thermoplastic acrylic resin; its stability is good and it has appropriate handling properties.) A 15% solution of Plextol B500 in deionised water was required when relaying large, distorted flakes where the paint layer was relatively thick; a 5–10% solution was adequate for securing the small thinner flakes. Following paint relaxation and pre-wetting, very small droplets of the adhesive solution were injected, through a fine syringe needle, behind individual paint flakes. Each flake was then pressed back into place with a small pad of dry cotton wool covered by Japanese tissue: the dry cotton wool immediately absorbed the majority of excess adhesive displaced as the flake was relaid. The cotton wool was removed and tissue was carefully peeled from the surface. Any residual adhesive on the surface following reattachment by this method did not significantly impair subsequent removal of surface dirt. This method was adapted slightly when it was discovered that by adding a small percentage of IMS to the adhesive solution it was usually possible to dispense with the pre-wetting process.

A different method was developed for re-laying distorted paint flakes underlying thick glue deposits. The glue had to be softened before the underlying paint flake became relaxed enough to be relaid. The best results were obtained by carefully dabbing the coated flake with a small piece of sponge to remove as much glue as possible; then, using the same sponge, delicately easing the relaxed flake back into position. Injecting Plextol B500 solution behind such flakes was less successful than relying on residual animal glue alone as the adhesive. There was some risk of failure on particularly distorted flakes because if the flake detached while the glue was being removed, any attempt to reposition it failed because the remaining surface glue stuck to the intervention layer. However, where the paint was only slightly cupped or lifted on one side the method was invariably successful.

Delaminating and lifting paint on nail heads was found to

be inflexible and brittle. First, up to two applications by syringe of Paraloid B72™ (10% in acetone) was required to secure the paint. (Paraloid B72 is an ethyl methacrylate co-polymer which through tests has been classed as one of the most stable synthetic resins available to conservators and is a preferred material for this treatment process.) Once the solvent had evaporated, a localised heat source (Preservation Pencil®) was applied to the flakes relaxing them sufficiently and enabling them to be gently pressed into place with a small spatula. Sufficient B72 was required to allow flakes (sometimes bent back at 90°) to be eased back into position.

In 2002, during the fire damage restoration works, we had the opportunity to revisit the east bays of the ceiling and assess the effectiveness of the paint reattachment over time. Generally, the paint was in the same stable condition as when treated: in the case of bay 1 four years beforehand, and in bays 2 and 3 three years. However, occasional individual paint flakes (28 recorded) were found and readhered using the same method as previously. Although the conservators were able to refer to the relevant condition surveys and treatment graphics, they were seldom able to determine if a particular flake had been treated in the past. Prior to the first treatment, delamination had occurred in clusters and these were plotted on the 1:15 scale graphics accordingly. Whether a particular flake within that cluster was overlooked during treatment or whether it had subsequently lifted again was impossible to tell. Only where there was a flake where none had been recorded on the graphic could we be sure it had not been treated before; gratifyingly these instances were few and far between.

Paint on the east end infill boards was adequately bound and required no further consolidation, with the exception of panel 40/III, much of which had a thin and very powdery layer of decoration painted directly on the softwood boards (Fig 196). Different dilutions of Paraloid B72™ in both xylene and acetone were trialled, with the consolidant applied by brush through Japanese tissue paper (the paper was carefully

Fig 196 Detail of powdering paint (40/III, bay 1)

peeled away from the paint surface immediately after application). A 5% solution of B72 in acetone was identified as the most appropriate solution. Generally, the powdery pigment was consolidated adequately after a single application and the process did not darken the paint or result in a shiny surface. It was found that more than one application of a similar strength solution of B72 in xylene was required to achieve the same effect; the less volatile solvent apparently caused the consolidant to penetrate further into the support where it was not required.

Tests had indicated there was no alternative but to use water to remove the animal glue film. Solvents had no effect; heat, rather than having a softening effect, made the glue brittle and contract further. The glue was more easily removed using warm rather than cold water, although, on vulnerable colours, the shorter contact time was not noticeably reflected by a lessening of surface blanch. Wherever glue was removed, the resulting 'lighter' or 'cleaner' paint was toned down with watercolour paints.

Thin deposits of the glue film were removed by swabbing with warm deionised water. Raised droplets and thick runs overlying delaminating paint would not be dissolved completely by this method. It was necessary to use the Preservation Pencil® on maximum moisture setting at 40°C and gradually stroke dissolved glue away with a small sponge. Using the smaller of the two round-ended nozzles confined the spread of the moisture. This advantage was somewhat offset as the moisture output was considerably reduced, thus slowing the process: the small area of paint surrounding the glue was subjected to less moisture but for a longer period.

SURFACE CLEANING

A 'dry' method of cleaning using Wishab™ sponges (cakes of synthetic rubber granules that collect the dirt and self-abrade when rubbed across a surface) produced good results and was preferable for a number of reasons (Fig 197). Some solvent-based solutions were ineffective; all proved difficult to control and produced different cleaning levels on the various colours and paints; most caused the paint surface to shine; in addition, much of the paint surface lightened after contact with water. By contrast, cleaning tests with Wishab™ sponges within the easternmost bay demonstrated it was relatively easy to achieve a uniform level of clean: the majority of the paint was stable and withstood the gentle surface abrasion necessary without need for preliminary consolidation; surface dirt could be removed without causing the paint surface to shine; and Wishab™ cleaning leaves no significant, potentially harmful residues on the paint surface (Harrison and Lithgow nd a, 57). The trial areas were examined on site using a video microscope and samples were taken for further testing in the laboratory. Howard recommended the following procedures for Wishab™ use on the nave ceiling:

  brush the surface with a soft sable brush before use of Wishab™;

  use a small, shaped piece of the sponge which can be applied with delicacy to a small area;

  monitor the cleaning process by regular checking at magnification;

  brush off the surface with a soft brush after application of Wishab™ to remove any residual particles.

The guidelines recommended by Howard for Wishab™ use on the nave ceiling were followed throughout. Loose surface dust particles and the soot layer resulting from the 2001 fire in the building were brushed from the surface, using small and very soft brushes; the dust was sucked into a vacuum cleaner nozzle held close by. Small, shaped pieces of the Wishab™ sponge were applied to the paint surface with gentle circular strokes, with constant attention to guard against surface shine as well as disruption of loose paint or raised, granular particles. The particles of Wishab™ remaining on the surface were removed with a soft brush. This method achieved a satisfactory and uniform level of clean, removing much of the efflorescence and bloom as well as most surface dirt; however, a slight surface discoloration remained. Cleaning with deionised water would have removed this surface deposit – as proved by previous tests and the paint surface where glue has been removed – but this was not an appropriate option given the extreme moisture sensitivity of the paint. As it is, the slightly yellowed deposit will serve to isolate the paint from future residues.

REMOVAL OF SURFACE STAINING

The approach adopted throughout the project was that stains considered to be particularly distracting and visible from the ground should be removed, reduced or disguised. Almost all stains were reduced rather than removed. On the original boards it was possible to reduce the smaller water stains using warm deionised water. Water alone was not effective in reducing the chemical stains or the more extensive water stains. For these a variety of materials or combination of materials was used, including a 2–5% solution of ammonium carbonate in IMS or acetone or a mixture of these two solvents (50:50). All categories of stains on the replacement boards were more difficult to reduce. None of the solvents mentioned above were effective in reducing these stains without affecting the paint layer. Cleaning with solvents causes a dark halo to appear around the stain which itself was then difficult to remove. In addition, attempts to remove stains on these boards resulted in a shiny surface.

REINTEGRATION

The 'lighter' or 'cleaner' areas of paint resulting from glue or stain removal were toned down with watercolour paints to match the surrounding Wishab™ cleaned paint (Fig 198; Fig 199). Similarly, some areas of distracting wood loss and unpainted gaps between ceiling boards were disguised by inpainting (retouching) the exposed edge of damaged board or underlying structural elements such as a softwood patch, hessian or the underside of noggins.

The policy for the reintegration of new timber inserts was

Fig 197 Removal of surface dirt using Wishab™ sponges provided a uniform level of clean across the ceiling: upper – cleaning the underside of the nave ceiling on the south side (39/III–IV, bay 1); lower – part-cleaned ashlar boards on the south side (adjacent to 30–31/IV, bay 3)

modified as the project progressed. In the first instance no attempt was made to recreate the missing figurative detail on the relatively large area of new timber inserted within the anthropophagus lozenge (Fig 200). The project team decided there would be too much conjecture involved (Fig 201); therefore the repair was painted to match the adjacent background colours. Subsequent timber inserts were all much smaller and for them it was agreed the painted detail of the border patterns and lozenge centres should be recreated, but in a manner that did not disguise the new

timber inserts under close inspection (above, 6.6; Figs 178–181). A white acrylic primer was applied to the new wood patches followed by numerous applications of differently toned resin and tempera paints applied as thin glazes. We found it necessary to use these different paint media on the new timber inserts to achieve the very matt appearance of the existing scheme.

Acrylic-based paints were used to reintegrate the repairs material (filler) used to consolidate the small areas of wood loss resulting from wet rot and/or insect damage (above). A

Fig 198 Examples of glue removal and reintegration (left, 27/IV, bay 4; right, ashlar board on south side adjacent to 9–10/IV, bay 8)

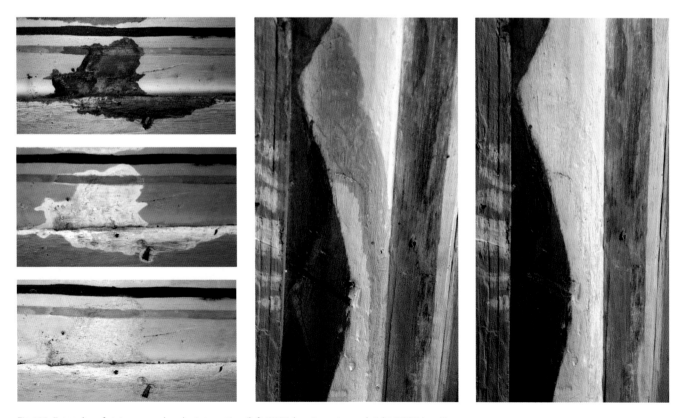

Fig 199 Examples of stain removal and reintegration (left, 21/III, bay 5; centre and right, 29/IV, bay 3)

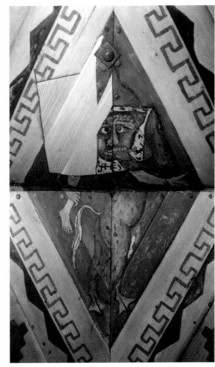

Fig 200 The 1926 patch repair in the anthropophagus lozenge (33–34/I–II, bay 2) (left to right): before treatment; with new oak insert; as it now appears with the insert painted in background colours

Fig 201 Digital reconstruction of the anthropophagus lozenge with the missing detail repainted (33–34/I–II, bay 2), prepared for a project team discussion of an appropriate reintegration approach

primer of Plextol B500 (20% solution in water) was used in some areas, otherwise two to three layers of paint were required to give adequate depth of colour.

All visible stainless steel fixings inserted during treatment were painted in neutral colours using acrylic-based paints. Following the removal of loose rust particles, a single coating of 10% B72 in acetone was applied as an isolation layer to all corroded metal exposed as a result of paint loss from metal fixings. No surface coating was applied to the painted decoration on the ceiling or ashlar boards.

The transept ceilings

Condition and treatment

Since very little paint has survived on the transept ceilings, the condition of the painted decoration formed only a minor part of the condition recording process. Nevertheless, a great deal of related information was photographed and recorded graphically on photogrammetric drawings of the ceiling boards. Analysis of that information, together with the findings of paint sample analysis and the research of archive documents, has culminated in the detailed descriptions of the ceilings and their physical history in the archive and here (Chapter 3; Chapter 5).

To inform the preliminary investigations and development of a treatment strategy samples of the dark residual coating and a sample of what may have been residual original ground were obtained from the south transept ceiling and sent to Catherine Hassall (Hassall 2002). It was necessary to investigate the nature of these materials to determine whether they were intended coatings or residue from the 1880s paint removal. Hassall found a resin content in both samples; the dark coating contained no pigment; the whitish material was on top of the dark coating and consisted of lead white, calcium carbonate and iron oxide. The materials and nature of the whitish layer suggest a residual 'mush' of paint and ground. The fact that it is over the dark coating indicates both are residues not properly cleared during paint removal. Sample 3 was obtained from a weathered original board that appeared to have possible residue from a preparatory layer within the grain. At that initial stage no other indications of paint had been found. The sample was of lead white paint tinted with a few particles of charcoal black and iron oxide. Very similar paint is present in samples analysed subsequently and considered to be from a 1740s repaint. Therefore analysis of the dark residual coating and the associated overlying semi-opaque whitish layer that had been smeared over 1880s boards adjacent to original boards established that they were simply residues not properly cleared during paint removal in the late 19th century.

Limited tests were carried out to determine whether it would be possible or desirable to remove this residue. The dark coating was not affected by water or white spirit but it, and the associated semi-opaque whitish layer, could be removed by swabbing with industrial methylated spirits (IMS) and/or acetone; this resulted in a slight lightening in the colour of the underlying wood surface. Although it would not have been technically difficult to remove the coating from the 1880s boards it would have more than doubled the time involved and therefore the cost of the surface cleaning process. For this reason, in consultation with the architect and conservation adviser, it was agreed the residual coating should be left in place.

As soot and surface dirt were removed from the ceilings, surviving traces of the original paint scheme became evident. In particular, this was found on original and 17th-century boards removed for tree-ring analysis in places protected by overlapping edges. Representative paint samples were obtained as treatment progressed and on completion of the work these were sent to Jane Davies for analysis (Davies 2003a). Jane Davies had carried out the paint sample analysis for phases 3 and 4 of the Peterborough Cathedral nave ceiling conservation project so was able to compare samples taken from the three ceilings, this being a particularly important aspect of the analysis and its interpretation given their closely linked physical histories.

Designs visible in shallow relief on some of the early boards – particularly the cross motifs at the centre of lozenge compartments – and the parallel grooves on some original board edges are the only indications remaining of the 13th-century scheme (Chapter 3.4). The shallow relief is thought to be due to the masking effect of the painted designs whereby the paint protected the underlying timber from a degrading factor such as weathering, while the surrounding, less protected timber has receded (cf Chapter 4.3).

Apart from paint discovered on overlapped edges, fragments of paint were found on only four boards across the two ceilings. The three instances found in the south transept were apparently brown/black 1740s paint from dog-tooth border patterns. In the north transept 1740s paint fragments were found on apparent original, linear 'bun' pattern decoration. All the surviving paint was stable. Dark shadowing indicating the 1740s paint scheme was recorded on 160 original south transept boards and eight original north transept boards.

Relatively few instances of graffiti were found on the ceilings; these included the pencilled signatures of 'Sam Buxton', dated 1888, in the north transept (panel J/8) and two by 'HS Burleigh' and 'HS Burleigh Whitesmith', dated 1924 and 1911 respectively, in the south-west corner of the south transept (panel N/0). Various pencil marks and incised lines appear to date from the 1880s intervention; most are simple lines or Xs, probably drawn to indicate the position of structural elements above the boards.

A preferential accumulation of dirt, indicative from below the ceiling of the position of some joists, was particularly noticeable on the north and south transept ceilings prior to the surface cleaning following the 2001 fire. Although there was very little paint remaining on the ceiling boards the guidelines recommended by Howard for Wishab™ sponge use on the nave ceiling (above) were followed throughout the transept.

Liquid glue used in the 1920s as an adhesive for the hessian backing material had in many places on both ceilings penetrated between the boards and through empty nail holes (as in the nave, cf above). The water-soluble animal glue formed thick dark globules as it dried on the timber surface and these deposits were recorded on the transept graphics. Having removed the thick layer of soot and surface dirt from the ceiling boards, the glue deposits were particularly distracting but, in addition, significant and widespread areas of different degrees of surface staining resulting from other liquids were noticeable on both ceilings. The time available was spent treating the most distracting stains.

Glue drips, surface stains, surface splinters and splits were treated as per the nave (above), and consolidation of wood loss, surface coating of corroded metal fixings and reintegration followed the pattern established for the nave ceiling. All visible stainless steel fixings inserted by Hugh Harrison's team to stabilise loose boards and to reposition boards that had been removed for tree-ring dating were painted in neutral colours using acrylic-based paints.

6.8 ENDNOTE

To commemorate the nine-year-long nave ceiling conservation project, an inscription was painted in red ochre watercolour on the reintegrated off-white background of the north side ashlar boards at the west end of the nave above the stone ledge (Fig 202).

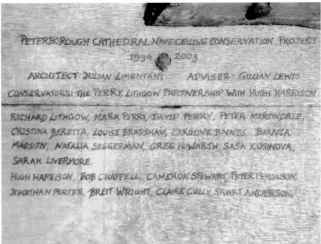

Fig 202 The completion of the conservation project marked by an inscription on the north side of the west end of the nave

Table 9 Paint samples from the nave and transept referred to in the text, where referenced by sample number/year taken (eg, 1/1997), as in the phase reports (Harrison and Lithgow nd a–e); the analysis report reference is also given (eg, Howard 1997, 1/2093) (for further details and for full lists of paint samples see Harrison and Lithgow nd e, i, appendix 23; nd f, appendix 5)

Sample no. by year	Board no. (if known)	Location/ board type	Description	Analysis sample no./accession no.
ann 1997				**Howard 1997**
1	-	lozenge	dulcimer player, instrument: pink/brown colour on wooden support	1/2093
2	-	lozenge	dulcimer player, cusped mandorla: green paint layer	2/2094
3	-	lozenge	dulcimer player, cusped mandorla: blue/green over green	3/2095
4	-	lozenge	dulcimer player, edge of instrument: purple with white line applied in impasto	4/2096
7	-	lozenge	dulcimer player, left proper cheek: pale flesh tone	7/2099
8	-	lozenge	dulcimer player, hair: metallic bloom on surface of brown hair	8/2100
9	-	lozenge	dulcimer player, top of head: dark line which appears to be beneath 'early green'	9/2101
16	-	lozenge	St Paul, cusped mandorla, inner area: bright yellow/green with darker green on surface	16/2108
17	-	stepped chevron	St Paul, stepped 'battlement' border around figure: brown/black	17/2109
19	-	wave	St Paul, chevron border: opaque rich black	19/2111
20	-	lozenge	St Peter, above left proper eye: flesh tone	20/2112
21	-	lozenge	St Peter, above right proper eye: flesh tone; consolidated by the Perry Lithgow Partnership, April 1997	21/2113
23	-	lozenge	St Peter, left proper temple: flesh tone with what appears to be an earlier consolidant on the surface	23/2115
24	-	lozenge	St Peter, right proper sleeve: dark blue lining of sleeve	24/2116
25	-	key border	St Peter, border with key pattern: shiny black paint with white bloom on surface	25/2117
27	-	extended chevron	St Peter, border with extended chevron pattern: ghost of trefoil pattern beneath chevron design	27/2119
28	-	grey chevron	St Peter, chevron border: impasto decoration beneath grey paint	28/2120

Table 9 (cont)

Sample no. by year	Board no. (if known)	Location/ board type	Description	Analysis sample no./accession no.
ann 1998				**Howard 1998b**
2	36/IV/ee	lozenge	centre of foliate motif: crude black and red overpaint on creamy-white ground	2/2348
3	36/IV/dd	lozenge	foliate motif: foliate scroll beneath creamy-white repaint	3/2349
5	36/III/w	grey chevron	black with bloom and extensive craquelure	5/2351
9	37/I/d	wave	chevron pattern in black on cream ground: salts along edge of black chevron	9/2355
11	37/III/r	extended chevron	extensive drips and staining of dark brown material	11/2357
ann 1999				**Kakoulli 1999**
10	32/II	replacement board, coloured bands	black-painted area of a replacement board with no traces of earlier decoration underneath the existing scheme	10/2704
13	28/III/c	key border	painted decoration of an earlier scheme showing in low relief through the key decoration of the existing painting	13/2707
14	29/III/b	lozenge	red-painted area overlapping a low-relief underpainting of an earlier scheme; the sample was taken near the harp of the ass	14/2708
15	33/III/b	lozenge	near the wing of the wyvern-like lizard/dragon: greenish-grey paint; this paint is overlapping an earlier scheme	15/2709
16	28/I/p	extended chevron	cream-coloured area overlapping an earlier scheme with trefoils showing in low relief beneath the existing painting	16/2710
17	29/III	baseboard	white blanching over black paint	17/2711
18	28/III/e	wave	cream-coloured paint overlapping an earlier scheme with wavy decoration showing in low relief beneath the existing painting	18/2712
19	28/I/d/e	bun	cream-coloured paint overlapping an earlier scheme showing in low relief beneath the existing painting	19/2713
20	33/III/cc	lozenge	the staff of Agnus Dei, an area showing an earlier painted scheme in low relief beneath the existing painting	20/2714
22	29–30/III	lozenge	red paint under ceiling bolt	22/2726
26	32/1/e	key border	red paint from groove in a key pattern board; the paint had been protected by an original nail head (now missing)	26/2730
30	33/III/y	stepped chevron	within stepped chevron	30/2734
31	33/III/y	stepped chevron	outer edge of stepped chevron	31/2735
34	30/IV/v	lozenge	apparent original design of tail and harness of ass visible in raking light	34/2738
35	32/IV/m	replacement board, coloured bands	black on board apparently repainted in the 1740s	35/2739
36	32/IV/m	replacement board, coloured bands	red on board apparently repainted in the 1740s	36/2740
37	30/III/x	grey chevron	black/brown with possible original paint: black and white (possible ?red traces) lines under a lost original nail head	37/2741
39	33/II/u	extended chevron	trefoil	39/2743
41	31/II/z	lozenge	St Peter	41/2745
44	33/III/a	lozenge	rear leg of original fox underlying the wyvern-like lizard/dragon overpaint	44/2748
45	31/III/d	wave	deep matt black	45/2749
47	29/IV/s	grey chevron	thick resinous coating	47/2751
52	34/III/e	replacement stepped chevron	black coating, resinous medium where it is in impasto	52/2756
55	34/IV/b	lozenge	design unclear, but it is on a reused board	55/2759

Table 9 (cont)

Sample no. by year	Board no. (if known)	Location/ board type	Description	Analysis sample no./accession no.
57	28/IV/o	grey chevron	white ?paint from original nail hole in grooves of the grey chevron board	57/2761
ann 2000				**Davies 2001**
1	22/III/o	coloured bands	original frieze decoration on oak replacement boards – suspected original ashlar decoration visible in relief on two repositioned oak ceiling boards: sample of paint from trefoil design	1 (2989)
2	22/III/o	coloured bands	original frieze decoration on oak replacement boards – suspected original ashlar decoration visible in relief on two repositioned oak ceiling boards: paint from tendril design	2 (2990)
3	22/IV/e	dog-tooth	exposed area of seemingly original linear dog-tooth pattern: white	3 (2991)
6	21/I/o	coloured bands	under original nail head (now missing): thin layer of white paint or preparation layer from within a groove	6 (2994)
7	21/I/o	coloured bands	under original nail head (now missing): black paint on raised area between grooves	7 (2995)
9	27/II/s	replacement grey chevron	red paint from frieze decoration underpaint on replacement softwood ceiling boards	9 (2997)
10	27/II/s	replacement grey chevron	black paint from frieze decoration underpaint on replacement softwood ceiling boards	10 (2998)
13	22/II/z	lozenge	head of angel with cornet: flesh tone on neck	13 (3060)
14	21/II/a	lozenge	head of angel with cornet: flesh tone on bridge of nose	14 (3061)
16	19/III/aa	lozenge	face and neck of archbishop: flesh tone below nostril	16 (3063)
20	19/III/m	baseboard	sample from raised scroll design through 1830s white paint	20 (3067)
21	22/III/a	lozenge	collar of archbishop: fragment of green paint within area of paint loss on collar	21 (3068)
ann 2001				**Davies 2002**
4	13/I/a	lozenge	under original nail head (now missing): red/brown on base of organistrum	4 (3073)
5	13/I/c	lozenge	under original nail head (now missing): green on drapery of organistrum player	5 (3074)
7	17/II/b	lozenge	under original nail head (now missing): green from background of Grammar	7 (3076)
9	11/II/j	coloured bands	under original nail head (now missing): red paint from outer groove	9 (3078)
10	11/I/s	grey chevron	under original nail head (now missing): red paint from middle groove	10 (3079)
11	11/I/f	grey chevron	under original nail head (now missing): red paint from middle groove	11 (3080)
13	15/I/q	extended chevron	small impasto circle/dot on 'body' of original trefoil	13 (3082)
14	14/III/t	extended chevron	small impasto circle/dot on 'body' of original trefoil	14 (3083)
15	9/I/f	stepped chevron	original linear stepped chevron decoration visible in relief under 18th-/19th-century paint: sample through white	15 (3084)
16	9/I/f	stepped chevron	original linear stepped chevron decoration visible in relief under 18th-/19th-century paint: sample through black	16 (3085)
17	9/I/f	stepped chevron	original linear stepped chevron decoration visible in relief under 18th-/19th-century paint: sample through white	17 (3086)
18	9/I/f	stepped chevron	original linear stepped chevron decoration visible in relief under 18th-/19th-century paint: sample through black	18 (3087)
19	9/I/f	stepped chevron	original linear stepped chevron decoration visible in relief under 18th-/19th-century paint: sample through white	19 (3088)
20	12/III/e	stepped chevron	original linear stepped chevron decoration visible in relief under 18th-/19th-century paint: sample through white	20 (3089)
21	12/III/e	stepped chevron	original linear stepped chevron decoration visible in relief under 18th-/19th-century paint: sample through black	21 (3090)

Table 9 (cont)

Sample no. by year	Board no. (if known)	Location/ board type	Description	Analysis sample no./accession no.
22	12/III/e	stepped chevron	original linear stepped chevron decoration visible in relief under 18th-/19th-century paint: sample through white	22 (3091)
23	17/IV/g	stepped chevron	under original nail head (now missing): white paint from raised linear stepped chevron decoration	23 (3092)
25	15/I/f	stepped chevron	under original nail head (now missing): white paint from raised linear stepped chevron decoration	25 (3094)
ann 2002				**Davies 2003a**
ST 2	M/5/f	south transept	white ground to black chevron on 17th-century board	2 (3106)
ST 3	M&N/4–M&N/5 junction	south transept	ceiling bolt and washer: black paint on washer	3 (3107)
ST 4	M/5/f M&N/5 junction	south transept	ceiling bolt and washer: white ground on washer	4 (3108)
ST 5	G/8/j	south transept	faint black chevron on original board	5 (3109)
ST 6	M/5/g	south transept	white paint under lost nail head in an original groove on detached original board	6 (3110)
NT 8	E/0/b	north transept	black paint under overlap on detached original board	8 (3112)
NT 9	E/0/b	north transept	brown/black paint on raised bun pattern	9 (3113)
ann 2002				**Davies 2003b**
32	joist 1	joist above ceiling	painted decoration found on a 2m section of the easternmost ceiling joist: black paint from pattern of circles and triangles	32 (3101, P4a:1)
33	joist 1	joist above ceiling	painted decoration found on a 2m section of the easternmost ceiling joist: white paint from pattern of circles and triangles	33 (3102, P4a:2)
34	joist 1	joist above ceiling	painted decoration found on a 2m section of the easternmost ceiling joist: red paint from pattern of circles and triangles	34 (3103, P4a:3)
ann 2003				**Davies 2004**
1	22/III/a	lozenge	under original nail head (now missing): flesh tone on neck of archbishop	1 (3105)
2	23/II/cc	lozenge	under original nail head (now missing): green with red stripe within hair of archbishop	2 (3106)
3	23/II/cc	lozenge	under original nail head (now missing): flesh tone with red edge on neck of archbishop	3 (3107)
4	22/III/a	lozenge	under original nail head (now missing): light red from within lower robe drapery of archbishop	4 (3108)
5	22/III/a	lozenge	under original nail head (now missing): light red from within lower robe drapery of archbishop	5 (3109)
6	22/III/a	lozenge	under original nail head (now missing): dark red from within lower robe drapery of archbishop	6 (3110)
7	23/II/cc	lozenge	under original nail head (now missing): off-white from white edging of drapery of archbishop	7 (3111)
8	23/II/aa	lozenge	under original nail head (now missing): white paint from mitre of archbishop	8 (3112)
9	21/III/e	wave	under original protruding nail head: black from an apparent black line on outer curved edge of board	9 (3113)
10	21/I/c	lozenge	under original nail head (now missing): red paint from within white background of angel with cornet lozenge	10 (3114)
11	18/I/ee	lozenge	under original nail head (now missing): green paint from within drapery of Grammar lozenge	11 (3115)

FRENCH, ITALIAN, GERMAN AND SPANISH SUMMARIES

Résumé

Madeleine Hummler

Le plafond de la nef de la cathédrale de Peterborough est un objet d'intérêt et d'importance immenses. Ce plafond en bois, construit et peint au XIIIe siècle, fut réparé et repeint par deux fois, dans les années 1740 et 1830. L'état des planches du plafond et des peintures devint critique durant les années 1990. On décida donc d'initier un projet de conservation et d'examen d'envergure, concernant non seulement le plafond mais aussi les vestiges tronqués du toit du XIIe siècle auxquels ce plafond est accroché. En 2001, alors que ce projet était au trois quart complet, un incendie s'est déclaré à l'intérieur de la cathédrale, recouvrant de suie toutes les surfaces de l'édifice. Il a fallu recommencer le nettoyage. Nous avons saisi cette occasion pour étendre nos recherches et travaux de conservation à l'ensemble des plafonds de la cathédrale.

Ce volume expose les nouvelles connaissances acquises sur le plafond de la nef, sur son histoire, et sur les structures qui y sont rattachées au sens propre du terme (le toit et les murs médiévaux de la nef), ainsi que sur les plafonds des transepts. Toutes les structures de bois importantes ont fait l'objet d'examens dendrochronologiques, ce qui a entraîné une révision significative de nos interprétations, en particulier des phases médiévales ; de plus, l'examen des documents écrits a fourni des données importantes sur le mode de construction au Moyen Age et sur les fréquentes réparations datant de l'époque postmédiévale. L'analyse des structures nous a également permis de comprendre le travail des artisans médiévaux et plus tardifs ; l'examen de la peinture a d'autre part donné des indices sur les techniques et pigments employés au Moyen Age, et sur les restaurations des XVIIIe et XIXe siècles. Dans la mesure du possible ces restaurations tardives ont préservé les schémas iconographiques du Moyen Age, qui sont réexaminés ici.

Nous documentons également le programme de conservation, pour donner une idée des meilleures pratiques appliquées lors de l'exécution du projet, à l'intention de conservateurs et architectes engagés sur d'autres bâtiments et dans des travaux ultérieurs à Peterborough. Les mesures de la température et de l'humidité au-dessus et en dessous du plafond, avant, durant et après un incendie qui aurait pu être catastrophique et qui, nous l'espérons, ne se reproduira pas, se révèlent de très grande valeur pour tous ceux qui ont la responsabilité de grandes et belles églises (à quelque chose malheur est bon).

Prefazione

Patrizia Pierazzo

Il soffitto della navata della Cattedrale di Peterborough ha immensa importanza e grande significato. La struttura in legno fu costruita e dipinta nel XIII secolo e fu restaurata in due occasioni, la prima volta tra il 1740 e il 1750 e in seguito tra il 1830 e il 1840. Negli anni '90 del secolo scorso, la struttura in legno del tetto ed il dipinto stesso erano in condizioni precarie, di conseguenza iniziò un esteso programma di studio e restauro, non riguardante solamente il soffitto ma anche ciò che rimaneva del tetto di secolo XII al quale il dipinto era appeso. Nel 2001, a progetto quasi ultimato, un incendio colpì parte della cattedrale e tutte le superfici furono coperte di fuliggine. La pulitura dovette essere effettuata nuovamente e, grazie a questa opportunità, lo studio ed il restauro vennero estesi ad altre parti del tetto della cattedrale.

Questa pubblicazione illustra la rinnovata comprensione dell'evoluzione storica del tetto della navata e delle strutture ad esso connesse direttamente, quali il tetto medievale della navata ed i muri, ed indirettamente, quale il soffitto del transetto. Tutte le maggiori strutture lignee sono state studiate con la tecnica della dendrocronologia, ottenendo così un significativo approfondimento della nostra preesistente conoscenza in special modo delle fasi medievali. Nel contempo la ricerca d'archivio ha permesso una migliore comprensione delle diversi fasi costruttive di epoca medievale e di molti dei restauri effettuati in epoca post-medievale. L'analisi strutturale ha rivelato le tecniche artigianali medievali e post-medievali utilizzate per la costruzione dell'edificio; l'analisi dei dipinti ha lasciato intravvedere pigmenti e tecniche pittoriche medievali oltre alle fasi di restauro del XVIII e XIX secolo, rispettose dove possibile dell'iconografia medievale, che sono state in questa occasione nuovamente studiate.

Il programma di restauro conservativo è stato accuratamente documentato in questa pubblicazione, cosicché le migliori tecniche artigianali e artistiche applicate al tempo possano essere esaminate, comprese e messe a disposizione di restauratori e architetti al lavoro in edifici simili e di coloro i quali saranno impiegati a Peterborough in futuro. Le registrazioni della temperatura e del tasso di umidità al di sopra ed al di sotto del soffitto eseguite prima, durante e dopo l'incendio, la nota positiva di un mancato disastro, hanno valore incomparabile per tutti coloro i quali si prendono cura di grandi edifici di culto e sono (si spera) da non ripetersi.

Zusammenfassung

Madeleine Hummler

Die Decke des Mittelschiffes der Kathedrale von Peterborough ist ein Objekt von hervorragender Bedeutung und Interesse. Diese Holzdecke wurde im 13. Jh. gefertigt und bemalt. Sie wurde zweimal erneuert und übermalt, in den 1740er und 1830er Jahren. In den 1990er Jahren hatte sich der Erhaltungszustand der Bretter und der Bemalung verschlechtert. Infolgedessen wurde ein Konservierungs- und Untersuchungsprogramm initiiert. Dieses betraf nicht nur die Holzdecke, sondern auch die abgeschnittenen Überreste des Daches aus dem 12. Jh., an welchen die Decke befestigt ist. Im Jahre 2001, zu drei Vierteln durch das Untersuchungsprogramm, brach ein Brand im Inneren der Kathedrale aus, und alle Flächen des Gebäudes wurden mit Ruß bedeckt. Am mindesten musste man das Ganze neu reinigen. Dies hat die Gelegenheit gegeben, die Untersuchungen und die Konservierungsarbeiten auf andere Decken der Kathedrale zu erweitern.

Dieser Bericht enthält die Ergebnisse der Untersuchung der Decke des Mittelschiffes und neue Erkenntnisse über ihre Geschichte sowie über die Strukturen, die (im echten Sinne des Wortes) damit verbunden sind – also die mittelalterlichen Mauern und Dach – und vergleichend über die Decken der Querschiffe. Alle größeren Holzstrukturen wurden dendrochronologisch datiert, und die Ergebnisse haben zu wesentlichen Umarbeitungen unserer Kenntnisse, vor allem der mittelalterlichen Phasen, geführt. Dazu hat die Untersuchung der schriftlichen Quellen ein Licht über die Bautätigkeiten des Mittelalters und über die späteren Reparaturen geworfen. Das Können der Handwerker des Mittelalters und der frühen Neuzeit wurde durch strukturelle Untersuchungen besser erfasst, und die Analyse der Bemalungen hat Einblicke in die Technik und Pigmenten, die im Mittelalter gebraucht wurden, gegeben, wie auch über die Übermalungen des 18. und 19. Jhs. Diese späteren Übermalungen haben die mittelalterlichen Darstellungen so weit wie möglich berücksichtigt; diese Bildnisse werden hier neu betrachtet.

Die Konservierungsarbeiten werden hier auch dokumentiert, sodass die aktuellen Verfahren offenlegen und den Denkmalpfleger und Architekten zur Verfügung stehen, sogleich für andere Gebäude wie auch für zukünftige Projekte in Peterborough. Die Aufzeichnung der Temperatur und der Feuchtigkeit unter und über der Decke, vor, während und nach dem Brand – ein Silberstreifen in beinahe verhängnisvollen Umständen, die sich hoffentlich nie wieder wiederholen dürften – sind ein unermesslich wertvolles Hilfsmittel für alle, die sich um bedeutende Kirchen kümmern.

Resumen

Juan José Fuldain

El techo de la nave de la catedral de Peterborough es un elemento de gran interés e importancia. Este techo de madera se construyó y pintó en el siglo 13; fue reparado y repintado dos veces, una vez en la década de 1740 y otra vez de nuevo en la década de 1830. En la década de 1990, tanto las placas de techo como la pintura misma se encontraban en un estado bastante frágil. Por lo tanto, se inició un importante programa de conservación y de investigación, no sólo en el techo, sino también en la parte restante cortada del techo del siglo 12 de la cual cuelga. Hechas tres cuartas partes del programa, en 2001, se produjo un incendio en el interior de la catedral, que cubrió todas las superficies del interior del edificio con hollín. La limpieza, al menos, había que hacerla de nuevo. Se aprovechó la oportunidad para realizar la investigación y conservación en los demás techos de la catedral.

Este libro hace referencia a nuestro nuevo modo de entender el techo de la nave y su historia, y de las estructuras conectadas a ella, literalmente, (la cubierta de la nave medieval y paredes) y comparativamente (los techos del transepto). Todas las grandes estructuras de madera fueron datadas por dendrocronología, lo que ha producido un ajuste significativo de nuestro conocimiento sobre todo de las fases medievales, mientras que la investigación documental ha arrojado luz sobre el programa de constructivo medieval y sobre muchas de las reparaciones post-medievales. El análisis estructural puso al descubierto técnicas medievales y post-medievales; el análisis de la pintura muestra pigmentos y técnicas medievales, con añadidos repintados en los siglos 18 y 19. En lo posible, estos trabajos posteriores mantuvieron el esquema iconográfico medieval, asunto este nuevamente estudiado.

También se documenta aquí el programa de conservación física, por lo que se examinan las mejores prácticas del momento y se ponen a disposición tanto de los conservadores y arquitectos de otros edificios como para los que trabajen en Peterborough en el futuro. Los registros de temperatura y humedad por encima y por debajo del techo, antes, durante y después del incendio (el lado positivo de un casi desastre) son de un valor incomparable para todos los que cuidan de grandes iglesias así como algo (esperamos) poco probable que ocurra de nuevo.

BIBLIOGRAPHY

MANUSCRIPTS

Cambridge University Library (CUL)

PDC MS 35   'Brief anals [sic] of it's [sic] modern history From Chapter Auditt Books, Ditto Minute Books, Etc., etc., etc., 1542–1891; James Thomas Irvine, 1890'

PDC MS 52   accounts 1611–71, unfoliated volume, although some of the individual accounts have their own foliation
  ann 1629, audit book
  ann 1640, accounts for bequests
  ann 1662, [repairs]
  ann 1664–5, 'Dr Howorth his booke of disburstments for the Cathedrall Church of Peterb' from August 2th 1664 unto August 1st 1665'
  ann 1668–9, disbursements from Lammas 1668 to Lammas 1669
  ann 1670–1, 'A book of reparations and other extraordinary expences for this last year from Lamas 1670 to Lamas 1671'

PDC MS 53   accounts 1671–80, unfoliated volume, although some of the individual accounts have their own foliation
  ann 1671, [repairs]
  ann 1672, 'A Booke of reparations and other extraordinary expences for this last yeare'
  ann 1674–5, 'A Booke of reparations & other extraodinary [sic] expences for this last yeare from Lady day 1674 to Lady 1675'
  ann 1676–7, 'A Book of reparations and other extraordinary expences for this last year from Lady-day 1676 to Lady-day 1677'
  ann 1677–8, 'A Book of repaires and other extraordinary expences for this last year from Lady-day 1677 to Lady-day 1678'
  ann 1678, [repairs]
  ann 1679–80, [repairs]

The Fitzwilliam Museum, Cambridge

MS 12   Peterborough Psalter

Koninklijke Bibliotheek van België – Bibliothèque royale de Belgique, Brussels (KBR)

MS 9961–2   Peterborough Psalter

New College, Oxford

MS 322   New College Psalter

Northamptonshire Record Office (NRO)

ML 869   Dean and Chapter accounts 1750–85, unfoliated
ML 872   Dean and Chapter accounts 1806–25, unfoliated
ML 874   Dean and Chapter accounts 1826–44, unfoliated
PD/DC/AP 2343   architectural plan of the south transept roof, Peterborough Cathedral, possibly by J T Irvine, 1880s
PDC Box X5051   vouchers for 1803–22, in bundles by years
PDC Box X5052   vouchers for 1823–32, in bundles by years
PDC Box X5053   vouchers for 1832–1845, in bundles by years
PDC Box X5054   vouchers for 1846–1863, in bundles by years
PDC Box X5055   vouchers for 1864–1881, in bundles by years
PDC Box X5096   letters and papers associated with cathedral works, late 19th century
  PDC RP18   'Specification of the Works required to be done in the Reparation of the Roofs of the North & South Transepts and in the underpinning of the walls of the Same by J L Pearson and a quotation for the same by John Thompson'
PDC Box X5097   letters associated with cathedral works, late 19th century
  PDC RP42   over 300 items/bundles including Restoration Committee minutes, including estimates
PDC Box X5098   letters and papers associated with cathedral works, late 19th century
  PDC RP121   63 items/bundles including Restoration Committee minutes
PDC Box X5157   assorted items, including one voucher:
ann 1761   'An Accompt between the Revd the Dean and Chapter of the Cathedral Church of Peterborough and Richard Tryce of Peterborough Esqr for Money Paid and Received by the said Mr Tryce on Account of taking down Rebuilding and Covering a [sic] of new Roof of the South end of the Cross Isle in the Cath. Church according to a Chapter Act 30th June 1761'
PDC/E. 211 [X505]   principal transactions of the Dean and Chapter from July 1822 to July 1830, compiled by J H Monk, DD, Dean, unfoliated

Peterborough Cathedral Library (PCL)

Irvine Papers   11 volumes of papers produced or gathered
    by J T Irvine, clerk of works 1883–1900
PDC MS 54   Peterborough Dean and Chapter Acts, 1
    August 1660 to 4 April 1814
PDC MS 57   Dean and Chapter audit book, 1814–70
Peterborough Advertiser   [newspaper clippings]

Society of Antiquaries of London (SAL)

MS 59   Peterborough Psalter (the Lindsey Psalter)

PRINTED AND OTHER SECONDARY WORKS

Andrews, D, 2003 *Measured and drawn: techniques and
    practice for the metric survey of historic buildings*, Swindon
The Architect, 1898 [view of the interior of the nave,
    Peterborough Cathedral], no. 136, no page
Ayers, T, and Sampson, J, 2000 The Middle Ages, in *Salisbury
    Cathedral: the west front* (ed T Ayers), 9–82, Chichester
Baillie, M G L, 1982 *Tree-ring dating and archaeology*,
    London
Baillie, M G L, 1984 Some thoughts on art-historical
    dendrochronology, *J Archaeol Sci* 11, 371–93
Baillie, M G L, and Pilcher, J R, 1973 A simple cross-dating
    program for tree-ring research, *Tree Ring Bull* 33, 7–14
Baillie, M G L, Hillam, J, Briffa, K R, and Brown, D M, 1985
    Redating the English art-historical tree-ring chronologies,
    Nature 315, 317–19
Baker, E, 1977 Peterborough Cathedral, [inspection report] 8
    August 1977, unpub rep
Bayliss, A, 2007 Bayesian buildings: an introduction for the
    numerically challenged, *Vernacular Architect* 38, 75–86
Bergendahl Hohler, E, 1999 *Norwegian stave church sculpture*
    (2 vols), Oslo
Binski, P, 2003 The painted nave ceiling of Peterborough
    Abbey, in *The medieval English cathedral: papers in honour
    of Pamela Tudor-Craig* (ed J Backhouse), Harlaxton
    Medieval Stud 10, 41–62, Donington
Binski, P, 2004 *Becket's crown: art and imagination in Gothic
    England 1170–1300*, London
Binski, P, and Massing, A (eds), 2009 *The Westminster
    retable: history, technique, conservation*, Painting Practice 2,
    Cambridge
Bomford, D, Dunkerton, J, Gordon, D, and Roy, A, 1990 *Art
    in the making: Italian painting before 1400*, London
Bonde, N, and Jensen, J S, 1995 The dating of a Hanseatic
    cog find in Denmark, in *Shipshape: essays for Ole Crumlin-
    Pederson* (eds O Olsen, J S Madsen and F Rieck), 103–22,
    Roskilde
Bonde, N, Tyers, I, and Wazny, T, 1997 Where does the
    timber come from? Dendrochronological evidence of the
    timber trade in northern Europe, in *Archaeological sciences
    1995: proceedings of a conference on the application of
    scientific techniques to the study of archaeology* (eds A

Sinclair, E Slater and J Gowlett), Oxbow Monogr Archaeol
    64, 201–4, Oxford
Brewer, A J, 1991 Effect of selected coatings on moisture
    sorption of selected wood test panels with regard to
    common panel painting supports, *Stud Conserv* 36, 9–23
Brewer, A J, 1998 Practical aspects of structural conservation
    of large panel paintings, in Dardes and Rothe (eds) 1998,
    448–78
Brewer, J A, 2000 Observations on wood effects for the nave
    ceiling of Peterborough Cathedral, November 2000, in
    Harrison and Lithgow nd e, appendix 4
Bristow, I, 1996 *Interior house-painting colours and technology
    1615–1840*, London
Britton, J, 1828 *The history and antiquities of Peterborough
    Cathedral*, London
Britton, J, 1997 (1828) *The history and antiquities of
    Peterborough Cathedral*, repr, Glossop
Bronk Ramsey, C, 1995 Radiocarbon calibration and
    stratigraphy: the OxCal program, *Radiocarbon* 37, 425–30
Bronk Ramsey, C, 2008 Deposition models for chronological
    records, *Quat Sci Rev* 27, 42–60
Brown, S, 1999 *Sumptuous and richly adorn'd: the decoration
    of Salisbury Cathedral*, London
Bryan, P G, and Andrews, D, 2001 The application of
    photogrammetric survey within the conservation of the
    great ceiling at Peterborough Cathedral, in *Surveying and
    documentation of historic buildings, monuments, sites –
    traditional and modern methods: Potsdam (Germany),
    September 18–21, 2001, proceedings of the 18th
    international symposium, CIPA 2001* (ed Jörg Albertz),
    93–9, Berlin
Bucklow, S, 2003 A summary of the technique, in Massing
    (ed) 2003, 28–46
Bunker, M, and Binski, P, 2006 *Peterborough Cathedral
    2001–6 from devastation to restoration*, London
Cal Close R   Calendar of close rolls, 1892–1975, London
Cal Pat R   Calendar of patent rolls, 1894–1974, London
Camuffo, D, Sturaro, G, Valentino, A, and Camuffo, M, 1999
    The conservation of artworks and hot air heating systems
    in churches: are they compatible? The case of Rocca
    Pietore, Italian Alps, *Stud Conserv* 44, 209–16
Carlyle, L, 2001 *The artist's assistant: oil painting instruction
    manuals and handbooks in Britain 1800–1900 with
    reference to selected 18th-century sources*, London
Cassar, M, 1995 *Environmental management*, Guidelines Mus
    Galleries Datasheet 4, London
Cave, C J P, and Borenius, T, 1937 The painted ceiling in the
    nave of Peterborough Cathedral, *Archaeologia* 87, 297–309
Caviness, M H, 1974 A lost cycle of Canterbury paintings of
    1220, *Antiq J* 54, 66–74
*Chron Majora   Matthaei Parisiensis, monachi Sancti Albani,
    chronica majora* (ed H R Luard), Chronicles Memorials Gr
    Brit Ir Middle Ages 57 (7 vols), 1872–83, London
Church, A H, 1915 (1901) *The chemistry of paints and
    painting*, 4 edn, London
Clarke, H, 1992 The Hanse and England: a survey of the

evidence for contacts between England and the Baltic in the Middle Ages, *Archaeol Elbingensis* 1, 135–8

Curteis, T, 2000 Peterborough Cathedral: environmental monitoring of the nave ceiling, Peterborough Cathedral, March 1998–May 2000, Tobit Curteis Associates, unpub rep

Curteis, T, 2001 Peterborough Cathedral: environmental monitoring of the nave ceiling, Peterborough Cathedral, June 2000–May 2001, Tobit Curteis Associates, unpub rep

Curteis, T, 2002 Peterborough Cathedral: environmental monitoring of the nave ceiling, Peterborough Cathedral, June 2001–May 2002, Tobit Curteis Associates, unpub rep

Curteis, T, 2003 Peterborough Cathedral: environmental monitoring of the nave ceiling, Peterborough Cathedral, June 2002–October 2003, Tobit Curteis Associates, unpub rep

Dardes, K, and Rothe, A (eds), 1998 *The structural conservation of panel paintings, proceedings of a symposium at the J Paul Getty Museum, 24–28 April 1995*, Los Angeles

Davies, J, 2001 Peterborough Cathedral nave ceiling: phase 3, investigation of painting materials and techniques, unpub rep

Davies, J, 2002 Peterborough Cathedral nave ceiling: investigation of painting materials and techniques, conservation phase 4, unpub rep

Davies, J, 2003a Peterborough Cathedral: scientific examination of the transept ceiling paint samples, unpub rep

Davies, J, 2003b Peterborough Cathedral nave ceiling roof space: investigation of painting materials and techniques, unpub rep

Davies, J, 2004 Peterborough Cathedral nave ceiling: investigation of painting materials and techniques, conservation phase 5, unpub rep

Davys, O W, 1846 *Historical and architectural guide to Peterborough Cathedral*, Peterborough

Dean, J S, Meko, D M, and Swetnam, T W (eds), 1996 *Tree rings, environment and humanity*, Arizona

Demus, O, 1970 *Romanesque mural painting*, London

Denninger, E, 1969 The examination of pigments and media from the painted wooden ceiling of St Michael's church at Hildesheim, West Germany, *Stud Conserv* 14, 91–5

Dollinger, P, 1970 *The German Hansa*, London

Dry, W, 1906 *Northamptonshire*, Little Guides, London

Eastlake, C, 1847 *Materials for a history of oil painting: Vol 1*, London

English Heritage, 1996 Peterborough Cathedral environmental monitoring, 2 November 1995 to 31 January 1996, unpub rep

Fedorowicz, J K, 1980 *England's Baltic trade in the early 17th century*, Cambridge

Fernie, E, 2000 *The architecture of Norman England*, Oxford

Fernie, E, 2003 The architecture and sculpture of Ely Cathedral in the Norman period, in *A history of Ely Cathedral* (eds P Meadows and N Ramsey), 95–111, Woodbridge

Field, G, 1835 *Chromatography: or, a treatise on colours and pigments, and of their powers in painting*, London

Fletcher, J M, 1980 Tree-ring dating of Tudor portraits, *Proc Roy Inst Gr Brit* 52, 81–104

Fletcher, J M, and Spokes, P S, 1964 The origin and development of crown-post roofs, *Medieval Archaeol* 8, 153–83

Foard, G, Hall, D, and Partilda, T, 2009 *Rockingham Forest: an atlas of the medieval and early modern landscape*, Northampton

Franzini, M, Gratziu, C, and Wicks, E, 1984 Patine ad ossalato di calcio su monumenti marmorei, *Rendiconti Società Italiana di Mineralogia e Petrologia* 39, 59–70

Friar, S, 1996 *A companion to the English parish church*, Stroud

The Friends of Peterborough Cathedral Journal, 1981 [photograph of the north transept ceiling at Peterborough Cathedral, prior to 1880s restoration work]

Gärtner, W, 1988 Peterborough Cathedral – painted ceiling – nave: inspection report, May 1988, unpub rep

Gilmour, B, 2003 Nails from the wood panelled nave ceiling of Peterborough Cathedral: technological investigation of nails, in Harrison and Lithgow nd c

Grout, R, and Burnstock, A, 2000 A study of the blackening of vermilion, *Zeitschrift für Kunsttechnologie und Konservierung* 14, 15–22

Groves, C, 2000a Belarus to Bexley and beyond: dendrochronology and dendroprovenancing of conifer timbers, *Vernacular Architect* 31, 59–66

Groves, C, 2000b Tree-ring analysis of oak timbers from Peterborough Cathedral, Peterborough, Cambridgeshire: boards from the painted nave ceiling, unpub Ancient Monuments Lab rep 10/2000, http://www.research.historicengland.org.uk/ (last accessed 12 May 2015)

Groves, C, 2000c Tree-ring analysis of oak timbers from Peterborough Cathedral, Peterborough, Cambridgeshire: boards from the painted nave ceiling – phase 2, unpub Ancient Monuments Lab rep 37/2000, http://www.research.historicengland.org.uk/ (last accessed 12 May 2015)

Groves, C, 2002 Tree-ring analysis of imported medieval timbers, in Hall, R A, and Hunter-Mann, K, *Medieval urbanism in Coppergate: refining a townscape*, The Archaeology of York 10/6, 826–35, York

Gunton, S, 1990 (1686) *The history of the church of Peterborough*, facsimile repr Stamford (London 1686)

Hall, J, 2008 Peterborough Cathedral: early memorials and a late medieval house discovered, *Church Archaeol* 12, 1–29

Hall, J, and Atherton, J, 2011 Devotion and image at Binham Priory: a 14th-century hexagonal stone pedestal, *Norfolk Archaeol* 46, 153–70

Halliday, T M, 2009 Select manuscripts relating to the abbey and cathedral of Peterborough: transcriptions, translations and notes, unpub rep

Hamilton, W D, Bayliss, A, Menuge, A, Bronk Ramsey, C, and Cook, G, 2007 Revd Thomas Bayes: get ready to wiggle – Bayesian modelling, radiocarbon wiggle-matching and the north wing of Baguley Hall, *Vernacular Architect* 38, 87–97

Haneca, K, Wazny, T, van Acker, J, and Beeckman, H, 2005 Provenancing Baltic timber from art-historical objects: success and limitations, *J Archaeol Sci* 32, 261–71

Harrison, H, and Lithgow, R, nd a Peterborough Cathedral nave ceiling, phase 1: rows 36–40, January–June 1998. Condition survey and conservation treatment: Vol I, Text and graphics; Vol II, Plates, the Perry Lithgow Partnership in collaboration with Hugh Harrison, unpub rep

Harrison, H, and Lithgow, R, nd b Peterborough Cathedral nave ceiling, phase 2: rows 28–35, May–July 1999. Condition survey and conservation treatment: Vol I, Text and graphics; Vol II, Plates, the Perry Lithgow Partnership in collaboration with Hugh Harrison, unpub rep

Harrison, H, and Lithgow, R, nd c Peterborough Cathedral nave ceiling, phase 3: rows 18–27, May–October 2000. Condition survey and conservation treatment: Vol I, Text and graphics; Vol II, Plates, the Perry Lithgow Partnership in collaboration with Hugh Harrison, unpub rep

Harrison, H, and Lithgow, R, nd d Peterborough Cathedral nave ceiling, phase 4: rows 8–17, May–October 2001. Condition survey and conservation treatment: Vol I, Text and graphics; Vol II, Plates, the Perry Lithgow Partnership in collaboration with Hugh Harrison, unpub rep

Harrison, H, and Lithgow, R, nd e Peterborough Cathedral nave ceiling, phase 5: rows 0–7, May–October 2003. Condition survey and conservation treatment: Vol I, Text and graphics; Vol II, Plates, the Perry Lithgow Partnership in collaboration with Hugh Harrison, unpub rep

Harrison, H, and Lithgow, R, nd f Peterborough Cathedral: the transept ceilings. Record of treatment and additional investigation following a fire in the cathedral on 22 November 2002, July–October 2002, the Perry Lithgow Partnership in collaboration with Hugh Harrison, unpub rep

Harrison, H, McNeill, J, Plummer, P, and Simpson, G, 2012 The presbytery vault at St Albans, *Antiq J* 92, 245–72

Harrison, S A, Morris, R K, and Robinson, D M, 1998 A 14th-century pulpitum screen at Tintern Abbey, Monmouthshire, *Antiq J* 78, 177–268

Hassall, C, 2002 Peterborough Cathedral, south transept ceiling, in Harrison and Lithgow nd f, appendix 4

Hauglid, R, 1970 *Norwegian stave churches* (trans R I Christophersen), Oslo

Hewett, C A, 1985 *English cathedral and monastic carpentry*, Chichester

Heymanowski, K, 1979 Niektore sortymenty drzewne w Polsce w XV w. w swiete materialow z 'miedziowca', *Kwartalnik Hostorii Kultury Materialnej* 27, 345–51

Hillam, J, 1998 *Dendrochronology: guidelines on producing and interpreting dendrochronological dates*, London

Hillam, J, and Groves, C, 1996 Tree-ring research at Windsor Castle, in Dean et al (eds) 1996, 515–23

Hillam, J, Morgan, R A, and Tyers, I, 1987 Sapwood estimates and the dating of short ring sequences, in *Applications of tree-ring studies: current research in dendrochronology and related subjects* (ed R G W Ward), BAR Int Ser 333, 165–85, Oxford

Hirst Conservation, 1995 Nave ceiling Peterborough Cathedral, unpub rep

Hoadley, R B, 1998 Chemical and physical properties of wood, in Dardes and Rothe (eds) 1998, 2–20

Horie, C V, 1987 *Materials for conservation: organic consolidants, adhesives and coatings*, London

Howard, H, 1997 Peterborough Cathedral, nave ceiling: scientific examination of the original decoration, September 1997, unpub Courtauld Inst Art rep

Howard, H, 1998 Peterborough Cathedral, nave ceiling: scientific examination of the original decoration of bays 36–9, September 1997, unpub Courtauld Inst Art rep

Howard, H, 2003a *Pigments of English medieval wall painting*, London

Howard, H, 2003b Scientific examination of the polychromy, in Tracy, C, and Woodfield, P, with Howard, H, Tyers, I, and Eastaugh, N, The Adisham 'reredos'. What is it?, *J Brit Archaeol Ass* 156, 65–9

Howard, H, and Sauerberg, M L, 2009 Polychrome techniques at Westminster 1250–1350, in Binski and Massing (eds) 2009, 290–318

Hughes, M K, Milson, S J, and Leggett, P A, 1981 Sapwood estimates in the interpretation of tree-ring dates, *J Archaeol Sci* 8, 381–90

Irvine, J T, 1894 Account of the pre-Norman remains discovered at Peterborough Cathedral in 1884, *J Brit Archaeol Ass* 50, 45–54

James, M R, 1896 On the paintings formerly in the choir at Peterborough, *Proc Cambridge Antiq Soc* 9, ns 3, 178–94

James, M R, 1950 *Pictor in carmine*, Archaeologia 94, 141–66

Jenkins, G J, Perry, M C, and Prior, M J, 2008 *The climate of the United Kingdom and recent trends*, Exeter

Kakoulli, I, 1999 Cathedral nave ceiling paintings: scientific examination phase 2, December 1999, unpub Courtauld Inst Art rep

King, E, 1973 *Peterborough Abbey 1086–1310: a study in the land market*, Cambridge

King, E, forthcoming *The Peterborough Abbey chronicle: Vol 2*, Northamptonshire Rec Soc

King, R J, 1862 *Handbook to the cathedrals of England: eastern division*, London

Knut, N, 1999 *The restoration of paintings*, Cologne

Lavier, C, and Lambert, G, 1996 Dendrochronology and works of art, in Dean et al (eds) 1996, 543–56

Laxton, R R, Litton, C D, and Howard, R E, 2001 *Timber: dendrochronology of roof timbers at Lincoln Cathedral*, Engl Heritage Res Trans 7, London

Leuschner, B, and Leuschner, H H, 1996 Plasticine imprints for recording tree rings, *Dendrochronologia* 14, 287–90

Lewis, E, 1995 A 16th-century painted ceiling from Winchester College, *Proc Hampshire Fld Club Archaeol Soc* 51, 137–65

Lewis, G, 1996 Peterborough Cathedral nave ceiling: updated

condition notes, February 1996, unpub rep

Lindblom, A, 1916 *La Peinture gothique en suède et en norvège*, Stockholm

Ling, R, 1991 *Roman painting*, Cambridge

Lithgow, R, 1997 Peterborough Cathedral, the nave ceiling: St Peter, St Paul and psaltery player lozenges, unpub rep

Litton, C D, and Zainodin, H J, 1991 Statistical models of dendrochronology, *J Archaeol Sci* 18, 429–40

Liversidge, M, and Binski, P, 1995 Two ceiling fragments from the painted chamber at Westminster Palace, *Burlington Mag* 137 no. 1109 (August), 491–501

Lower, A R M, 1973 *Great Britain's woodyard: British America and the timber trade, 1763–1867*, Montreal

Lynn, J, 1995 Appendix: preliminary technical report on the Westminster panels, in Liversidge and Binski 1995, 498–501

Mackreth, D F, 1994 Abbot Benedict and Canterbury, *Friends of Peterborough Cathedral*, 4–9

Massing, A (ed), 2003 *The Thornham Parva retable: technique, conservation and context of an English medieval painting*, Cambridge

Mellows, W T (ed), 1941 *The Peterborough chronicle of Hugh Candidus* (trans C Mellows and W T Mellows), Peterborough Mus Publ ns 1, pt 1, 1–11

Mellows, W T (ed), 1949 *The chronicle of Hugh Candidus, a monk of Peterborough*, Oxford

Mellows, W T (ed), 1966 (1941) *The Peterborough chronicle of Hugh Candidus* (trans C Mellows and W T Mellows), Peterborough Mus Soc, rev edn, Peterborough

Meteorological Office, nd UK climate, http://www.metoffice.gov.uk/climate/uk/averages/ ukmapavge.html (last accessed 23 October 2014)

Miles, D, 1997 The interpretation, presentation and use of tree-ring dates, *Vernacular Architect* 28, 40–56

Miles, D, 2002 The tree-ring dating of the roof carpentry of the eastern chapels, north nave triforium and north porch, Salisbury Cathedral, Wiltshire, unpub Engl Heritage Res Department Rep 94/2002, http://www.research.historicengland.org.uk/ (last accessed 12 May 2015)

Miles, D, 2005 The tree-ring dating of the nave roof at Salisbury Cathedral, Wiltshire, unpub Engl Heritage Res Department Rep 58/2005, http://www.research.historicengland.org.uk/ (last accessed 12 May 2015)

Miles, D, 2006 Refinements in the interpretation of tree-ring dates for oak building timbers in England and Wales, *Vernacular Architect* 37, 84–96

Miles, D, and Bridge, M, 2005 The tree-ring dating of the early medieval doors at Westminster Abbey, London, unpub Engl Heritage Res Department Rep 38/2005, http://www.research.historicengland.org.uk/ (last accessed 12 May 2015)

Miles, D, and Bridge, M, 2010 The chapter house doors and their dating, in *Westminster Abbey chapter house: the history, art and architecture of 'a chapter house beyond compare'* (eds W Rodwell and R Mortimer), 251–60, London

Millard, A, 2002 A Bayesian approach to sapwood estimates and felling dates in dendrochronology, *Archaeometry* 44, 137–43

Mills, C, and Crone, A, 1998 Tree-ring evidence for the historic timber trade and woodland exploitation in Scotland, in *Dendrochronology and environmental trends* (eds V Stravinskiene and R Juknys), 46–55, Kaunas

Møller, D F, 1996 *Music aloft: musical symbolism in the mural paintings of Danish medieval churches*, Copenhagen

Moore, L, 1925 Peterborough Cathedral roof and its repair, *Architect's J*, 262–5

Monte, M del, and Sabbioni, C, 1986 Chemical and biological weathering of an historical building: Reggio Emilia Cathedral, *Sci Total Environment* 50, 165–82

Morgan, N J, 1982 *A survey of manuscripts illuminated in the British Isles: Vol 4, Early Gothic manuscripts (I), 1190–1250*, London

Morgan, N J, 1988 *A survey of manuscripts illuminated in the British Isles: Vol 4, Early Gothic manuscripts (II), 1250–85*, London

Munby, J, 1996 Cathedral carpentry, in Tatton-Brown and Munby (eds) 1996, 165–82

Neal, D S, and Cosh, S R, 2002 *Roman mosaics of Britain: Vol 1, Northern Britain, incorporating the Midlands and East Anglia*, London

Nordström, F, 1955 Peterborough, Lincoln, and the science of Robert Grosseteste: a study in 13th-century architecture and iconography, *Art Bull* 37, 241–72

Norton, E C, 1996 The medieval paintings in the chapter house, in *Friends of York Minster 67th Annual Report*, 34–51, York

OxCal, 2014 Oxford radiocarbon accelerator unit, University of Oxford, http://c14.arch.ox.ac.uk/oxcal (last accessed 23 October 2014)

Peers, C, 1906 Peterborough minster, in *VCH* 1906, 431–56

Pevsner, N, and Cherry, B, 1973 (1961) *The buildings of England: Northamptonshire*, 2 edn, Harmondsworth

Pevsner, N, and Wilson, B, 1997 *Norfolk: Vol I, Norwich and north-east*, Buildings of England, London

Plummer, C (ed), 1952 (1892) *Two of the Saxon chronicles parallel: with supplementary extracts from the others* (a revised text, on the basis of an earlier edition by John Earle), reissue (2 vols), Oxford

Poole, G A, 1855 On the abbey church of Peterborough, *Ass Architect Soc Rep Pap* 3, 187–221

Powicke, F M, and Cheney, C R (eds), 1964 *Councils and synods with other documents relating to the English Church II: AD 1205–1313*, Oxford

Pownall, T, 1789 Observations on ancient painting in England: in a letter from Gov Pownall to the Revd Michael Lott, DDUPAS, *Archaeologia* 9, 141–56

Rackham, O, 1990 (1981) *Trees and woodland in the British landscape*, 2 edn, London

Rackham, O, 2006 *Woodlands*, London

Reeve, M M, 2008 *Thirteenth-century wall painting of Salisbury Cathedral, art, liturgy, reform*, Woodbridge

Reilly, L, 1997 *An architectural history of Peterborough Cathedral*, Oxford

Rickerby, S, 1991 Heat alterations to pigments painted in the fresco technique, *Conservator* 15, 39–44

Rickman, T, 1817 *An attempt to discriminate the styles of English architecture, from the Conquest to the Reformation*, London

Saiz-Jimenez, C, 1989 Biogenic versus anthropogenic oxalic acid in the environment, in *The oxalate films: origin and significance in the conservation of works of art, proceedings, Milano, 25–26 octobre 1989, Centro Congressi Cariplo*, 207–14, Milan

Salzman, L F, 1952 *Building in England down to 1540*, Oxford

Sampson, J, 1998 *Wells Cathedral west front: construction, sculpture and conservation*, Stroud

Sandler, L F, 1970 Peterborough Abbey and the Peterborough Psalter in Brussels, *J Brit Archaeol Ass* 33, 36–49

Sauerberg, M-L, 2013 The polychromy of the coronation chair, in Rodwell, W, *The coronation chair and the Stone of Scone: history, archaeology and conservation*, 77–104, Oxford

Sauerberg, M-L, Roy, A, Spring, M, Bucklow, S, and Kempski, M, 2009 Materials and techniques, in Binski and Massing (eds) 2009, 233–51

Schama, S, 1995 *Landscape and memory*, London

Schweingruber, F H, 1990 *Anatomy of European woods*, Berne

Simpson, W G, and Litton, C D, 1996 Dendrochronology in cathedrals, in Tatton-Brown and Munby (eds) 1996, 183–209

Sørensen, A C, 2001 *Ladby: a Danish ship-grave from the Viking Age*, Roskilde

Sparke, J (ed), 1723 *Historiæ Coenobii Burgensis scriptores varii*, London

Stopford, J, and Wright, S M, 1998 A group of late medieval inscribed tiles from Bordesley Abbey, *Antiq J* 78, 307–22

Strickland, W, 1849 *Lithographic drawing of the ancient painted ceiling in the nave of Peterborough Cathedral*, Peterborough

Stubbs, W (ed), 1879 *The historical works of Gervase of Canterbury: Vol 1*, Chronicles Memorials Gr Brit Ir Middle Ages 73, London

Stukeley, W, 1887 *The family memoirs of the Revd William Stukeley, MD, and the antiquarian and other correspondence of William Stukeley, Roger and Samuel Gale, etc: Vol. 3*, Publ Surtees Soc 80, Durham

Swanton, M (ed), 2000 *The Anglo-Saxon chronicles*, London

Sweeting, W D, 1898 *The cathedral church of Peterborough: a description of its fabric and a brief history of the episcopal see*, Bell's Cathedral Ser, London

Sweeting, W D, 1932 (1899) *The cathedral church of Peterborough: a description of its fabric and a brief history of the episcopal see*, Bell's Cathedral Ser, 3 edn, London

Tatton-Brown, T, and Munby, J (eds), 1996 *The archaeology of cathedrals*, Oxford Univ Comm Archaeol Monogr 42, Oxford

Thomson, G, 1986 (1978) *The museum environment*, 2 edn, London

Thurlby, M, 1994 The Romanesque apse vault at Peterborough Cathedral, in *Studies in medieval art and architecture presented to Peter Lasko* (eds D Buckton and T A Heslop), 171–86, Stroud

Thurlby, M, 2006 Stone vault or painted wooden ceiling? The question of how to cover the nave of Peterborough Abbey church, *Ecclesiol Today* 36, 77–90

Topham, J, 1998 A dendrochronological investigation of British stringed instruments of the violin family, *J Archaeol Sci* 25, 1149–57

Tracy, C, 1997 An English painted screen at Kingston Lacy, *Apollo* 146, no. 425 (July), 20–8

Tristram, E W, 1944 *English medieval wall painting: the 12th century*, Oxford

Tristram, E W, 1950 *English medieval wall painting: Vol 1, Text: the 13th century*, Oxford

Tyers, C, 2008 Bayesian interpretation of tree-ring dates in practice, *Vernacular Architect* 39, 91–106

Tyers, C, and Tyers, I, 2007 *Peterborough Cathedral, tree-ring analysis of the nave ceiling*, unpub Engl Heritage Res Department Rep 4/2007, http://www.research.historicengland.org.uk/ (last accessed 12 May 2015)

Tyers, C, Arnold, A J, and Howard, R E, forthcoming Dendrochronological analysis of conifer timbers from Millers House and House Mill, Three Mills Lane, Bromley by Bow, London, unpub Engl Heritage Res Department Rep

Tyers, I, 1987 Dendrochronology report: Deptford Wharf, unpub MOL DGLA Dendrochronol Rep 02/87

Tyers, I, 1996 Appendix 1: dendrochronology of shipping from London, 12th to 17th centuries, in Marsden, P, *Ships of the port of London: 12th to 17th centuries AD*, Engl Heritage Archaeol Rep 5, 185–98, London

Tyers, I, 1998a Beech dendrochronology, in Nayling, N, *Magor Pill medieval wreck*, CBA Res Rep 115, 123–8, York

Tyers, I, 1998b Tree-ring analysis and wood identification of timbers excavated on the Magistrates Court site, Kingston upon Hull, East Yorkshire, unpub ARCUS Rep 410

Tyers, I, 1999 Tree-ring analysis of oak timbers from Peterborough Cathedral, Peterborough, Cambridgeshire: structural timbers from the nave roof and north-west portico, unpub Ancient Monuments Lab Rep 9/99, http://www.research.historicengland.org.uk/ (last accessed 12 May 2015)

Tyers, I, 2002 Tree-ring analysis of the Westminster retable, unpub ARCUS Rep 499

Tyers, I, 2003 Appendix 1: the eastern Baltic timber trade, in Massing (ed) 2003, 219–21

Tyers, I, 2004 Tree-ring analysis of oak boards and structural timbers from the transepts, presbytery and tower of Peterborough Cathedral, City of Peterborough, unpub Engl Heritage Res Department Rep 77/2004, http://www.research.historicengland.org.uk/ (last accessed 12 May 2015)

Tyers, I, 2009 Tree-ring analysis of the Westminster retable, in Binski and Massing (eds) 2009, 215–21

Tyers, I, 2010 Aspects of the European trade in oak boards to England 1200–1700, in *Trade in artists' materials, markets and commerce in Europe to 1700* (eds J Kirby, S Nash and J Cannon), 42–9, London

VCH, 1906 *The Victoria history of the county of Northampton: Vol 2* (eds W R D Adkins, D Ryland and R M Serjeantson), London

Wadum, J, Microclimate boxes for panel paintings, in Dardes and Rothe (eds) 1998, 497–524

Ware, S, 1809 *A treatise of the properties of arches and their abutment piers: … also concerning bridges, and the flying buttresses of cathedrals*, London

Warncke, J, 1912 Mittelalterliche Schülgerate im Museum zu Lübeck: ein Kloakenfund vom Grundstück der alten Lübecker Stadtschule, *Zeitschrift für Geschichte der Erziehung und des Unterrichts* 2/4, 277

Wazny, T, 1990 Aufbau und Anwendung der Dendrochronologie für Eichenholz in Polen, unpub PhD thesis, Hamburg Univ

Wazny, T, 2002 Baltic timber in western Europe: an exciting dendrochronological question, *Dendrochronologia* 20, 313–20

Wazny, T, and Eckstein, D, 1991 The dendrochronological signal of oak (*Quercus* spp) in Poland, *Dendrochronologia* 9, 35–49

West Fitzhugh, E, 1997 Orpiment and realgar, in *Artists' pigments. A handbook of their history and characteristics: Vol 3* (ed E West FitzHugh), 47–80, Oxford

Wilson, A, nd Letter from Lt Col A Wilson, OIC, the weapons collection, HQ small arms school corps, Warminster, in Harrison and Lithgow nd e, appendix 14